Innovation in Professional Education

Richard E. Boyatzis
Scott S. Cowen
David A. Kolb
and Associates

INNOVATION IN PROFESSIONAL EDUCATION

*Steps on a Journey
from Teaching
to Learning*

The Story of Change and Invention
at the Weatherhead School
of Management

Jossey-Bass Publishers • San Francisco

Substantial discounts on bulk quantities of Jossey-Bass books are available to corporations, professional associations, and other organizations. For details and discount information, contact the special sales department at Jossey-Bass Inc., Publishers. (415) 433-1740; Fax (415) 433-0499.

For international orders, please contact your local Paramount Publishing International office.

Manufactured in the United States of America. Nearly all Jossey-Bass books and jackets are printed on recycled paper that contains at least 50 percent recycled waste, including 10 percent postconsumer waste. Many of our materials are also printed with vegetable-based inks; during the printing process these inks emit fewer volatile organic compounds (VOCs) than petroleum-based inks. VOCs contribute to the formation of smog.

Library of Congress Cataloging-in-Publication Data

Boyatzis, Richard E.
    Innovation in professional education : steps on a journey from teaching to learning / Richard E. Boyatzis, Scott S. Cowen, David A. Kolb, and Associates. — 1st ed.
        p.   cm. — (A joint publication in the Jossey-Bass management series and the Jossey-Bass higher and adult education series)
    Includes bibliographical references and index.
    ISBN 0-7879-0032-X
    1. Professional education — United States.   2. Master of business administration degree — United States.   3. Universities and colleges — United States — Graduate work.   I. Cowen, Scott S.   II. Kolb, David A., date.   III. Title.   IV. Series: Jossey-Bass management series.   V. Series: Jossey-Bass higher and adult education series.
LC1059.B69   1994
378'.013'0973 — dc20   94–28010
                                                                          CIP

FIRST EDITION
HB Printing   10 9 8 7 6 5 4 3 2 1   *Code 94113*

Dedication

*This book is dedicated to our colleagues —
the faculty, staff, and students of
the Weatherhead School of Management —
who created, designed, and implemented
the program about which this book is written.*

*This is our story;
thank you for making it happen.*

CONTENTS

ix

Part Two: Outcome Assessments and Results

Part Three: Key Learnings and Dreams

PREFACE

Higher education is undergoing a significant and traumatic change. Driven by people from within our educational institutions as well as by stakeholders outside of them — such as prospective students, parents, employers, and funding agents — this process of transformation is likely to leave few areas of the academic world untouched. The consequences may be hopeful, surprising, or merely disappointing.

Innovation in Professional Education is about curriculum innovation in management education. It focuses on the processes that bring about innovation and on possible outcomes. The book conveys a message of hope.

Our intention in writing this book has been to share with you, as honestly as we can, the story of the Weatherhead School of Management (WSOM) at Case Western Reserve University. We hope that this account will be useful to other educational institutions embarking on a similar process of change. We make humble validity claims for our story, since in every case there are different perspectives to be taken and untold stories to be heard. We are also probably guilty of selling ourselves and our "product," because we believe in them. By examining our experiences closely, we also hope to stimulate questions and offer one set of answers about the current wave of innovations in professional education — in particular, in schools of management. Are these innovations old wine in new bottles? Or have we rediscovered the soul of our educational institutions?

Who Should Read This Book?

Several groups of professionals should find this story useful. They include faculty, administrators, deans, and researchers involved in management education — or, more generally, all those seeking to explore new and better ways of developing people. The same groups in other areas of professional education, such as in schools of architecture, education, engineering, dentistry, law, medicine, nursing, social work, and so forth, will also profit from the material that we have brought together in this book. In addition, human resource development professionals, corporate recruiters who hire MBAs, and consultants involved in management, executive, and leadership development should find this account intriguing. A group who will find the outcome assessment studies to be of interest are psychologists and other social scientists studying adult development, adult self-directed learning, and educational processes, as well as those conducting policy analyses and making educational and training policy recommendations.

These professionals will, we hope, find the book useful in three major ways. First, it provides an approach and perspective on learning, curriculum revision, and adult development that the reader can adapt to a particular situation and institution or organization. The concept of guiding innovation with a vision, mission, or philosophy is not new, but we stress the need to develop a philosophy of learning as a basis for curriculum innovation. This approach moves us beyond superficial measures such as developing or adding courses and increasing requirements as the remedies for educational deficiencies.

Second, the processes used in establishing the strategy, vision, philosophies, methods, outcome studies, and formative review and evaluation of progress are outlined step by step. We have attempted to avoid the arrogance of "assumed expertise"; therefore, you will not find "how-to-do-it" lists in the book. But you will find clearly delineated processes.

Third, professionals intrigued with assessing their impact within the context of an outcome orientation and/or conducting outcome studies will find the designs, methods, and procedures for such studies described in detail. In addition, we describe ways of utilizing raw data and analyzed results as part of the innovation process.

Overview of the Contents

Chapters One through Seven examine the early parts of the journey—that is, the processes used and the design of the new WSOM MBA program. In each chapter, the authors identify observations and learnings about graduate, professional, and management education, as well as about institutional change. In Chapters Eight through Ten, we examine the consequences and impact of the new program. Some of the chapters appear in narrative form, and others present data and investigate statistical significance. We have attempted to portray the contributions of several epistemologies to our journey. We hope that the reader will find at least several chapters addressing their "way of knowing," and that the other chapters will be of interest as well.

Chapter One sets the stage for the journey. In Chapter Two, the topic of strategic planning within a professional school is explored. Rather than describing neat, seemingly rational steps in an idealized process, the chapter reviews some of the learnings from the multiyear process of the Weatherhead School of Management. In Chapter Three, the process of discovery and design of the new MBA program is described. Chapter Four provides a detailed description of the Managerial Assessment and Development course—one of the key elements of the new program and a driving force for the self-directed learning of students. Results of years of job competency studies in management were incorporated into the identification of the characteristics to be assessed. The outcome model for the WSOM MBA is described in this chapter. It was based on the results of years of job competency studies.

Chapters Five through Eight report results from various outcome assessment studies. The WSOM has engaged in the five different types of outcome assessment studies relevant to professional schools. Some schools have focused on alumni and employer studies. In the discussion of results and design of the new program, we focused on faculty- and student-change outcome assessment studies, using information collected during alumni, employer, and job competency studies.

Since outcome assessment is central to many of the processes, discoveries, and events described in this book, a brief review of the five types of outcome assessment studies relevant to professional schools may be helpful. Listed in order of increasing difficulty, they are as follows:

1. *Alumni studies.* How are alumni doing in their careers? What do they think of the program?
2. *Employer studies.* What do prospective employers desire in our graduates? What do employers of recent graduates think of their performance?
3. *Faculty studies.* What kind of impact do faculty hope to have on students? How would they like students to be when they graduate? How would they like students to have changed as a result of the program?
4. *Student-change studies.* How are students different when they graduate than when they entered our program?
5. *Professional competency studies.* What are the characteristics of the superior performers among managers, doctors, lawyers, nurses, and so on? What characteristics may be important in the future that are not recognized or appreciated currently in organizations?

In Chapter Five, results are reported from two years of student-change outcome studies of the old MBA program, looking at effects on full-time and part-time students as well as native English-speaking and nonnative English-speaking students. Chapter Six reports results from the study of faculty objectives and compares the intention of the faculty with the student outcome. Although not described in this book, the results of the studies reported in Chapters Five and Six were reviewed with alumni and prospective employers. Discussions of the discoveries incorporate the conclusions from additional alumni and employer outcome studies. Chapters Five and Six establish a baseline with the examination of the old MBA program.

The largest segment of students entering MBA programs who are different from the traditional students of earlier decades are women. In Chapter Seven, differences between female and male MBA students at the point of entry into the program are explored. Their Life Stories, Career Histories, and individualized Learning Plans are examined.

In Chapter Eight, results are reported on two graduating groups in the new MBA program. These are student-change outcome studies of the new program; therefore, they can be used to examine the effectiveness of the innovations as compared to the student-change information from the old program.

In Chapters Five through Eight, numerous statistical tables are provided in appendixes. They are available for the interested researcher or faculty member but have been removed from the text to minimize distractions for the reader primarily interested in curriculum innovation and with limited quantitative patience.

In Chapter Nine, the reactions of various stakeholders during the early implementation years are described. Returning to the objectives of the design as described in Chapter Three, the question of whether or not the program is meeting those objectives is addressed. Combined with the data from Chapter Eight, the observations and discussion in Chapter Nine constitute an evaluation of the new program's efficacy.

In Chapter Ten, we have taken the liberty of dreaming. We have asked ourselves what an ideal professional program would involve. Although focused on management education, our experiences and discussions with faculty from schools of dentistry, education, engineering, law, medicine, nursing, and social work lead us to believe that their journeys are similar to the one we describe. With this observation, we hope the processes, ideas, results, and learnings described in this book are useful in provoking thought in all professional education programs.

The journey from teaching to learning is not abstract. Once begun, it denies you the comfort of sitting in your office or a library

or in your favorite reading chair at home and tracing someone
else's itinerary on a map. We have found that this journey ig-
nites the wonder, excitement, and awe of visiting exotic lands
and learning with new friends.

Cleveland, Ohio   Richard E. Boyatzis
August 1994   Scott S. Cowen
                                               David A. Kolb

ACKNOWLEDGMENTS

Hundreds of faculty, staff, students, alumni, recruiters, executives, and managers contributed to the processes and ideas described in *Innovation in Professional Education*. A number of them made special contributions to the creation and implementation of the new MBA program at the WSOM. We would like to thank all those serving on the MBA Objectives Committee during its six years: Theodore Alfred, John Aram, David Bowers, Fran Cort, Stan Cort, John Drotning, Dale Flowers, Paul Gerhart, Marian Hogue, Rettamarie Holdorf, Miles Kennedy, Kamlesh Mathur, Thomas Morrissey, Eric Neilsen, Larry Parker, William Peirce, John Ruhl, Paul Salipante, and J. B. Silvers. The department chairs, Faculty Council, MBA Curriculum Committee, and many task forces played a vital role in conducting meetings and creating the forum for many of the ideas to be discussed, argued, and debated. In addition to some of those already mentioned, we would like to thank Robert Baird, Diana Bilimoria, Richard Boland, David Campbell, Susan Case, David Cooperrider, Pat Davis, Hamilton Emmons, Assim Erdilek, Ronald Fry, Michael Ginzberg, David Hammack, Jamie Hobba, Terri Justofin, Leonard Lynn, Robert Mason, William Pasmore, Gary Previts, Mohan Reddy, Daniel Solow, Suresh Srivastva, and Donald Wolfe. In addition, we would like to thank the following doctoral students for their help in collecting and analyzing data in the studies reported here: Christine Dreyfus, Deborah Griest, Tojo Thachankery, and Xiaoping Tian.

Numerous colleagues at other institutions have provided guidance and support for us during these exciting but difficult years. We would like to honor and thank Sister Joel Read, Austin Doherty, Georgine Loacker, Marcia Mentkowski, and Kathleen O'Brian from Alverno College. Their pioneering work in the 1970s and continued efforts through the 1980s were an inspiration to us.

Encouragement in the early and vulnerable stages came from many sectors. We would like to thank William Laidlaw, executive director of the American Association of Collegiate Schools of Business, and William Broesamle, president of the Graduate Management Admission Council (GMAC), for creating visibility and recognition of our efforts. We would also like to thank Ellen Machan of the WSOM and Chas Withers of Case Western Reserve University for communicating the message, and to industry watchers and chroniclers, such as John Byrne of *Business Week* and Elizabeth Fowler, formerly of the *New York Times,* for early enthusiasm. We would like to express our appreciation to Becky Barker, Louella Hein, and Rettamarie Holdorf for their help in preparing this manuscript and coordinating our efforts. Many colleagues have helped by commenting on this book or segments of it. Our thanks go to William Hicks, David Justice, and Ronald Sims.

Writing a book is not an individualistic exercise, nor does it only affect our professional lives. It involves the whole person and their family system. We would like to thank our wives, Sandy Boyatzis and Marjorie Cowen, for their patience, unrelenting belief in us, and unconditional love and support as we journeyed down the path from teaching to learning. David Kolb says "ditto" for his cat, Jack.

R.E.B.
S.S.C.
D.A.K.

THE AUTHORS

RICHARD E. BOYATZIS is professor of organizational behavior at the Weatherhead School of Management, Case Western Reserve University. His current research focuses on adult development of abilities and values. His prior publications have addressed self-directed change and learning, power and affiliation motivation, alcoholism and aggression, and leadership and management competencies and development. Boyatzis is author of *The Competent Manager: A Model for Effective Performance.* He received his B.S. degree (1968) from the Massachusetts Institute of Technology in aeronautics and astronautics and his M.A. degree (1970) and Ph.D. degree (1973) from Harvard University in social psychology.

SCOTT S. COWEN is dean and Albert J. Weatherhead III Professor of Management at the Weatherhead School of Management. He is currently the vice president/president-elect of the American Assembly of Collegiate Schools of Business. His current research focuses on the process of value creation, in its many forms within organizations. His prior publications have addressed financial planning and control systems, corporate governance, strategic planning, and educational change. He received his B.S. degree (1968) from the University of Connecticut in accounting and his M.B.A. (1972) and DBA (1975) degrees from George Washington University.

DAVID A. KOLB is the DeWindt Professor in Leadership and Enterprise Development at the Weatherhead School of Management. His current research focuses on learning and the role of conversation in learning. He is best known for his research on experiential learning and learning styles. His other research has addressed self-directed change and learning, achievement motivation, professional development, and leadership and management development. He is author of *Experiential Learning: Experience as the Source of Learning and Development* and coauthor of *Organization Behavior: An Experiential Approach to Human Behavior in Organizations and Leaders* (with I. Rubin and J. Osland) and *Changing Human Behavior: Principles of Planned Intervention* (with R. Schwitzgebel). Kolb received his B.A. degree (1961) from Knox College in psychology and his M.A. degree (1964) and Ph.D. degree (1967) from Harvard University in social psychology.

Ann Baker is completing her doctorate in organizational behavior at Case Western Reserve University. Her current research focuses on the factors promoting collaboration and "good conversation" as a way of building bridges across individual differences. She received her M.P.A. degree (1975) from the University of Tennessee.

Susan S. Case is an assistant professor in organizational behavior at the Weatherhead School of Management. Her research focuses on gender dynamics in work organizations and managerial development in the multicultural workforce. She received her Ph.D. degree (1985) from the State University of New York, Buffalo, in organizational administration and policy.

David Leonard is completing his doctorate in organizational behavior at Case Western Reserve University. His current research focuses on competencies and competency development of project managers. He received his M.A. degree (1990) from the University of Richmond in psychology.

Anne Renio-McKee is an adjunct assistant professor at the Wharton School of the University of Pennsylvania, teaching primarily in the Leadership Program. Her research focuses on creating programs and environments for diverse students to engage in self-directed learning in graduate programs. She received her

Ph.D. degree (1990) from Case Western Reserve University in organizational behavior.

Kenneth Rhee is completing his doctorate in organizational behavior at Case Western Reserve University. His current research focuses on the rhythms and patterns of self-directed change and learning during a two-year MBA program. He received his M.B.A. degree (1989) from Boston University.

Lorraine Thompson is completing her doctorate in organizational behavior at Case Western Reserve University. Her current research focuses on the impact of learning goals and learning plans in stimulating changes on the part of students in graduate management programs. She received her M.B.A. degree (1987) from the University of New Hampshire.

Innovation in Professional Education

One

INTRODUCTION: TAKING THE PATH TOWARD LEARNING

Richard E. Boyatzis, Scott S. Cowen, and David A. Kolb

Managing change in the academic curriculum, in what is taught and how it is learned, must rank among the top twenty-first-century management challenges for higher education. Universities today often find it easier to construct buildings and increase endowments than to bring about fundamental improvements in the teaching and learning processes. The University of Michigan's National Center to Improve Postsecondary Teaching and Learning states that curriculum revision takes an average of five years to complete (Genthon, 1989). If we assume that the programs thus revised are not revised again for five to twenty years, we see that the fundamental knowledge base communicated to students changes in a ten- to fifteen-year cycle. This is too slow for the pace of the twenty-first century.

A shorter curriculum revision cycle is not enough, however, to respond to the learning requirements of individuals in the world society of the twenty-first century. There is a need for innovation in the learning process. Ernest Boyer (1987), president of the Carnegie Foundation for the Advancement of Teaching, has imagined the sorry state of the telephone if AT&T had invested as little in communications research and development as higher education has invested in R&D on learning.

Increased productivity in learning is essential if higher education is to keep its leadership role in developing human potential.

We cannot, in this book, offer a review of curriculum change processes in the many disciplines and professions and unique university settings that comprise higher education, nor can we catalogue the many innovations now occurring in the educational process. Instead, we present our attempt and that of our institution to grapple with these issues as a case study of some of the opportunities, problems, and dilemmas we have experienced. Our purpose is to reflect on the process of curriculum innovation as it occurred in our institution to see if there are any lessons to be learned that might apply in other areas of higher education. We have viewed ourselves as travelers on a path from a traditional focus on teaching to a focus on learning — or more accurately, to a focus on learning and teaching. We offer the story of our process, successes and failures, strides and stumbles.

This journey of the Weatherhead School of Management (WSOM) began in 1979, when the dean and faculty began discussions about the school's future. In 1984, a series of discussions about the strategy of the school focused these efforts. An early attempt to change the nature of the MBA program failed in 1984. A series of studies about our processes, objectives, and accomplishments began in 1987 and continue today. Another attempt to change the MBA program in early 1988 failed to win faculty support. They said, "Let's not tinker. The proposal is not a sufficiently dramatic change." New curriculum design efforts began in early 1988 and were completed in early 1990, resulting in pilot testing of elements of the new MBA program in 1989–90 and full-scale implementation in August 1990. Now, in the fifth year of implementation, we find ourselves continuing to make significant changes and discovering new destinations for our journey.

The Crisis Facing Management Education

The criticisms of graduates of MBA programs in recent years (Porter and McKibbin, 1988) and declining enrollments are matters of concern for faculty and deans of graduate schools of management. Similar waves of increasing and then rapidly decreasing enrollments have faced other professional schools recently, such as dentistry, nursing, and law. The shock of "losing favor" and experiencing decreasing enrollments after years of steady increases adds a sense of urgency to other forces affecting professional education.

The cost of a graduate education has increased dramatically while, at the same time, degreee escalation (that is, the need to have a graduate degree, whereas years ago merely a college degree was thought to be sufficient for success in life) has reached many occupations. Embarrassing statistics on the comparative performance of U.S. high school graduates have added to the growing frustration with the plight of public schools.

Parents, students, educators, prospective employers, and politicians have joined in a call for accountability from the educational system. Sometimes the spirit of quality improvement has infused an institution. Sometimes a desire to get more recognition and competitive advantage or a sense of desperation in trying not to lose students is driving schools to change. Even accrediting bodies have joined in the increased demands, and with recent changes in federal educational policies and practices, they have begun to demand evidence of continuous improvement in accreditation reviews of institutions. For example, outcome studies showing evidence of student change are now requested in such reviews of professional programs.

Regardless of the driving forces, professional programs are exploring change to meet these new demands. Deans and faculty have turned their attention to the educational objectives and processes in their programs.

Graduate management (that is, MBA) programs are changing to meet these new demands (Albanese and others, 1990; William Laidlaw, personal communication, August 1992); some are changing dramatically. Programs are experimenting in a variety of ways. Some are trying the least disruptive change of adding a course on ethics or electives on international management. Others are trying complicated changes involving elements such as integrated modules to deliver basic knowledge, assessment and development courses or workshops, international projects, internships, and so forth. Will the changes produce sufficient benefit to warrant the expense of time, energy, and money in developing and implementing them? Will they be durable?

Six common criticisms of MBA graduates seem to be expressed in books, newspapers, and magazines ("B-Schools Are Failing the US," 1988; Muller, Porter, and Rehder, 1988; Porter and McKibbin, 1988; Fuchsberg, 1990; Louis, 1990). MBA graduates are viewed as: (1) too analytical, not practical and action oriented; (2) lacking interpersonal, and in particular, communications skills; (3) parochial, not global in their thinking and values; (4) having exceedingly high expectations about their first jobs after graduation—wanting to enter middle-level management and move into vice-presidential positions quickly; (5) not oriented toward information resources and systems; and (6) not working well in groups. MBA graduates vary tremendously, but these criticisms have been made by too many different types of people (including employers, recruiters, alumni-MBAs themselves later in life, educators, administrators, and parents) to be a shared delusion.

The criticisms of graduates of other professional programs often appear similar. Medical schools are concerned about infusing a sense of compassion, caring for patients as human beings and not merely as disease-bearing problems to be solved, and formulating new guidelines for ethical practices. Law schools are worried about producing trial attorneys who can present their client's case, rather than embarrass the judge and bore the jury. They are also turning attention to client management, diversity, and globalization. Dental and nursing schools are attempting to prepare people for more activist roles in society, assuming more responsibility for the wellness or health of the whole person and family.

In the past twenty to thirty years, the challenges to professional schools have typically been in pursuit of other objectives, such as research productivity or professional certification of individuals. As a result, the current state of professional education is comfortable, but vulnerable. Forces threatening the future of professional education include decreases in the available jobs. For example, the number of managerial jobs in large corporations has declined significantly in the last fifteen years. Similarly, health care reforms have raised the question of whether there are too many physicians. Dentistry has already sustained a prolonged period of oversupply in the marketplace and the resulting closing of dental schools.

At the same time, an increasing number of older and experienced people are pursuing new interests or trying to make career changes. Whether they are seeking to broaden their perspectives or hoping for another chance at a new career, many are turning to institutions of higher education to help them realize these goals.

Some of these individuals already have professional degrees but are attending management schools to sharpen their skills at managing others, whether the others are physicians, lawyers, engineers, or salespeople. Some are trying to start over again, especially after being laid off, downsized, deselected, early retired, or any of the other polite ways of saying cast aside.

Therefore, graduate management programs and management continuing education have an opportunity to position themselves for the future. The graduates of management programs should be better able to address the challenges of their organizations and of an increasingly complex society than the entrants to our programs are. Their increased capability should be reflected in: (1) a greater base of knowledge related to management; (2) a broader range of abilities or more sophisticated levels of abilities related to effectiveness in management; and (3) an awareness of their values as well as of alternative viewpoints in a diverse world. These increased capabilities are building on a wide range of existing talent, which needs to be respected and incorporated into the development process. As the students entering professional programs — and, in particular, management programs — become more sophisticated, or at least more experienced, each brings to the educational program a rich array of experiences, models and theories developed to make sense of their world, and observations, beliefs, and practices nurtured by their past work environments.

We believe that to have a place in the future and turn the

threats into opportunities, graduate management education will have to make the transition from a teaching perspective to a learning perspective. Actually, the perspective will need to incorporate both teaching and learning, but since the past and current situations are embedded in one perspective, we feel a need to emphasize learning. As Newmann and Archbald (1992, p. 72) point out, professionals and managers "face the primary challenge of producing, rather than reproducing knowledge." This act of creation requires the full capability of the individual, combined with curiosity and eagerness — the processes involved in learning.

None of the ideas about to be presented are new. The challenge is that we must do them! Like collaborating with others for peaceful resolution of conflict, we often "know what" to do, have concepts for "how" to do it, and even may "want" to do it, but we do not do it, or do not do it consistently! This is the serious and complex challenge to graduate management education, indeed, all professional education, for the twenty-first century. Can we create environments in which students can learn? Can they acquire the knowledge, abilities, and values important to their organizations in the future?

Getting Lost on the Path from Teaching to Learning

Most faculty began their careers with a passionate commitment to learning. Many faculty also started out with a desire to work with students and affect, if not inspire, their learning. A variety of factors have turned many of us from our path. *It has been easy for us to become victims of our socialization within academic disciplines and institutions rather than masters of our vision.*

As Figure 1.1 shows, three factors in our environment encourage a focus on teaching:

1. The tendency to view faculty as experts — that is, as unique sources of wisdom
2. The reward system for faculty, which stresses research rather than teaching, and values papers about teaching and learning less than papers about the concepts within the discipline

3. The emphasis on faculty autonomy (if students were viewed as customers or clients, faculty would have to surrender some of this autonomy)

Figure 1.1. Factors That Encourage Teaching.

The view of faculty as experts

Faculty reward systems

Drive to maximize autonomy

TEACHING

One consequence of these forces is that educators tend to assume learning rather than promote it. Teaching and learning are then viewed as the same thing. Promoting learning from the teaching perspective almost always occurs within the confines of the educational "black box."

In research-oriented universities, a preoccupation with research crowds out eagerness for teaching. Acquiring research funding can become the primary objective of faculty members. While attending to the research process and acquiring research funding, faculty may revert to the use of traditional teaching practices (for example, using a lecture format and reusing old lectures) as a way to pursue quality in their educational activities with a minimal use of energy. It is not surprising that in this type of setting, with all of the potency of institutional and professional socialization forcing attention on research objectives, a focus on traditional approaches to teaching (that is, with the faculty as an expert dispensing wisdom) would emerge as a common practice and then become embedded as the norm.

Efforts to increase productivity and halt the skyrocketing costs of higher education have, because of this orientation, focused on teaching productivity. The initial reaction to these pressures for increased efficiency is often to try to increase the number of students per class or the number of classes taught by each faculty member. Faculty reluctance to embrace these moves, as well as their ingenuity in resisting such changes, often result in the perception that faculty represent obstacles to educational reform. It seems that "faculty bashing" is a logical consequence of the focus on teaching. Johnstone (1993, p. 4) offers a different perspective: "The more substantial and sustainable productivity gains in higher education lie in measures that lead to more learning from the students rather than merely to increased workloads of the faculty or of administrative and professional staff."

Meanwhile, as Figure 1.2 illustrates, three factors in our environment force a focus on learning:

1. Our original commitment to education and helping others
2. Realization that students are in control of what they learn, no matter what we say or do
3. Increased demands for accountability of educational institutions and programs

Experiments and innovations in higher education in the past forty years have shown that colleges can create environments focused on learning. Well-known examples include Antioch College and Alverno College. These colleges can sustain the energy and commitment of the faculty and stakeholders in creating a focus on the students' learning. The durability of this atmosphere and commitment appears to transform the institution so that it becomes focused on learning — learning about education, learning about organizational processes, and learning about institutional development.

Figure 1.2. Factors That Encourage Learning.

LEARNING

Original commitment to education
and helping others

Realization that students
are in control

Increased demands for
accountability

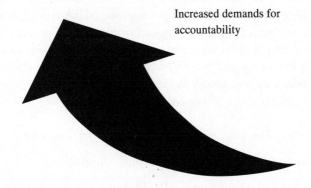

The focus on teaching incorporates an input orientation. A focus on learning requires an output orientation. As professors, we have been socialized and are continually resocialized into an input orientation as the only framework or epistemology of learning during our week-to-week and semester-to-semester academic life. An input orientation is easier and more convenient for us. The faculty member can say, "I control the input and determine it and evaluate how much material is sufficient to teach." Also, an input orientation is typically content specific; we can focus on narrowly defined, specialized knowledge.

An output orientation is difficult. It requires attention to the relationship between faculty and student. Both content and process must be examined to effect the desired output or explain progress or the lack of progress toward the desired output. An output orientation also requires discovery and determination of what the student is learning.

The curriculum is typically organized and communicated through a menu of courses defined, labeled, and organized by discipline. Since disciplines are often equated with departments, disciplines are also the basis for the organizational structure of universities. Both of these factors may result in a further emphasis on teaching.

The discipline-based conceptualization of the curriculum and the school reflects the faculty's framework for knowledge, not necessarily the student's. Although doctoral students will readily accept this approach because of their desire to be admitted to the professoriate or the profession, MBA students and others may prefer a problem-centered organization of concepts and curriculum. *A focus on learning would adopt the student's way of organizing knowledge and probably be less discipline defined and more problem-centered and contextually defined. The following list contrasts a learning-centered with a teaching-centered approach:*

Focus on Teaching	*Focus on Learning*
Input orientation	Output orientation
Discipline-defined knowledge	Problem-centered or contextually defined knowledge
Faculty's way of knowing	Student's way of knowing
Stakeholders: faculty and specialized field	Stakeholders: faculty, students, employers, alumni, and so on

Similarly, the pace and flow of understanding, logic, and "way of knowing" should be centered on the students' capability, not the faculty's orientation. This would result in a greater focus on learning rather than teaching.

When you take a learning perspective, you are forced to consider all the stakeholders—such as students, faculty, administrators, potential employers, alumni, the community, and so forth—because you must consider the entire environment or context in which learning occurs.

When we were students, we learned in our own way. But success in learning the material was profoundly affected by the methods used by faculty, their style, the nature of the material, and its perceived relationship to our experiences and academic goals. A focus on learning is nothing more or less than returning to the behavior, attitudes, and techniques we used or experienced as students. Adding to our own experiential background, we should incorporate the ways others around us learn. With a diversity of approaches to learning, we will be equipped to focus on our students' learning. Otherwise, we may be seduced by the powerful forces of socialization as well as by our desire to belong to and be viewed as a respected member of our reference group—the professoriate, our institution of higher education, and our department.

Conclusion

When we began this journey toward an increased focus on learning, we did not know what to pack. It was difficult to feel prepared because we were not sure where it would lead. The journey has been as stimulating as reaching the destination; actually, the destination as conceived earlier is, clearly, only a stop along the way. The first part of the book describes the processes and experiences resulting in the design of the new MBA program. The second part of the book reports results from outcome studies examining the impact of the old and new MBA programs. The third part of the book explores the observations, learnings, and dreams for professional education emerging from these experiences.

Part One

PROCESSES
AND DESIGNS

Two

LESSONS LEARNED: GUIDING STRATEGIC CHANGE IN HIGHER EDUCATION

Scott S. Cowen

In the academic organization, successful curriculum change represents one objective of an organization's total change initiative. Promoting awareness of the need for curriculum change, as well as generating the initiative to begin the process and see it through to fruition, are most effectively accomplished within the context of a comprehensive long-term strategy for transforming the organization. Developing such a strategy, securing its acceptance by the faculty, and transferring its ownership to them are the key elements in properly preparing the academic organization for any type of change — especially change relating to the core faculty activities of teaching and research. Strategy formulation should be a process of dialogue, in which the faculty engage in discourse with one another on the future of their organization and eventually articulate the philosophy and vision that will guide the development of the academic enterprise. Such a framework provides the organizational context for evaluating specific change recommendations.

It is often difficult to identify the origin of the process of strategy formulation and to determine the time when an organization is prepared to implement the key components of a new

An earlier version of this chapter appeared as "Preparing the Organization," *Selections*, 1994, *10*(3), 1–7.

strategy. At the Weatherhead School of Management (WSOM), seven years had passed before we were able to seriously consider instituting a significant change in our MBA curriculum. This was an exceptionally long period, even for an institution of higher education.

In our view, six factors were responsible for this lengthy preparation period. First, ours was the first attempt in the history of the school to engage the entire faculty in the development of a comprehensive, long-term strategy. Second, the faculty experienced perceptual difficulty in making the transition from a discipline-based mentality to a schoolwide perspective. Third, related to this shift was the faculty's difficulty in making the commitment to transformative as opposed to evolutionary change. (In fact, the initial reaction of the faculty to our strategic planning effort was that the organization simply ought to do more of what it had done in the past, rather than adopt new and significantly different modes of thinking and acting.) Fourth, the number of faculty and administrators willing to assume leadership of the planning effort was inadequate. Fifth, the planning process was not initially linked to the entire faculty, but was delegated to "position-related" faculty. Consequently, the strategy formulation process was viewed as an administrative activity rather than as a core task of the faculty. Sixth, no stakeholders outside of the organization were involved in the strategic planning effort.

Even under ideal conditions, the process of developing a reasonably well-articulated and well-accepted organizational strategy would probably require two to three years of effort before serious attention could be focused on the process of curriculum change. We believe, however, that the amount of time spent on the strategy formulation stage is proportional to the savings in time and frustration later in the process, as well as to the increased potential for developing a plan for significant and successful curriculum change. Based on our experience at the WSOM, an organization engaged in the first cycle of significant change should expect to devote three to five years to preparing itself for transformation and another five years to implementing its strategy — that is, a total of eight to ten years!

We believe that subsequent change cycles will require less total time because the organization has already experienced the "planning-learning cycle" of strategy formulation and experiential learning throughout its initial cycle of change.

Principles for Developing a Strategy-in-Context

It is not our intention to describe here how the strategic planning process was conducted at the WSOM in preparation for curriculum change, nor to describe in general how strategic planning should be carried out in institutions of higher education. (The academic and practitioner literature is replete with studies regarding strategic planning for the for-profit and not-for-profit sectors.) Instead, we intend to share some of the lessons learned at the WSOM that may be helpful to others contemplating or actively developing a plan for significant organizational change. These lessons take the form of six principles that we believe will increase the probability of developing a strategy-in-context for successful organizational change:

> *Lesson 1:* Adopt an outside-in perspective
> *Lesson 2:* Build on the seeds of vision and strategy that lie within
> *Lesson 3:* Develop a collaborative attitude
> *Lesson 4:* Challenge convention and tradition
> *Lesson 5:* Focus on substance rather than form
> *Lesson 6:* Provide multifaceted leadership

In the remainder of this chapter, each lesson is explored in detail.

Lesson 1: Adopt an Outside-In Perspective

Change in higher education may be difficult to implement because those who often control the change process — that is, the faculty — are most likely to be significantly affected by the end results. Naturally, to willingly and collectively take action that is likely to significantly alter one's professional life is a stressful, though bold, undertaking. At the WSOM, the faculty's ability to recognize the need to change, as well as to implement change, was greatly enhanced by their willingness to listen and respond to the needs of the school's key external and internal stakeholders. As we reflected on this positive attitude and receptivity to the needs of the school's constituents, we realized that our faculty had succeeded in adopting an "outside-in" perspective toward strategic planning.

Early in the WSOM's planning effort, a group of senior faculty and administrators identified the school's key stakeholder groups. These included graduates, current students, prospective students, donors, organizations that hire our graduates, other members of the academic community, the community-at-large, and the faculty. We then engaged groups of these stakeholders in dialogue regarding their expectations of the WSOM, the school's success in meeting these expectations, and the actions we might take to close the gap between the stakeholders' expectations and what we were actually providing to them. In retrospect, this experience proved invaluable in determining the key issues to be addressed and providing a justification for change. The most vivid example of the value of this identification process occurred in 1984, when the WSOM conducted an opinion survey of corporate and civic leaders in our local community. While this activity was undertaken primarily to determine the feasibility of mounting a capital campaign, the results provided the school with a dramatic illustration of the need for significant change. As part of this opinion survey, an independent firm conducted in-depth interviews with fifty organizational leaders to ascertain their views of the WSOM, its programs, and its impact on and value to the local community. Most of us at the school approached the survey process with a comfortable feeling about the results, especially since we had a relatively high regard for our impact and contributions to our community. To our surprise, the survey results not only failed to reflect our self-image but also clearly indicated that we had a lot of work to do to gain the respect, recognition, and support of the community. This feedback was the starting point for our recognition that change was needed and for our initial activities to ascertain the views and expectations for the WSOM from other key stakeholder groups.

That 1984 opinion survey marked the beginning of what has become a systematic and periodic effort to collect and analyze feedback from the school's stakeholders and to provide these data to the faculty as part of an ongoing process of continuous improvement. To make the best use of stakeholder feedback, however, it is critical to assign priority to each of these groups and their views. Such priority setting can be the most interesting and controversial aspect of the outside-in perspective.

Stakeholder priority setting is necessary because of the various and often contradictory views of an organization's constituencies. Furthermore, it is not possible for any organization to be all things to all people. Setting priorities and making choices are vital to effective strategic planning and change processes, and key decisions must reflect the expectations and aspirations of the stakeholders if the organization is to achieve appropriate recognition for its efforts. But how does an institution establish stakeholder priorities?

This fundamental question immediately gives rise to others: Why does our institution exist? To whom are we most responsible? Realistically, the number of answers to these questions will be positively correlated with the number of people asked. In the end, however, an organization must come to a consensus regarding the ordering of stakeholder priorities. (This ordering may be different with regard to the various educational programs or institutional activities offered.) In our particular setting, and in the context of the WSOM's professional portfolio of programs, we are most influenced by the views and expectations of the organizations that are most likely to recruit our graduates. This perspective dictates clear answers to questions regarding the context and content of our professional programs. For example, the WSOM's innovative MBA program is heavily influenced by themes such as outcome assessment, managerial skill development, integration of knowledge, and a liberalizing perspective on management education. In our discussions with organizational stakeholders, these themes were cited most frequently as being critical to the development of future leaders and managers. Yet, if one were to have similar discussions with students, it is unlikely that these themes would be deemed significant. Whose point of view should prevail? We believe that the organizations' perspective should prevail because, in the context of our professional programs, they are the ultimate purchasers of our product: professional degree graduates.

Another issue related to identifying and prioritizing stakeholder expectations is the time frame implicit in those expectations. For example, individual stakeholder expectations for the near term may be heavily influenced by prevailing environmental conditions relevant to that stakeholder group. Such expectations can rapidly and profoundly change along with evolving circumstances and concerns. Clearly, therefore, the short-term perspective does not provide guidance for institutional change. At the WSOM, we recognized that an integral part of our stakeholder priority analysis was to separate their long-term expectations from those that appeared to be short-term and transitory. Institutional changes oriented toward the long-term view are likely to be more sustainable, innovative, and substantive and to create longer-term value for stakeholders. Changes made in response to short-term trends are likely to be "faddish" and consequently unlikely to deliver sustainable value over time.

Lesson 2: Build on the Seeds of Vision and Strategy That Lie Within

Successful planning and change efforts in institutions of higher education are likely to occur when there is a close alignment between the needs and expectations of external stakeholders and the competencies, interests, and aspirations of the faculty. From our perspective, this alignment is critical to the development of an effective institutional strategy for change.

As previously mentioned, accomplishing change in an academic organization is difficult because of the unique character of the university faculty. The concepts of security, stability, academic freedom, and tenure — which are fundamental to the life of the academy — may limit a faculty's ability to adapt to changes in the external environment. Therefore, an essential component of effective strategy formulation in higher education is the institution's ability to build on its intrinsic strengths and aspirations and align these with the interests of external stakeholders.

The success of this alignment increases the probability that the faculty will become committed to strategic change rather than sabotaging the effort because it threatens their autonomy and collective vision.

A change in strategy that reflects the alignment of external and internal constituencies will also assist an institution in developing a sustainable, distinctive character that clearly differentiates it from others. One study analyzed ten institutions with reputations for distinctiveness and concluded that distinctiveness resulted from an institution's ability to adapt its strengths and values to an available market niche (Townsend, Newell, and Weise, 1992). Such an adaptation is sustainable, the authors stated, because it builds on the prevailing value system of the faculty and clearly satisfies the needs of a segment of the institution's stakeholders.

In the case of the WSOM MBA program, the alignment between our stakeholders' needs and the values, strengths, and vision of our faculty is expressed through a unique philosophy of MBA education built on the themes of value creation, competency-based education, and a liberalizing perspective on management. Because these themes were intrinsic to the educational philosophy held by our faculty, the curriculum change process was possible and, ultimately, successful.

As a prelude to the strategic planning process, institutional leaders must seek and recognize these seeds of vision that may be found within its internal constituencies. When aligned with the needs of external stakeholders, this vision can become a powerful catalyst for change and institutional differentiation. Without such an alignment, the effort is likely to fail, and the resulting frustration may derail further attempts at significant organizational change.

Lesson 3: Develop a Collaborative Attitude

Any strategic planning process must be designed and conducted in partnership among the organization's key stakeholders in order to be successful. This lesson, which is an outgrowth of Lessons 1 and 2, tells us that the effective strategic planning process is not dominated by any particular stakeholder group. Instead, the process is a collaborative effort among external and internal stakeholders, involving a series of dialogues and interactive activities that create a give-and-take atmosphere.

It is not uncommon in organizations for strategic planning to become a one-way process. This is often described in terms such as "top-down" or "bottom-up" or "internally focused" or "externally driven" planning. The temptation to fall into a one-way process must be resisted; otherwise, the institution's key stakeholders cannot develop a sense of ownership and a continuing commitment to the outcome of the planning process.

At the WSOM, the development of an interactive process involving key stakeholders was a priority in planning for significant change in our organization. For example, as an integral part of our MBA curriculum change process, we regularly consulted with stakeholders regarding the design of the planning process as well as the potential outcome. These dialogues helped to legitimize the process and, therefore, affirm its outcome at the completion of the planning effort.

To assist us in maintaining an interactive, collaborative planning process, the WSOM has adopted the construct of the "perpetual draft document," which incorporates ideas and actions under discussion. This construct openly conveys that the school welcomes the introduction of new ideas and feedback and that we view a strategic plan as a living document that is subject to change. Of course, in developing a new strategic plan, there does come a time for closure so that implementation can begin; however, it is important that this does not occur prematurely. One of the challenges of leading such a change process lies in determining the time to move from the planning stage to implementation of the plan.

During the course of our experience with the change process at the WSOM, it became evident that corporate vision and strategy represent the end products of the shared experiences and aspirations of the organization's key stakeholder groups. In contrast, a unilateral approach to the creation of a strategic plan for an organization will likely lead to compliance, not to commitment.

Lesson 4: Challenge Convention and Tradition

It is not unusual for a strategic planning process to encourage the maintenance of the status quo rather than to stimulate the exploration of a significantly different path for an organization. This tendency is especially likely in highly successful organizations or in those where nothing is obviously in need of overhaul. In these situations, the prevailing attitude of "if it ain't broke, don't fix it" often impedes the creation of an innovative atmosphere. To maximize the possibility of developing such an atmosphere, it must be made clear at the beginning and reinforced throughout the planning process that participants are expected to challenge convention and tradition in their exploration of future directions for the organization.

In the early discussion stages of the WSOM MBA curriculum reform effort, faculty constantly raised the question, "Why should we make any changes in our curriculum? After all, enrollments are healthy, student quality is high, and the school's reputation is solid and growing locally, regionally, and nationally." Since crisis was on the horizon but was not yet confronting us directly, the faculty had some difficulty in understanding the need to significantly alter the school's current mode of operation.

Of course, this attitude began to shift as we gradually gathered feedback about the WSOM's performance from external stakeholders. As mentioned above, that process indicated a cognitive dissonance between the faculty's views of the institution and those of the school's other constituencies. However, even after they were supplied with this survey data, the faculty continued to wonder why we were attempting to reinvent the MBA curriculum rather than merely improving on what already existed. Fortunately, one segment of the faculty strongly advocated our taking a more expansive, creative, and revolutionary view toward the curriculum reform effort. Their perspective was based not only on intuition, but also on their interpretation of the stakeholder survey data, which indicated that the philosophy of management education inherent in the school's existing MBA curriculum was rapidly becoming obsolete. Armed with these attitudes and beliefs, these faculty members were able to convince their colleagues that the "old ways" should be seriously challenged before we invested more time and resources in making incremental changes to what was apparently an obsolete curriculum design.

Challenging convention and tradition should be a theme that underlies any strategic planning effort. It is especially important that this perspective be emphasized in the early stages of the planning effort to ensure that the end result is based on sound assumptions about the future rather than on the staid practices of the past.

This lesson is one of the characteristics of what today's management theorists refer to as a *learning organization.* For example, in a recent report focused on innovations in higher education (Curry, 1992), the author describes innovative organizations as learning organizations that have the capacity to change as a result of alterations in the external environment, encourage a norm of innovation, promote systemic self-study, evaluation, and development, and encourage shared leadership. This "learning" perspective of organizations is the most effective mechanism for ensuring that the strategic planning process is robust and challenging and reveals valuable new ways of knowing and doing.

Lesson 5: Focus on Substance Rather Than Form

The *process* of strategic planning often becomes more dominant than the substance and creativity resulting from the planning dialogue. Early in the WSOM's planning efforts, we experimented with various methodologies for developing a strategic plan. Many of these methodologies were adapted from processes used by corporations or from the experiences of other institutions of higher education. We had hoped that these approaches would help us to maintain discipline in our planning efforts as well as ensure that the plan was properly developed.

As it happened, however, many of our early planning discussions focused more on how we were approaching the task than on the substance resulting from the planning dialogue. We found ourselves guilty of one of the cardinal sins of planning: being more concerned with form than with substance. Fortunately, we recognized this problem early in the process and thus were able to avoid the frustration, discord, and, worst of all, indifference that can set in among participants. All too often, observers of and participants in planning efforts come to realize that the process and methodology of planning are stifling creativity, innovation, and change and thus fostering status quo thinking and a "let's-just-get-this-done" mindset. These attitudes often lead to a hollow planning effort, which creates little long-term value for the organization.

Once the WSOM faculty realized our "form-over-substance" error, we moved quickly to alter our process so as to devote more time to discussing ideas and aspirations rather than to developing five-year, pro forma statements and well-articulated strategic objectives and strategies, or attempting to clarify in great detail each potential strategic path to be explored. Instead, we focused on broad, nonfinancial issues related to our external stakeholders' views of the WSOM; the macro trends likely to impact on the field of management in the future; and the school's existing strengths, weaknesses, interests, and desires. Thus, our planning process came to focus on idea generation and evaluation, continuous dialogue among stakeholders, and, ultimately, the articulation of strategic intent and strategic initiatives for the school.

The articulation of the WSOM's strategic intent involved the identification of where we, as a school and a management faculty, aspired to be in ten years, as compared to other regional and national schools of business or management. This intent was expressed in terms of a set of outcome measures of performance and achievement, addressing such areas as student quality, faculty profile, resource availability, research productivity and impact, community involvement and visibility, and academic program characteristics. The strategic initiatives that were subsequently identified represented the means by which the school's strategic intent would be accomplished. These initiatives were expressed as broad, directional statements of desired actions. We did allow for some ambiguity in the description and proposed implementation of these initiatives so as to minimize the likelihood of becoming prematurely mired in details and slowing our forward progress. We also embraced the concept of the "perpetual draft" of our strategic plan in order to communicate to the school's constituents that this was a living document, open to periodic review, discussion, and renewal. This perspective has allowed us to obtain ongoing input regarding the completed strategic plan, while at the same time providing the WSOM with a defined path to follow.

Admittedly, the process just described does not reflect the traditional concept of how strategic planning ought to be accomplished in an organization. Yet this process fit well with the culture and needs of our school and ultimately resulted in a strategic plan that was understood and accepted by our constituents and implemented with relative ease. Our ability to place substance over form and not allow ourselves to become overwhelmed by attempts to comply with the traditional methodology of strategic planning resulted in a desirable outcome for the WSOM.

Lesson 6: Provide Multifaceted Leadership

In most organizations involved in planning for significant change, leadership is the key ingredient for success. The WSOM's situation was no different. In reflecting on the role of leadership in our planning and change processes, at least four forms of leadership were required for success: idea leadership, inspirational leadership, process leadership, and political leadership. These four facets of leadership may be expressed by a single individual or by many people in an organization. The latter scenario, which is the most common, was the case at the WSOM.

Idea leadership is provided by those in the organization who offer the important ideas and concepts that direct planning and change efforts. Without this type of leadership in an academic institution, these efforts can be devoid of content, academic rigor, and philosophical justification. In the WSOM's case, idea leadership came primarily from three individuals who had strongly held beliefs and ideas about what was needed to create a truly innovative MBA program. These idea leaders emerged early in the process, were persuasive advocates for change, and did not hesitate to advance, justify, or revise their ideas as necessary. Eventually, these ideas — a value-creation orientation, competency-based education, and a liberalizing perspective — formed the foundation for successful curriculum change. In the end, the intellectual input of an institution's idea leaders will determine the quality, significance, and longevity of any curriculum change.

Inspirational leadership is required to build enthusiasm for the need for change. The WSOM's inspirational leaders were always able to articulate why change was needed, how we and others would benefit from the effort, and why the effort was worthy of the faculty's investment of time and energy.

We found that the change process can be frustrating and unrewarding when great effort is being expended if there is little visible progress. It was especially at those times that our inspirational leaders kept the faculty focused and maintained a level of excitement so as to ensure the continuation of progress. They were our "cheerleaders" who kept us in the game when it did not appear to be worth our while to keep playing.

Process leadership involves the responsibility for organizing and implementing the planning process. Our process leaders made sure that we followed a process acceptable to the school's stakeholders (especially the faculty) so that the end product would not be challenged or undermined for lack of adherence to "due process" during the planning effort. Such leaders must have the necessary skills for designing a process that is inclusive, focused on ideas, and oriented toward consensus building and team building. In addition, process leaders must have the capability to obtain closure at the appropriate point in the planning process. This is particularly important to the planning effort because it will ensure that the need for continuing dialogue does not override the need for closure.

As faculty members, we tend to enjoy the debate and dialogue that accompany any decision-making process and occasionally delay an end to our discussion for fear of subverting the flow of our colleagues' ideas, thoughts, and feelings. In fact, the more important the decision, the more likely we are to keep the dialogue going. However, there does come a time in the process where this good intention can become dysfunctional and jeopardize the ability of a group to move forward. Process leaders are often the individuals to whom we look for help in determining the time for closure. Their sense of timing is critical to ensuring that appropriate closure is ultimately achieved.

Effective strategic planning also requires *political leadership* from individuals who, by virtue of their position or personality, can actually get a strategy or change approved. As educators and academics, we believe in participatory, democratic processes for decision making and acknowledge that important decisions require the support of all faculty. Reaching a consensus about the institution's strategic direction — especially in sensitive areas of faculty interest — often requires that a few faculty "sell" a decision to their colleagues by spending considerable time in private conversation in order to garner the necessary support to arrive at a consensus. These political leaders must possess the respect and trust of their colleagues and be viewed as devoted to the best interests of the institution rather than to their own parochial interests. Without political leaders, it is often difficult, if not impossible, to obtain approval for a proposal for change, especially one focused on significant change to an existing curriculum.

The four forms of leadership described above are often required simultaneously throughout the planning process. Ideally, leadership is distributed among many faculty rather than a few, and the various leaders share a conviction about the need for change. In addition, it was our experience at the WSOM that all four forms of leadership are essential in order to make significant change. A deficiency in any area of leadership is likely to retard or jeopardize the entire process of planning for change.

Strategy-in-Context in Higher Education: Is It Unique?

The principles embodied in these six lessons are not unique to institutions of higher education. In reality, they might apply across a wide range of organizations. In higher education, however, their perceived value may be quite different — that is, they may be considered unimportant to an effective strategic planning process in an academic environment. It must be kept in mind that the value of these principles to higher education lies in the weight given to them during the planning process. For example, Lessons 1 and 2 encourage institutions to "adopt an outside-in perspective" and "build on the seeds of vision and strategy that lie within" — needs that often are either overlooked in planning efforts in higher education or are overtly resisted.

The value of the outside-in perspective is readily accepted in the for-profit sector, where it is incumbent on companies to maintain an external market orientation and customer focus in order to be successful. In higher education, however, the outside-in approach may be dismissed as overly commercial, crass, and limited in scope, and a customer focus as antithetical to the mission of a university. This extreme position results in an insular mindset and a disconnection from social reality. Of course, on the other hand, becoming excessively customer focused may lead to faddishness and short-term thinking. Our experience leads us to believe that institutions of higher education need to embrace an outside-in perspective to counteract a built-in bias for inside-out thinking. The built-in bias is an extension of one of the assumptions inherent in the focus on teaching. Faculty are experts whose role is to dispense insight to others who listen. Therefore, this approach would say, faculty should be the sources, and are the best sources, of insight and strategic planning for the institution.

Educators who worry that the outside-in perspective may lead academe too far afield in curriculum reform can take comfort in the message presented in Lesson 2. In the for-profit sector, it is possible for a company to reengineer or restructure itself in order to exploit new market and product opportunities. Therefore, in an extreme case, a customer focus could lead to a comprehensive transformation of an organization, encompassing issues related to leadership, the workforce, product lines, and financial status. This type of comprehensive restructuring is simply not possible in higher education, which is built on a foundation of stability and consistency through the tenure system. Any strategies adopted by a university must be consistent with the strengths and interests of its faculty; otherwise, such strategies are bound to fail. The key to successful strategic planning in higher education is to *balance* the outcomes of Lessons 1 and 2. An overabundance of one or the other in an academic institution is a prescription for disappointment, whereas in the for-profit sector, considerably more latitude exists for change in the short term.

Finally, the multiple leadership roles necessary for an effective planning process are somewhat unique to higher education, which places a premium on process and the intrinsic quality of ideas. These are also valued in the for-profit sector, of course, although not with the same passion as in higher education. For example, lack of adherence to process can defeat a good idea in higher education, a result that would be less likely to occur in the for-profit sector. Therefore, process and idea leadership are particularly important to successful strategic planning in higher education. Likewise, political leadership in the egalitarian university environment is the key to making sure that progress is achieved, since the hierarchical system that often drives change in the for-profit organization does not do so in universities.

Conclusion

The six principles outlined in this chapter, shown on page 31, represent the core lessons learned at the WSOM as the faculty engaged in an effort to create a strategic plan for growth and change. These lessons emerged from an examination of what we accomplished as well as the process by which we accomplished our objectives, and they are being used to guide the school's current planning efforts. We believe that our past experience, as reflected in these six lessons, has enabled our subsequent planning efforts to be more efficient and effective.

Principles for Developing Strategy-in-Context

Lesson 1: Adopt an outside-in perspective
Lesson 2: Build on the seeds of vision and strategy that lie within
Lesson 3: Develop a collaborative attitude
Lesson 4: Challenge convention and tradition
Lesson 5: Focus on substance rather than form
Lesson 6: Provide multifaceted leadership

Three

MANAGEMENT OF KNOWLEDGE: REDESIGNING THE WEATHERHEAD MBA PROGRAM

Richard E. Boyatzis, Scott S. Cowen, and David A. Kolb

Program Design Principles

The new Weatherhead School of Management (WSOM) MBA program emerged over a five-year period, culminating in critical faculty votes in May and December of 1989. Throughout the process, a number of principles guided our discussions. These principles emerged from the strategy formulation process and early faculty discussions about the MBA program revision. They were endorsed by a unanimous faculty vote as the design principles or objectives for the program in December 1988. This chapter tells the story of our journey during the five years of curriculum design from our perspective at the time of full-scale implementation (that is, fall 1990). The seven design principles are listed below, followed by a discussion of each.

An earlier version of this chapter appeared as "Reflections on Curriculum Innovation in Higher Education: The New Weatherhead MBA Program," in R. Sims, and S. Sims (eds.), *Managing Institutions of Higher Education in the 21st Century: Issues and Implications,* Westport, CT: Greenwood Press, 1991; it also appeared as "Curricular Innovations in Higher Education: The New Weatherhead MBA Program," *Selections,* 1991, *8*(1), 27–37.

Design Principles

1. The objectives of the new program should reflect the concept of "added value" from all stakeholders' perspectives.
2. Focusing on desired learning outcomes facilitates discussion within and among stakeholder groups.
3. Faculty should see themselves as "managers of learning" rather than teachers.
4. Professional graduate education should be liberalizing for the students, getting them to think about issues and situations in novel ways and to develop habits of the mind that stretch and expand their capacity to think and act creatively.
5. The new program should use state-of-the-art adult learning technologies.
6. The curriculum change process should be led by the faculty.
7. The proposed program should be resource-consistent with the current program.

1. *The objectives of the new program should reflect the concept of "added value" from all stakeholders' perspectives.* The value-added concept, which assumes that the program can contribute more to students' development and growth than the old, caused faculty to emphasize what students were learning, rather than what faculty were teaching. This perspective focused on how the WSOM MBA experience was contributing to improving students' knowledge and skills. It did not assume that the current program did not add value to students' capability, but that we could aspire to have an even greater impact. This was a major departure from the conventional wisdom exemplified by the expression, "If it ain't broke, don't fix it!"

There were many stakeholders whose views needed to be considered in the process of revising the MBA program: potential applicants, students, alumni, faculty, administrators, prospective employees of graduates, community supporters, and donors. While the perspectives of each stakeholder group were different, it was assumed that all stakeholder groups would have to be excited about the changes and perceive their added value. For example, students and prospective students are interested in the impact of the changes on their employment prospects.

Donors, on the other hand, are more concerned with community and national reputation. All stakeholder groups consider educational goals, outcomes, and responsibilities as important.

A challenge during the process was to avoid settling for the lowest common denominator of changes that all groups would accept and to strive for a design that was exciting, distinctive, and effective. Frustration with previous attempts at change and horror stories from colleagues at other institutions created a heavy blanket of low expectations that threatened to extinguish the fires of innovation. The "me-too" approach toward an MBA education was discarded, and a concerted effort was made to develop a truly distinctive MBA program.

2. *Focusing on desired learning outcomes facilitates discussion within and among stakeholder groups.* An orientation toward learning outcomes encourages viewing students and their potential from a holistic perspective. It focuses attention on the student's knowledge and abilities (that is, skills and personal characteristics) at the point of graduation. Desired learning outcomes become a focal point for discussions among people from different groups with different values and different responsibilities concerning the student. The orientation and discussion of outcomes often lead to a discussion of outcome assessment. The following questions are raised: What are the capabilities of our graduates in terms of knowledge and abilities? Are they prepared to enter, or reenter, the workforce? Are they capable of continuing the learning necessary for the world of tomorrow? As soon as the measurement of outcomes appears in discussions, measuring these same characteristics at the point of entry into the program becomes an issue. The outcome assessment approach thereby leads to an acknowledgment and respect for the students' expertise and experience at the time of entrance into the program.

3. *Faculty should see themselves as "managers of learning" rather than teachers.* This principle requires a shift of control from the faculty as sole director of the educational process to a student-centered approach to learning. When students' learning becomes the primary objective, students must have more control over the learning process. They will want to move at a pace and direction appropriate to their individual backgrounds, past experiences, personal learning styles, and so forth. Respecting this

diversity of capability and allowing for the diversity of future career interests require that the program be responsive to the unique learning needs of each individual.

The shift of attention from what is taught to what is learned encourages an overview of the whole MBA program, not merely the courses in it. The shift of the role of faculty members from teachers to managers of learning leads to a shift in the faculty members' thinking, from an exclusive focus on their discipline to a focus on the role their discipline plays in management jobs. The program involves courses but also relationships with students and other faculty members, extracurricular activities at school, and activities at work. All of these experiences are opportunities for learning and development. Although we encourage an individualized program, students should experience membership in the WSOM and Case Western Reserve University learning community.

This shift in perspective also raises the need for integrative learning. Courses are often effective vehicles for specialized learning, but they may not be appropriate vehicles to foster integration of learning. In the new program, we sought to help students find perspectives to integrate what they are learning in different courses, activities to link theory and practice, and opportunities to understand themselves and articulate their career direction. Vehicles for integrative learning are especially useful for employed MBA students. Whether full time or part time, students often do not have the time or the opportunity to explore what they are learning in their jobs.

4. *Professional graduate education should be liberalizing for the students, getting them to think about issues and situations in novel ways and to develop habits of the mind that stretch and expand their capacity to think and act creatively.* Many of us are concerned about the increasingly vocational and specialized nature of not only professional education but of higher education in general. As the world becomes more and more complex, and as organizations operate in vastly different markets, cultures, and economies, managers must be able to think in highly complex, global ways. The natural tendency of professional education is to socialize the person into the profession. This process involves learning to think and act like a person in the field and learning the values and

norms of the profession. While this socialization is a valuable aspect of becoming a professional and the goal of every eager aspirant, any profession can become so specialized in its jargon, values, and norms that it excludes innovative thought, sensitivity to new situations, and the learning skills necessary for continued professional growth and development. Since managers must work with people, and the workforce is becoming increasingly diverse in most countries, management education should be liberalizing and expand students' views about the global society in which we live.

5. *The new program should use state-of-the-art adult learning technologies.* Eight adult learning technologies were considered by the faculty during the curriculum change process: competency-based assessment, learning contracts, learning teams, experience-based learning, lifelong learning, machine technology (computers, video), credit for prior learning, and advanced professional studies. As described in other portions of this chapter, the faculty ultimately used all of these technologies except for the last two. The early discussion of new program possibilities began with the acknowledgment that the faculty should strive to adapt and adopt new methods of learning, especially those developed for use with adult students. Adult students have some, or often a great deal of, work and life experience. They have well-developed values, opinions, and thought processes for dealing with issues at work or at home. To learn a different way of thinking, these students must be given the opportunity to examine their current way of thinking; assess its value, costs, and benefits; explore the new way; and determine its relevance or potential to their lives or work. In professional education, the aim is to help them interpret their experiences and learn new and hopefully better ways to approach these situations in life and work. They must unlearn some past practices, or possibly relearn approaches discarded earlier in life.

6. *The curriculum change process should be led by the faculty.* Of all of the stakeholders, faculty are involved in the school and program for the longest duration and have the greatest impact on student learning. If faculty do not see the benefits and feel the excitement of the change process and the new program, it will be doomed to death from apathy. Faculty must be the

primary leaders of change in the new program to ensure that substantive change is implemented. To operationalize this, the faculty leadership—the elected Faculty Council—appointed a fifteen-member MBA Objectives Committee (MBAOC) comprising senior faculty and representatives of the school's six departments. Its charge was to develop a consensus program proposal in coordination with other stakeholder groups for approval by the Faculty Assembly.

7. *The proposed program should be resource-consistent with the current program.* Since no increase in enrollment was expected or desired, the school's budget would remain relatively the same. In addition, with two-thirds of the faculty tenured, it was clear that whatever program components were identified and developed, they would be implemented primarily by the current faculty. Thus, the current budget and the current faculty would have to be capable of implementing the new program.

Description of the New Program

This section touches on the intellectual theme as well as on the components of the program.

Intellectual Theme

The design principles reflect a number of philosophical beliefs guiding the new MBA program. In addition, we developed an intellectual theme connecting our courses, other developmental activities, and the learning environment within the WSOM. The theme is "creating economic, intellectual, and human value." This is pursued through four subthemes: managing in a complex, diverse, and interdependent world; innovating in the use of information and technology; developing the manager as leader and team member; and stimulating professionalism, integrity, and social responsibility.

Components of the Program

The new MBA program has six key elements: the managerial assessment and development course, the Learning Plan, the core courses, Executive Action Teams, perspectives courses, and advanced electives. Every entering MBA student is required to begin with the managerial assessment and development course, which teaches students a method for assessing and developing the knowledge and abilities relevant to management throughout their careers (see Chapter Four). The output of this course is distinctive from other "assessment centers" in three ways. First, current level of knowledge (that is, the subject matter of the eleven disciplines in the WSOM) and current abilities (the twenty-two abilities related to managerial effectiveness), as outlined in Boyatzis (1982) are assessed.

Second, students are engaged in the assessment activities for about two weeks, followed by seven weeks in feedback and interpretation activities; they then spend four or five weeks developing their Learning Plan. Classes are held once a week for three hours per class, in contrast to most assessment programs, which spend several intensive days in assessment and less than half a day in feedback processes.

Third, the assessment and feedback process is most effective when experienced in a psychologically safe, social context. In the first week of the course, students are formed into Executive Action Teams of twelve randomly assigned students, with an advanced doctoral student as facilitator. Most of the course activities are conducted in their team.

The Executive Action Team continues to meet during the following semester as a vehicle for integrating across-course learning and learning from other types of experiences, such as internships, mentorships, and clubs. It also engages in skill development workshops. Each Executive Action Team has a Cleveland-area executive as an advisor. It is expected that involvement in the team will develop the ability to work with others in groups.

The eleven required core courses, covering the range of knowledge areas typical in management education within a discipline, are as follows: accounting, labor and human resource policy, management information and decision systems, managerial economics, managerial finance, managerial marketing, managerial statistics, operations management, organizational behavior, policy, and quantitative methods in management. Each of these courses was revised to reflect the integrative, intellectual theme and subthemes of the program, as described earlier.

There are three perspectives courses in the program; students are required to take at least two of them. They are: managing in a global economy, the history of industrial development, and technology management. The courses are multidisciplinary, developed and taught by a team of faculty from at least two departments within the WSOM and one department from another school within the university. One of the objectives of these courses is to provide students with a liberalizing experience by exposing them to modes of thought and materials not typically covered in professional management programs.

Table 3.1 provides an overview of the new WSOM MBA program. This table, in contrast to the typical listing of courses taken each semester, reflects the way we think about our program. Riordan (1993, p. 6) comments on coherence in curriculum reform as follows: "It is important to assure that students experience not just a collection of courses, but a developmental and coherent curriculum. This means that the conceptual work of education extends beyond the domain of our respective disciplines to reflecting on and creating an undergraduate (or graduate) curriculum in general. . . . Faculty can accomplish this only through a common coherent vision of undergraduate (or graduate) learning." We take into account the whole program experience and its impact on various desired outcomes.

Observing the Process of Change

Developing the concept and implementation of change appeared to be successful in that all stakeholders were excited and almost unanimously in favor of the new program, implementation proceeded on schedule, and all stakeholders were still excited about the new program, as of fall 1990. A chronology of events is shown in Table 3.2.

Participation was a key factor in the process. Multiple efforts were made to involve all of the faculty in discussions, including the MBAOC meetings, meetings within each department, every WSOM faculty assembly meeting, and meetings of the numerous task groups. Nine task groups were formed to develop the components identified and endorsed by the faculty in their unanimous vote in May 1989. All stakeholder groups

Table 3.1. Overview of the New WSOM MBA Program.

Desired program outcome	Activities engaged in		
	First year	*Summer*	*Second year*
Create development plan	Managerial Assessment and Development course		
Develop liberalizing perspective on management			Perspectives courses
Attain general management knowledge and expertise	Required core courses	Internship	
Attain specialized knowledge and expertise		Internship	Elective courses
Build relationships with senior executives in various organizations	Mentoring program, Executive Action Teams, student activities	Internship	Student activities, field projects
Develop a value orientation	All courses, orientation program		All courses
Acquire team-building and team-functioning skills	Course projects, student clubs and activities, community projects		Course projects, student clubs and activities, community projects
Enhance skill development across twenty-two different abilities	All of the above, development workshops, progress on Learning Plan	Internship progress on learning plan	All of the above, development workshops, progress on Learning Plan
Job placement	All of the above	Internship	All of the above, placement activities and functions, interviewing and networking

Table 3.2. Chronology of Key Events.

1979–80	Formation of a Strategic Planning Committee; effort failed.
1983–85	Series of meetings of full faculty regarding planning, resulting in a draft position paper on the WSOM's vision, aspirations, and strategic initiatives; new dean and department chairs take office during this time.
1985–87	Discussions begin on desire for change; tone set for thoughtful and comprehensive discussions.
Jan. 1988	MBAOC formed to conduct study of faculty objectives.
May 1988	Curriculum committee proposal not endorsed in favor of more dramatic changes.
Aug. 1988	Subgroups begin brainstorming and identify possible changes.
Sept. 1988	Management education conference held; feedback of faculty objectives study obtained.
Nov. 1988	Visiting committee endorses concepts and activities as impressive.
Dec. 1988	Objectives of new program written and endorsed by full faculty.
Feb. 1989	Plan for May 1989 faculty vote on new program established; progress reports to faculty begin; departments' reactions to concepts first solicited.
May 1989	Eleven core required courses decided; informal meetings about proposed program; full faculty vote to endorse new program.
Jun. 1989	Nine task groups formed to develop new program components; intellectual themes developed.
Dec. 1989	Final faculty vote to implement the new program in August 1990.

were engaged in various discussions at each stage in the process. The style used for all such discussions was open, allowing people to state objections and ideas. Faculty, staff, and administrators were invited to participate in any MBAOC and task-group meetings. An important aspect of participation was the use of methods of discussion that suited the faculty culture at WSOM. Discussion would always proceed with analysis of raw data and then determination of conclusions. Most of the analyses began with the collection of data. Given the quantitative orientation of the faculty at WSOM, this approach proved inviting and provocative and allowed for full participation.

Patience and perseverance went hand in hand as key elements in the process. Patience was required to wait for people to join the process and become engaged in the excitement. There were many meetings; MBAOC met formally thirty-three times, involving approximately 1,050 hours of faculty time. Task groups, departments, other stakeholder groups, and full faculty meetings involved an immense amount of time. Everyone who wanted to be heard and every idea or issue were given attention. In this process, efficiency is an enemy. A misplaced sense of objectives might have resulted in merely discovering what was to be done in the new program (that is, design changes) and developing these changes, rather than considering the involvement and commitment of all stakeholders, which is the most important objective.

Perseverance with regard to the overall objectives was vital. Deadlines created internal benchmarks. Using whatever momentum was available was also an important element of perseverance. Momentum was provided by the reaction of WSOM's Visiting Committee (an advisory board of chief executive officers) to initial efforts; it was impressed and encouraged continued progress. A management education conference held in September 1988 was crucial in providing momentum as well as a wider perspective for our deliberations. Deans and senior faculty members from many highly regarded schools of management presented their thoughts, praise, and criticism of MBA programs. The conference ended with a half-day discussion of the WSOM faculty's objectives regarding knowledge and abilities in our courses using data collected in an outcome study (see Chapter Six). This discussion was led by the MBAOC, which reported on the study of faculty objectives. The conference made the WSOM faculty aware of the possibility of being different and distinctive from other schools. Another source of momentum was a pilot program begun in August 1989 involving a small number of entering part-time students. It provided encouraging information about their reactions to participation in elements of the new program. Another large boost to momentum was generated by the *Business Week* book and article on business schools, in which WSOM was cited as one of the three most innovative programs in the country and as one of the schools likely to break into *Business Week*'s top twenty business schools in coming years.

The politics of knowledge was essential to consider in the process. Efforts were made repeatedly to work within the existing power structure of the departments. Within the MBAOC, faculty and administrators learned and respected each other's epistemologies and autonomy. Department chairs were often asked to discuss particular proposals or ideas within their departments and to report their reactions and thoughts back to the MBAOC. The politics of knowledge was a factor that could also explain several compromises. There was a lengthy debate regarding the number of required core courses, with groups of faculty wanting to reduce the number to five, six, nine, or eleven. All positions involved a reduction from the fourteen core courses then required. The compromise consisted of each department or division having one required course in the new program.

Another compromise was the development of the concept of two MBA programs: the regular program requiring sixty hours of course work, and a short program requiring forty-two hours. Previously, students could waive any required course if they proved to the faculty of the department or the admissions committee that they had taken a comparable course at another accredited business school. This resulted in numerous negotiations as to length and cost of a student's program. Given the most frequent patterns of courses taken, it was determined that most of the students fit into the sixty- or the forty-two-hour programs. Now if a student waives any required course, he or she is able to take an additional elective. This decision takes the discussion out of the context of negotiations regarding time and money and replaces it with a discussion about learning and career appropriateness.

A number of operational practices helped the work of the MBAOC. The objectives of the entire effort were often repeated as a touchstone for meetings and discussions. Staff work was conducted to facilitate discussions at each meeting. A memo would be issued with minutes of the prior meeting, covering any decisions or assignments made or ideas generated. A memo was also issued to all committee members prior to each meeting highlighting the agenda items and providing documentation or thought pieces for their consideration. These memos provided a group memory and helped to minimize rediscussion of issues already covered. Since the committee meetings tended to be two or three hours long, lunch was provided to induce prompt attendance and create the impression that the meetings were not intruding into protected time.

The committee often broke into subgroups to conduct various studies or brainstorm ideas for discussion at future meetings. The staff work involved at least three studies of student and alumni views, two studies of other schools' approaches to issues, two studies of student-change outcomes (see Chapter Five), a study of graduation patterns, and the study of faculty objectives (see Chapter Six).

Information about the progress of the committee was made available to all faculty and administrators through progress memos and presentations at all faculty meetings. These progress memos and presentations were also a stimulus to the MBAOC to bring deliberations to a temporary close and take positions on various issues.

Generalization and Comparison

Throughout our efforts to revise the MBA program, we have been encouraged by the similar work of our colleagues around the world. Before we began, we were inspired by the model of Alverno College. Through its innovative use of assessment in the liberal arts curriculum, this small women's college has, in less than twenty years, moved from the brink of extinction to one of five U.S. institutions most frequently cited by academic deans as having a successful general education program (Mentkowski and others, 1991; Magner, 1989; Mentkowski and Strait, 1983).

Later, we searched for models applying state-of-the-art methods of adult learning to management education. The International Management Center in Buckingham, England, gave our faculty the model of an MBA curriculum based on the principles of action learning (Revans, 1982). Other institutions that had gone through a process of curriculum innovation in graduate professional education similar to what we were attempting helped confirm that we were on the right track. DePaul University's School for New Learning had created a liberal arts professional degree based on self-assessment, learning plans, and group-based learning (Justice and Marineau, 1988). In Australia, the Royal Melbourne Institute of Technology had built an MBA program using competency-based learning, learning teams, learning contracts, and experiential learning (Prideaux and Ford, 1988a, 1988b). Hawksbury Agricultural College had reorganized its entire curriculum according to the principles of experiential learning (Packham, Roberts, and Bawden, 1989).

Faculty from these schools have written extensively on their programs and in some cases about their process of curriculum revision. In the list that follows and in this concluding section are six tentative generalizations about the process of curriculum innovation in higher education based on these writings, our personal familiarity with their efforts, and our experiences at Case Western Reserve University up to fall 1990.

Tentative Generalizations About Curriculum Innovation

1. Curriculum innovation seems to be initiated by strong environmental signals from stakeholders.
2. The view that the faculty have primary responsibility for the academic curriculum is accepted widely in higher education.
3. Strong leadership is necessary to manage the change process — not only vision-oriented, involved leadership at the top, but broad and deep leadership in the system.
4. All of the curriculum innovations mentioned involved moving from a teaching to a learning perspective on education.
5. Curriculum innovation is enhanced by the creation of integrative mechanisms in the learning process.
6. Successful curriculum innovation results in movement toward a norm of continuous improvement.

1. Curriculum innovation seems to be initiated by strong environmental signals from stakeholders. Linking curriculum innovation to a strategic planning process is one way to sharpen and clarify these signals. Indeed, curriculum change may be difficult, if not impossible, without an established and reasonably well-accepted strategic context. Ideas, aspirations, and vision, no matter how vague, are the point guards for change, providing a focal point for dialogue among stakeholders.

Curriculum innovation as opposed to revision may require a transformative, distinctive strategy, rather than the common "me-too" strategy of modeling after the top schools in one's field.

2. *The view that the faculty have primary responsibility for the academic curriculum is accepted widely in higher education.* Successful curriculum innovation requires that this responsibility be translated into responsible, effective action. Collective, cooperative faculty involvement across disciplinary lines is essential for this to occur. Management processes that give voice to diverse viewpoints and promote consensus decisions work best. This takes time, so patience, perseverance, a positive attitude, and tolerance of politics are key.

3. *Strong leadership is necessary to manage the change process — not only vision-oriented, involved leadership at the top, but broad and deep leadership in the system.* Strategy formulation and curriculum change require the cooperation of the entire faculty and are dependent on the existence of a diverse group of leaders. These leaders play a variety of important leadership roles, such as idea champion, process leader, political negotiator, or cooperative team member. Leadership must also represent the formal departments and the informal coalitions in the school. Trustworthiness and credibility are important assets for anyone involved in leading the curriculum change process.

4. *All of the curriculum innovations mentioned involved moving from a teaching to a learning perspective on education.* The key aspects of this transition involved moving toward an outcome orientation, toward individualized learning, and toward the creation of a productive social context for learning. An outcome-oriented perspective on curriculum definition has two advantages. First, by defining the curriculum by learning outcomes, the processes for achieving those outcomes are freed for innovation. Current

practice controls the curriculum by controlling the process—through the academic credentials of the teachers and the number of contact hours with them. The fact that, in most universities, student contact hours are used to determine faculty workload and department size introduces tremendous rigidity in the curriculum, since fears of job security and departmental survival are easily raised by suggestions of change. Second, curriculum outcome models such as those developed through competence assessment (Boyatzis, 1982) provide a language for dialogue among stakeholders in the educational process about the purposes of education.

Individualized learning is particularly important for the diverse student population of the future. In the new WSOM MBA program, student learning goals and learning methods are individualized through developmental assessment and learning plans or contracts. The student's social context in the teaching perspective often inhibits rather than enhances student learning. The hierarchical one-way communication of the traditional classroom is not as efficient as structures like learning teams that enhance peer learning and two-way communication between faculty and students.

5. *Curriculum innovation is enhanced by the creation of integrative mechanisms in the learning process.* In current practice, the curriculum is fragmented and specialized, with many pieces often coming from different puzzles. Integration of learning is left to the student. Examples of integrative mechanisms in the new WSOM MBA program are the intellectual theme and subthemes, the perspective courses, the assessment and development course, the Learning Plan, and the Executive Action Teams.

6. *Successful curriculum innovation results in movement toward a norm of continuous improvement.* We and our colleagues feel the new WSOM MBA program that emerged from our consensus-oriented faculty deliberations marks a considerable improvement over the old program. We are also aware that political compromise, market realities, and the failure of some good ideas to gain acceptance prevented the new program from being even better. While there is some concern that the new program will

be cast in concrete for ten years as institutional attention shifts to other programs and priorities, we see a new spirit and attitude emerging to resist this ossification.

We borrow the powerful concept of continuous improvement from the quality movement to highlight this encouraging result of curriculum innovation efforts. The idea that curriculum revision and innovation is a continuous process is our best hope for coping with the pace and growth of twenty-first-century knowledge. We have seen this spirit of continuous improvement on the energetic and exciting campuses of other schools we have mentioned, particularly at Alverno College and Hawksbury Agricultural College.

Conclusion

We are not as far along as our sister institutions. As of the original writing of this piece in fall 1990, the new MBA program had not yet begun, but the spirit of continuous improvement was definitely present as we went about operationalizing our decisions in pilot courses and program plans. The lines of communication that opened during the change process across departments, between faculty and administrators, and among stakeholders made dialogue more frequent and easier. The sense of accomplishment we felt and the positive acceptance of the new MBA program by our stakeholders (based on advance publicity about the new program, applications were up 90 percent) stimulated a we-can-do-it-better attitude. The idea that the promotion of learning is the mission of higher education is itself an inspiration toward continuous improvement. Learning is not just for students anymore. Our future requires that we also promote organizational learning and continuing professional development for ourselves and our colleagues.

Summary of Design Principles and
Learning About Curriculum Innovation and Institutional Change

Design Principles:
1. The objectives of the new program should reflect the concept of "added value" from all stakeholders' perspectives.

2. Focusing on desired learning outcomes facilitates discussion within and among stakeholder groups.
3. Faculty should see themselves as "managers of learning" rather than teachers.
4. Professional graduate education should be liberalizing for the students, getting them to think about issues and situations in novel ways and to develop habits of the mind that stretch and expand their capacity to think and act creatively.
5. The new program should use state-of-the-art adult learning technologies.
6. The curriculum change process should be led by the faculty.
7. The proposed program should be resource-consistent with the current program.

Tentative Generalizations About Curriculum Innovation

1. Curriculum innovation seems to be initiated by strong environmental signals from stakeholders.
2. The view that the faculty have primary responsibility for the academic curriculum is accepted widely in higher education.
3. Strong leadership is necessary to manage the change process — not only vision-oriented, involved leadership at the top, but broad and deep leadership in the system.
4. All of the curriculum innovations mentioned involved moving from a teaching to a learning perspective on education.
5. Curriculum innovation is enhanced by the creation of integrative mechanisms in the learning process.
6. Successful curriculum innovation results in movement toward a norm of continuous improvement.

Four

CORNERSTONES OF CHANGE: BUILDING THE PATH FOR SELF-DIRECTED LEARNING

Richard E. Boyatzis

There appear to be no images, metaphors, or models for management from natural life. Although being a manager has been identified as similar to being a warrior, task master, coach, technician, juggler, parent, or facilitator, none of these is adequate to capture the complexity of the management job, or what it means to be a manager. Therefore, we may conclude that management is an unnatural act, or at least there is no "natural" guidance for being a manager.

If management is an unnatural act, then development and preparation to be a manager must be intentional. Unfortunately, most people and most organizations have used the "life experience" or "sink-or-swim" approach to management development: a congratulatory letter from the boss, a handshake, and a new title. Early preparation and lifelong development are increasingly pointed to as crucial to the development of managers (Kotter, 1988; McCall, Lombardo, and Morrison, 1988; Dreyfus, 1991).

The role of graduate management education (that is, an MBA program) can be to help people explicitly begin this process,

An earlier, briefer version of this chapter appeared in the *Journal of Management Education,* 1994, *18*(3), 304–323. I would like to thank Harry Evarts, formerly vice president of the American Management Associations, for his support and colleagueship in developing the first version of this course in 1979 for the AMA Competency Development Program.

regardless of their earlier experiences in high school, college, or work. But do MBA programs help prepare people for management jobs?

Given that the primary mode of teaching in graduate management schools has been the traditional, academic transmission of knowledge, we must question whether knowledge is enough. Studies of effective managers (Boyatzis, 1982; Luthans, Hodgetts, and Rosenkrantz, 1988; Kotter, 1982; Campbell, Dunnette, Lawler, and Weick, 1970) suggest that knowledge is necessary but not sufficient for superior performance as a manager. Graduate management programs based on the approach of building knowledge in the student are not adequate to prepare people for management.

Managerial Assessment and Development Course

The Managerial Assessment and Development course sets individuals on their path to development throughout the MBA program. Unlike a typical academic course, it stimulates students to consider drawing from all of their courses, noncourse developmental experiences, work experiences, and leisure efforts for learning and progress on their personal, developmental goals. Therefore, it seems particularly important to examine this course in detail.

Goal

The goal of the Managerial Assessment and Development course is to learn a method for assessing one's knowledge and abilities relevant to management and for developing and implementing plans for acquiring new management-related knowledge and abilities throughout one's career. Emphasis is also placed on becoming aware of one's values and the values of others. A detailed class-by-class syllabus appears in Exhibit 4.1.

Philosophy and Theory of Self-Directed Learning

The course is based on the belief that people learn most effectively when they are in control of the learning process and can

Exhibit 4.1. The Managerial Assessment
and Development Schedule.

Class	Topic	Activities
Residency	Intro	Introduction and Overiew of course Learning Style Inventory and Exercise Form Executive Action Teams In EATs (with Facilitators): Getting to know each other exercises
	Homework	1. Complete Individual Interview 2. Read Louis article and Syllabus 3. Complete paper: My Expectations About Learning
1	Setting Expectations	Review of Syllabus, course objectives and written assignments, Core Requirements self-assessment Workbook and waiver process, the importance of the EATs, and the role of the Executive Advisor In EATs: Discuss articles, learning styles, plan for meeting with Executive Advisor
	Homework	1. Complete paper: Projection to 2004, My Life Story, Model and Philosophy of Management 2. Complete Individual Interview
2	Assessment	Group Discussion Exercise (videotaped); Completion of Learning Skills Profile
	Homework	1. Prepare presentation for the Presentation Exercise 2. Complete paper: Written analysis of Business Case 3. Read career Dalton, Gallos, Thomas and Alderfer articles
3	Assessment	Presentation Exercise (videotaped); Discussion of personal career directions Complete Technology Applications and Personal Orientation Questionnaires
	Homework	1. Read assigned chapters from Boyatzis and Spencer and Spencer 2. Schedule and begin viewing faculty videos on careers and electives 3. Complete Adaptive Styles Inventory
4	Abilities	Introduction to the model of abilities, the codebook, discussion of video cases (*Working Girl, Executive Suite*)
	Homework	1. Complete the Abilities Self Assessment Questionnaire 2. Start collecting Others' Views of My Abilities

Exhibit 4.1. The Managerial Assessment
and Development Schedule, Cont'd.

Class	Topic	Activities
5	Abilities	Review of the model, discussion of video case studies
	Feedback	Review all assessment instruments and coding methods, and coded examples
		In EATs: View and code two of the Presentation Exercises to model giving feedback, discussion of feedback concepts
	Homework	1. In small groups, code *Star Trek* episode assigned
		2. Complete paper: Relevance of Abilities to My Desired Career
6	Feedback	In EATs: Return of assessment information, review of Group Discussion Exercise video, focus on Goal and Action Management Abilities
	Homework	1. Listen to audiotape of Individual Interview and review the coding of the Interview
		2. Complete My Goal and Action Management Abilities paper
7	Feedback	In EATs: Review Individual Interview coding, focus on People Management Abilities
	Homework	Review faculty videos
8	Feedback	In EATs: Review Presentation Exercise videos and code them
	Homework	Complete My People Management Abilities paper
9	Feedback	In EATs: Discuss readings, focus on Analytic Reasoning abilities
		Complete My Analytic Reasoning Abilities and Knowledge paper
10	Feedback	Review values and value orientations, self-directed change, learning goals concepts
		In EATs; Review values and learning goals, return LSP and ASI information
	Homework	1. Write a draft of My Learning Goals
		2. Review LSI/LSP/ASI information
11	Learning Plan	Review Learning Styles, Learning Skills, and Learning Flexibility
		In EATs: discuss learning goals and learning orientation, review and discuss group development of EAT
	Homework	Complete Learning Goals paper

Exhibit 4.1. The Managerial Assessment
and Development Schedule, Cont'd.

Class	Topic	Activities
12	Learning Plan	In EATs: Discussion of learning goals and implications of LSI/LSP/ASI to learning plans
	Homework	Begin drafting personalized actions and evidence for inclusion in learning plans
13	Learning Plan	In EATs: Discuss resources and actions other than courses
	Homework	Complete Learning Plan paper
14	Learning Plan	In EATs: Discuss learning plans
		Entire Class: Course Evaluation and Research Permission Letter

choose developmental activities best suited to their personal situation. We assume that people learn most effectively when they build on their current capabilities and experiences and do not repeat material they already know. We also take it for granted that feedback is necessary as a basis for planning growth and development. The course has a built-in assumption that participants in the graduate management program should add value to themselves as an asset and grow in their abilities and knowledge related to the management role.

The theory of self-directed change, which leads to self-directed learning, proposes that people initiate a self-perpetuating change process (Kolb and Boyatzis, 1970a, 1970b; Kolb, 1971; Boyatzis and Kolb, 1969; Boyatzis, 1982). Change and learning occur when individuals:

1. Articulate an image of where they are with regard to a particular characteristic (that is, The Real); and
2. Articulate an image of where they would like to be with regard to that same characteristic (that is, The Ideal); then
3. Perceive and experience a discrepancy between the Real and the Ideal, which is
4. Converted into a goal; this is

5. Translated into a plan to achieve the change, or learning goal; and then
6. Action and feedback with respect to progress occurs, and
7. Feed back information to the ongoing assessment of the Real and Ideal states, which begins the cycle again.

Using the theory of self-directed change as the guiding principle, you place control of the change process in the hands of students. After all, they are in control of the change process anyway. This approach merely avoids the delusion of faculty control.

Through the use of self-directed change and learning, students can use all of their experiences during the months or years of the MBA program as opportunities for learning. It is potentially far more efficient to access *all* of their experiences and to have them feel responsible for linking them into their agenda for learning than to have faculty responsible for creating the complete experience.

Faculty typically conceptualize and then deliver only one type of experience: a course. Students typically spend about 2,500 hours in classes and doing homework for classes in a two-year, full-time MBA program. Allowing for an average of seven hours of sleep each night, they are awake for approximately 10,500 hours during the same time period. *What are they learning during the other 8,000 hours?* Arousing and beginning the self-directed change process and guiding it through the use of the individualized Learning Plan makes all 10,500 hours opportunities for self-directed learning.

To engage self-directed change, the process should provide three components: (1) an assessment process and not merely a self-assessment process — otherwise the determination of the current state is more a function of social desirability and reference-group expectations than performance capability, (2) the generation of Learning Plans to help students focus their efforts and energy, and (3) vehicles for the reflection and integration from experiences to create learning.

A part of the philosophy on which the course is based

requires respecting the individual, especially in terms of individual experiences, theories, views, affect, values, and so forth. Since MBA students have worked and developed theories, or at least images, of themselves and how others should function, their personal theories or implicit images should be elicited prior to working on examining them (Hunt, 1987). Early in the course, students are asked to write several essays. One essay concerns their expectations about learning, including the role of students and faculty. Another concerns their philosophy of management. A third concerns their ideas about an ideal model of management (that is, the way a manager should act).

Building the Model of Management

Students determine their own learning agenda (or goals) on the basis of assessment on the WSOM management model. Although not limited to the characteristics in the model (that is, students are encouraged to add other characteristics of interest to them or relevant to their intended career), the model has twenty-two abilities, and eleven knowledge areas and also allows for preferences among value orientations and values. The abilities are subdivided into three groups:

Goal and Action Management Abilities

1. Efficiency orientation
2. Planning
3. Initiative
4. Attention to detail
5. Self-control
6. Flexibility

People Management Abilities

7. Empathy
8. Persuasiveness
9. Networking
10. Negotiating
11. Self-confidence
12. Group management

13. Developing others
14. Oral communication

Analytic Reasoning Abilities

15. Use of concepts
16. Systems thinking
17. Pattern recognition
18. Theory building
19. Using technology
20. Quantitative analysis
21. Social objectivity
22. Written communication

A detailed description of the abilities (that is, the codebook for determining when an ability is shown) appears in Appendix 4.1. The knowledge areas are as follows:

1. Accounting
2. Banking and finance
3. Economics
4. Labor and human resource policy
5. Marketing
6. Management information and decision systems
7. Operations research
8. Operations management
9. Organizational behavior
10. Policy
11. Managerial Statistics

As noted in the previous chapter, the program's overall theme is "creating economic, intellectual, and human value." This theme is divided into the following four subthemes:

1. Managing in a complex, diverse, and interdependent world
2. Innovating in the use of information and technology
3. Developing the manager as leader and team member
4. Stimulating professionalism, integrity, and social responsibility

The model of knowledge was constructed from analysis and discussions of the declarative, procedural, and metacognitive knowledge required for performance as a manager or for performance in the individual contribution jobs (for example, financial analyst, salesperson) that some of our graduates enter following the MBA program. It parallels the eleven disciplines the faculty view as reflected in the Weatherhead School of Management (WSOM) staff. The American Assembly of Collegiate Schools of Business (AACSB) (1987) established seven knowledge areas: accounting; business environment and strategy; finance; human resources and organization theory; marketing; management information systems; and quantitative analysis, operations research, production, and operations management. The WSOM model separates human resource policy and organizational behavior. It also separates operations research and quantitative methods and operations management. In addition, our model incorporates economics as separate from finance. All of these expansions reflect areas of distinctive strength within the school's history and current faculty.

The model of abilities was constructed from empirical studies of superior performance in management and related individual contributor jobs. An ability is defined as an underlying characteristic of the person that leads to or causes superior or effective performance in the job or jobs of interest to the model. Each ability is defined as having *behavioral indicators* (the various behaviors that "indicate" the demonstration of the ability in a setting) and the *intent* as to why the person is using the ability in the particular setting. The intent component is crucial in conceptualization and definition of the abilities because often similar actions are used for substantially different purposes.

Beginning with Boyatzis's (1982) model of managerial competencies, additional abilities were incorporated based on others' findings (Kotter, 1982; Howard and Bray, 1988; Luthans, Hodgetts, and Rosenkrantz, 1988; Campbell, Dunnette, Lawler, and Weick, 1970; Thornton and Byham, 1982). We also relied on work by colleagues (in particular, Boyatzis, Lyle Spencer, Murray Dalziel, and Richard Mansfield) at McBer and Company in the mid 1980s, which produced a generic competency dictionary for managerial and professional occupations. This dictionary eventually appeared in Spencer and Spencer (1993). Faculty reviewed and discussed these various abilities as well as future needs not evident in the workforce or organizations today and shifted the emphasis in the definitions of some of the abilities.

This model is different from the model of skills, abilities, and personal characteristics identified by the AACSB (1987). Their model included leadership, oral communication and presentation skills, written communication, planning and organizing, information gathering and problem analysis, decision making, delegation and control, self-objectivity, and disposition to lead. Sometimes models differ in the way they label a capability; an example would be self-objectivity versus perceptual objectivity versus social objectivity — all of which appear to reflect a similar, if not the same, capability.

Sometimes models differ in definition. The WSOM emphasizes the capabilities of individuals, regardless of the specific setting in which they work (Boyatzis, 1982; Spencer and Spencer, 1993; McClelland, 1985). From this perspective, the use of a capability, ability, or competency in a model depends on empirical validation relating the demonstration of the capability to superior performance in a job, but the capability is defined as part of the person. The AACSB model emphasizes an individual's behaviors as they appear in application to specific managerial tasks or job demands. This perspective focuses on behavior demonstrated during task completion and derives its definition, as well as labeling, from the tasks of the job (Thornton and Byham, 1982; Bray, Campbell, and Grant, 1974).

Models can be identified and constructed in various ways. The WSOM model seeks to identify and work on specific abilities, not clusters of abilities. Sometimes models differ in degree of specificity. A cluster of abilities might be called interpersonal communications. In the WSOM model, this cluster is broken into oral communications, written communications, empathy, and networking.

Another example of a model developed at the cluster level is described by Adair (1990) for pediatric dentistry. Among other models, he cites work by Stark, Lowther, and Hagerty (1986) identifying six aspects of professional competence for pediatric dentistry: conceptual competence, contextual competence, technical competence, interpersonal communications, integrative competence, and adaptive competence.

While "cluster" models may be useful in some settings, the increased specificity of the WSOM model is important because it is the framework around which students build an individual learning plan. To guide development efforts regarding abilities, students need behavioral specificity and situational guidance as to when and where to best use the ability. This is guidance through "intent."

The model of value themes was generated through faculty discussions. They represent shared concerns and perspectives most highly valued by the faculty and staff.

The entire model—including knowledge, abilities, and value themes—was discussed and altered through numerous discussions with all of the stakeholders, as described in Chapter Three. They are the shared view of what we—the stakeholders of the WSOM MBA program—hope our graduates will have and will be like when they graduate. It does not limit students, and in that sense is not a "cookie cutter" describing specification for standardized parts. Students are encouraged to place different weighting on the various characteristics in the model according to their personal dreams, aspirations, and careers. They are encouraged to add other characteristics that may be appropriate as well.

Determining Strengths and Weaknesses

An essential aspect of the assessment is determining strengths and weaknesses. The designation levels are: consistently and frequently shown (indicating a strength), occasionally shown, and rarely shown or not known. The latter may occur because of lack of prior opportunity to determine possession and use of the ability or knowledge area or lack of adequate information on which to make a judgment. The emphasis is placed on the degree to which the person "demonstrates" the ability or knowledge, avoiding the elusive issue of whether the person has, or possesses, the ability or knowledge but does not use it.

Another output of this determination is the level of priority of each ability and knowledge area for students' future jobs and careers. From the first class, through the various papers and assignments, and into the construction of their learning goals and learning plan, students are asked to anchor their thoughts and plans on the job, or types of jobs, career, type of organization, and life that they see as a desirable future. Therefore, when determining the third output — the level of priority for future development — students are viewing themselves in the context of their desired future.

Students use three sources of information about their abilities, knowledge, and values during the course to determine their strengths and weaknesses:

1. Their own view of where they stand on each ability, where they stand with regard to each body of knowledge, and where their preferences are regarding value orientations and values
2. The views and reactions of others (for example, the members of their Executive Action Team, colleagues and/or a manager at work, family and friends)
3. Coded assessment instruments and exercises

The students are told that no one of these sources of information is inherently more or less accurate than any other. Each source adds different information, and each has different vulnerabilities to distortion and error. Students are responsible for figuring out what it means, with the guidance provided by the course structure, faculty, and facilitator. Some students have found it useful to think about each of these sources of information as a different voice. In this case, a major activity of the course is for students to have a dialogue among the three voices and seek a consensus among them. We believe that people develop a more accurate view of current strengths and weaknesses by considering all three sources of information rather than one alone. The course methods and activities are designed to communicate and reinforce the message that students are in charge of interpreting and integrating all of the information provided.

Commitment to Growth: The Ladder of Commitment

To achieve the maximum benefit of this course and the entire MBA program, students must confront a series of questions about their development and future. They are informed that their growth during the program depends on their commitment to learning and change. They are told that people do not change unless they want to change and perceive the benefit of a change. The following questions are presented to the students as representing the logical development of commitment to learning and growth. It is difficult to seriously consider the answer to the second question, and continue learning in the MBA program, until the first has been answered, and so forth. In other words, progress in the course requires that students confront each question and arrive at an answer before proceeding. The questions are:

1. Are abilities and knowledge relevant to success in management or my intended future career?
2. Do I believe abilities can be developed? Do I believe knowledge can be acquired?
3. Do I think the specific abilities addressed in MGMT403 and the particular knowledge areas addressed at the WSOM are important?
4. Do I think I have little of this ability or knowledge area, or seldom use it? (At this point, each ability and each knowledge area requires separate commitment.)
5. Do I want to change my use of this particular ability or knowledge area in the next few years?
6. How can I pursue my goals to change and grow?

Components of the Course

The course is designed to incorporate five basic elements. These are as follows: (1) assessment of abilities, knowledge, and values; (2) feedback and interpretation as to levels of these abilities and knowledge areas; (3) documentation of current capability and past performance in these areas; (4) development of a Learning Plan for the period of the person's program; and (5) formation of Executive Action Teams.

Approximately one week is devoted to introductory activities, including exercises to help the students get to know each other in their Executive Action Team. Two weeks are devoted to assessment exercises. One week is spent on a lecture and case studies explaining the model of management used in the course (that is, the twenty-two abilities, eleven knowledge areas, and the associated value themes) as well as on preparation for the feedback. Six weeks are spent on feedback and interpretation. Two weeks are devoted to the development of one's learning agenda (that is, learning goals) in the context of one's life and career goals. Two to three weeks are devoted to development of the Learning Plan. This includes homework watching videos of faculty from each department describing potential career paths, their electives, and faculty members' interests. Other developmental resources within the university and community are identified and discussed and students are encouraged to seek resources in their current workplace; this is particularly appropriate for the evening MBA students. In addition, students review a set of tests designed to help them identify their preferred learning style, learning skills, and learning flexibilities. This information is considered essential in developing a realistic and personalized Learning Plan.

The assessment of abilities involves collecting information from three sources: assessment instruments and exercises, self-assessment, and views of others. The assessment instruments and exercises require students to directly demonstrate the ability being examined. The assessment exercises and instruments include:

1. Group discussion exercise (videotaped)
2. Critical incident interview (audiotaped)
3. Presentation exercise (videotaped)
4. Learning Styles Inventory (LSI), Learning Skills Profile, and Adaptive Style Inventory (ASI)

5. Technology Applications Questionnaire
6. Personal Orientation Questionnaire on value orientations
7. A value survey
8. Written comparative analysis of business case studies

The LSI is a measure of a person's learning preferences (Kolb, 1984). It asks respondents to rank nine sets of four descriptors that characterize how they learn. Four learning modes are assessed with this measure: (1) Concrete Experience, (2) Reflective Observation, (3) Abstract Conceptualization, and (4) Active Experimentation.

The Learning Skills Profile is a card sort in which students are asked to describe themselves by sorting seventy-two statements of skills in various categories reflecting different levels of skill acquisition and mastery (Boyatzis and Kolb, 1991; Boyatzis and Kolb, in press). Based on the underlying theory of experiential learning (Kolb, 1984), the items are organized into twelve skill scales. A respondent is asked to sort seventy-two cards into as many stacks as appropriate corresponding to seven categories: (1) I have no skill or ability in this area; (2) I am now learning this skill or activity; (3) I can do this with some help or supervision; (4) I am a competent performer in this area; (5) I am an outstanding performer in this area; (6) I am an exceptional performer in this area; or (7) I am a creator or leader in this area.

Each of the seventy-two cards has a statement describing a specific skill or activity. The respondent can form one stack, two stacks, or so on up to a maximum of seven. The statements are scored according to the stack into which the respondent places each card. Twelve scales result from the scoring: Leadership Skills, Relationship Skills, Help Skills, Sense-Making Skills, Information Gathering Skills, Information Analysis Skills, Theory Skills, Quantitative Skills, Technology Skills, Goal Setting Skills, Action Skills, and Initiative Skills. The reliability and validity data available suggest that each scale is an appropriate measure of the skills it represents (Boyatzis and Kolb, 1991; Boyatzis and Kolb, in press).

The ASI is the third part of a system of tests assessing learning dispositions and skills (Boyatzis and Kolb, 1993). While the LSI assesses people's preference for ways of learning, the ASI assesses the degree to which they can respond to the opportunities for learning in various types of settings. That is, the ASI shows whether individuals can adapt and be flexible in their way of learning (Kolb, 1984). It is scored in terms of a total score indicating Integrative Flexibility (that is, the ability to integrate learning from all possible ways of learning). It also provides scores assessing students' flexibility in responding to situations that offer learning through Concrete Experience, Reflective Observation, Abstract Conceptualization, and Active Experimentation — in other words, the four modes of the experiential learning cycle assessed in the LSI (Kolb, 1984).

The Presentation Exercise is primarily an assessment of students' Oral Communication ability. In the exercise, students are asked to prepare and make a ten-minute presentation on an organization for which they would like to work. They are provided with a two-page list of issues to consider in identifying their "ideal work organization." If they are not sure about the type of organization or industry in which they want to work, they are asked to identify an organization that intrigues them. They are instructed to approach the presentation as if they were recruiting MBA students to work for the organization. The presentation is followed by a five-minute question-and-answer period. The entire presentation and question-and-answer period are videotaped for later coding and analysis.

The Oral Communication ability is composed of six indicators. Each indicator can be coded as a 0, 1, or 2 (see Appendix 4.1 for a detailed description of these indicators). A total Oral Communication ability score is the sum of the person's scores on each of the six indicators. The Presentation Exercise is conducted with half of the person's Executive Action Team present, or about six people. Each person takes a turn making a presentation and answering questions.

The Group Discussion Exercise is a forty-five-minute exercise conducted with half of the Executive Action Team. The group is given three business problems and asked to discuss each and make a recommendation to top management as to how to respond to the situations. The exercise is videotaped for later coding and analysis. The Group Discussion Exercise is coded for the following attributes: Efficiency Orientation, Planning, Initiative, Attention to Detail, Flexibility, Empathy, Persuasiveness, Networking, Negotiating, Group Management, Developing Others, Systems Thinking, Pattern Recognition, and Social Objectivity. A person can be coded for having shown each ability once per business case. Self-Confidence is coded for each person at the end of the one hour; participants are assessed as to how consistently and clearly they demonstrated Self-Confidence according to the codebook.

The individual interview is a one-hour critical incident interview (Flanagan, 1954; Boyatzis, 1982; Spencer and Spencer, 1993; Raven, 1992; Rhee, 1992). It involves an in-depth reconstruction of three to five recent events in which the student felt effective or ineffective at work or during school projects and internships. An attempt is made to have half of the incidents reported represent effective events and about half represent ineffective events. The interview is coded for all of the abilities except Use of Concepts, Theory Building, and Written Communication.

The students are given the raw data or information (for example, the audiotape of the semistructured interview), the scoring keys, and the coding of these exercises. The audiotapes and videotapes have been coded by advanced doctoral students and faculty who have taken a graduate seminar on Thematic Analysis and participated in approximately twelve days of training through a computer-based, coder training program. At the end of the training, the prospective coders take a test, and only those who have passed the interrater reliability test beyond the .70 level of agreement on the fifteen frequently coded abilities become coders for the course.

The self-assessment has three components: abilities, knowledge, and values. The self-assessment on knowledge occurs through a *Core Requirements Self-Assessment Workbook.* It provides the outlines of each of the eleven required courses, corresponding to the eleven disciplines covered in the WSOM program. Students are asked to determine the degree to which they recognize, understand, and have past formal education or work experiences using these concepts. For example, for any concept identified, students are asked to list examples of events or times at work where they used the concept. If students determine, or believe, that they have such familiarity with more than 50 percent of the concepts in a particular required course, they are encouraged to either take a test to waive the course or meet with a faculty member from that department to determine the possibility of a waiver. Students who waive one of the required courses can take an extra elective at any point in their program.

The second self-assessment occurs through the *Self-Assessment of Abilities Workbook*. Students are asked to assess themselves on each ability prior to receiving the information from the assessment instruments and exercises.

The third self-assessment involves values. Students examine their value orientations through the Personal Orientation Questionnaire. They then develop a personal vision statement and determine the relative importance of various specific values through a survey.

Obtaining others' views of their abilities and knowledge is encouraged and required for their written analysis (that is, through the various homework assignments requiring interpretation of the "three voices" of information). Students are asked to solicit information from members of their Executive Action Team, colleagues at work, family, and friends about their strengths and weaknesses. A version of the *Self-Assessment of Abilities Workbook* is provided, without labels and the detail requested from the student, for collection of this information from others.

The feedback and interpretation component is designed to allow students to set their own pace. Discussion in the Executive Action Team is among a group of students all going through the same process, at the same time. The faculty and facilitators take steps to ensure that individuals can determine when, if, and how they discuss or invite discussion of their information. The only exception to this involves the discussion of observations of information generated in "public settings" and videotaped, such as the Group Discussion Exercise or the Presentation Exercise.

The scores and assessments are provided only to the student. The only others aware of the information are the facilitators and faculty of the course. No one is allowed to see or examine the information without the student's invitation and permission. The process allows for individual students to seek out the facilitator and faculty for separate conversations, if desired.

The Executive Action Teams are groups of ten to twelve students. The students are randomly assigned to the teams to maximize diversity, prevent people from forming groups with others they already know, and avoid groups composed of people who are comfortable with their similarity to each other. Each team has a facilitator and corporate executive advisor. The facilitator is typically an advanced doctoral student, or sometimes a faculty member, with expertise in small-group settings, career counseling, stimulating learning, and guiding structured experiences. The corporate executive advisor is a CEO, president, or executive director of an organization or reports to someone with that title if the organization is sufficiently large. The executive advisor may be from the private, public, health care, or education sector and is not to be confused with the executive or manager in the Mentor Program, in which each student develops a relationship with a middle-level manager or advanced professional. The team assignments during the first semester include work during the Managerial Assessment and Development course and other selected activities. One of the objectives of the Executive Action Teams is to help build a sense of belonging to a peer group, considered the most potent source of influence on growth and development during college years (Astin, 1992).

During the second semester, team assignments may include special developmental activities to be decided by the team members, such as oral communications workshops, negotiating workshops, and so forth. It is also expected that team assignments during the second semester will include discussion and integration of material students have been exposed to in the various courses taken and in experiences in their own work organizations.

Toward the end of the course, each student develops an individualized Learning Plan to maximize use of the resources and course offerings at the WSOM and to stimulate a process of self-directed learning. The Learning Plan is reviewed and approved by the facilitator and faculty to ensure compliance with the MBA degree requirements. It builds on the student's previous academic and work experiences and current capabilities and knowledge, to ensure the most effective and efficient use of the MBA experience.

The Learning Plan should become the student's document and guide. It is hoped that the student will modify the Learning Plan each semester. These modifications might include changing plans, adding learning objectives not previously identified, deleting learning objectives already accomplished, and so forth.

At the last class, students are asked to complete a course evaluation and provide their permission to allow the use of their information in research and/or in the training of future faculty and facilitators of the course. The information for students who do not give permission is destroyed after completion of the course. If students give permission, steps are taken to protect their confidentiality for the duration of the studies, which is currently conceived as fifty years.

Relationship to the WSOM Themes

Within the WSOM overall theme of "creating economic, intellectual, and human value," the primary purpose of this course is to develop human and intellectual value. By helping students learn how to increase their own capability and learn how to help others add to their current capability, we are helping them add to their value and others' value as human resources. Since people create economic and intellectual value, we believe that helping people increase their capability and the capability of others is a prerequisite to the establishment of economic and intellectual value.

The course helps students learn about and actually create, or add, value through helping them learn a method for assessing and developing knowledge, abilities, and values. This method will be useful to them throughout their careers as a stimulus to lifelong learning.

The course experiences help to create human value by directly addressing a number of key abilities. Working in the Executive Action Teams gives students many opportunities to give and receive feedback and to offer help and guidance to each other. The students work on communications skills while discussing the various topics and aspects of the course. Since the Executive Action Team is composed of twelve diverse students, they learn about the differences in how people from different backgrounds, cultures, genders, and other social groups hear, interpret, and act on information from and actions by others. Interactions with their executive advisor, as well as interactions with their colleagues in the Executive Action Team, provide practice enhancing their ability to build and use social networks. Creating their own Learning Plan and helping others create their Learning Plans enhance their planning ability.

Working with others in the Executive Action Team also addresses the WSOM theme of "developing the manager as leader and team member." The WSOM theme of "stimulating professionalism, integrity, and social responsibility" is an integral part of the course at several levels. First, students learn and confront integrity in terms of learning about themselves. The courage to candidly engage in self-examination and question beliefs and assumptions previously held about yourself requires integrity. Second, the theme of social responsibility is discussed from the standpoint of a person's responsibility to other students in terms of giving and receiving feedback.

Reactions to the Course

Reactions from several sources merit attention.

From Students

While the impact of the course will be determined with outcome assessment (that is, testing students just prior to graduation and in three- to five-year segments after graduation—see Chapter Eight), reactions at the end of the course provide some insight. In the first three semesters of full implementation, preceded by a year of pilot testing, a number of results were notable. Applications increased 85 percent in the first two years of the program. Even with changes in the enrollment policies, actual enrollments have increased by 15 percent (Boyatzis, Cowen, and Kolb, 1992; also see Chapter Nine). The program formerly allowed graduation with any combination of credit hours from thirty-six to sixty; in the new program, students must enter a sixty- or forty-two-hour program based on past experience and formal education. The years-of-work experience requirement was increased by the admissions committee.

Students evaluate the Managerial Assessment and Development course on a five-point scale ranging from "dissatisfied" to "satisfied." Although many students valued the course, their frustration and difficulty in coming to terms with information about their abilities from all sources led too many to question the usefulness of the course in the first semester of full implementation in the fall of 1990. Experiences during the term as well as in-depth evaluation information collected at the end of the course resulted in a number of substantial changes in the design of the course and the role of the facilitator. The results from the second semester were more encouraging. As shown in Table 4.1, 75 percent of the students in the spring 1991 semester rated

Table 4.1. Comparison of Course Evaluation for
Fall, Spring, and Summer of the 1990–91 Academic Year.

	Fall 1990	*Spring 1991*	*Summer 1991*
Number of students	231	70	19
Number of students completing evaluation form	215	65	19
Overall course rating	3.3	3.8	4.2
Percent rating course 4 or 5	44%	75%	100%
Percent rating course 1 or 2	22%	13%	0
Overall faculty rating	3.7	4.0	4.4
Overall facilitator rating	4.1	4.1	4.2
Course workload	2.3	3.9	4.7
Number of Executive Action Team activities outside of class	4.3	5.6	9.1
Number granting permission for research	89%	88%	89%

the course a 4 or 5 on a five-point scale, and 100 percent of the students in the summer 1991 semester did so. In subsequent semesters, the course evaluation form was changed so that the five-point scale extended from "poor" to "excellent." The percentage of full-time students appreciating the course, in terms of the course evaluations at the last day of class, have increased, with about 50 percent rating the course a 4 or 5 in 1991–92 and about 65 percent in 1992–93. Meanwhile, among the part-time students, about 70 percent have typically rated the course a 4 or 5 in 1991–92 and 1992–93. In addition, numerous students tell faculty during their second year, or last semester, that they have finally understood the importance of this course and the information generated through it. Recent alumni, in giving recruiting presentations to current students about their organizations, have often commented on the importance of the issues raised and addressed in this course, and how their appreciation of it increased as they reentered the workforce.

Regression analysis on the rating of the course showed that although the rating of the faculty was important, the significant loadings of the rating of the facilitator and Executive Action Team activities confirmed student comments. The role of the facilitator is critical in creating and stimulating group development and a constructive focus on course activities. The quality and preparation of the facilitators is essential in enabling the course to meet its objectives and the students' needs.

Student activism has increased. The number of student clubs has increased from five to eight, with three more beginning. Students asked to become involved in faculty deliberations and are now serving on three key faculty committees. Previously, students participated in only one of those committees, even though the policies of the WSOM provided for participation on all of these committees. Students also initiated and developed a Student Honor Code—that is, a code of ethics.

From Faculty

Faculty have continued to show enthusiasm and support for the new program. Although not every faculty member is excited about this new course, and some still quietly question its appropriateness in higher education, the overall mood is supportive. For example, in spring 1991, the faculty approved a new course evaluation form for all WSOM courses that includes a checklist for students to indicate which of the twenty-two abilities and five value themes have been "addressed or enhanced during the course" (shown in Appendix 9.1).

Two faculty committees have been formed to address two new efforts: (1) increased developmental opportunities for abilities and (2) the "second transcript." The first effort is straightforward. Following the development of their Learning Plans, students are choosing to participate in ability development workshops at a greater rate than previously and are demanding that more such workshops be offered than previously.

The second new effort is called the *second transcript* or *portfolio development*. The idea is for a student to provide recruiters with a second transcript or portfolio, along with the usual academic one indicating courses and grades. This second transcript will offer documentation as to the person's possession and use of the various abilities. While some of these abilities may be apparent during the first interview, many will not be. Typically, recruiters have twenty or so minutes to conduct an initial interview, assuming of course that the student has passed the "paper screen." It is expected that recruiters will view this second transcript as a significant aid in accomplishing their task.

Although a thorough exploration of the reactions to the new MBA program has been provided elsewhere (Boyatzis, Cowen, and Kolb, 1992; also see Chapter Nine), several other challenges were encountered by faculty and staff specific to MGMT403. In the earlier stages of design of the course, faculty brought their differing models of abilities or competence into the discussions of which abilities should be in our model. Discussions of empirical validity, appropriateness to a desired future world, and epistemological preferences took time. At the same time, there were still faculty who did not believe in the power of abilities to affect performance as a manager. Differences in work experience and academic discipline as well as epistemological differences resulted in some intellectually exciting discussions about these and other issues.

Once the pilot of this course was complete, preparations for the "scale-up" for full implementation were a logistical nightmare. Recruiting and training twenty facilitators, eight coders, seven faculty, and twenty executive advisors in the spirit of the course as well as the mechanics took a great deal of effort. Acquiring the appropriate equipment for the new level of videotaping and audiotaping activity, as well as the dilemma of finding secure places to store equipment and student files — including large numbers of tapes — became organizationwide issues. Finding rooms to conduct the course, with each Executive Action Team needing a room large enough for thirteen people plus equipment, involved numerous staff members and an expanding number of "discussions" with faculty whose classes had to be moved from their typical classrooms.

The initial implementation of the course, described in this chapter, was clearly not the end of the story but merely a stage in the process. Continuous improvement is needed in the course structure, materials, training for faculty and others, and integration into the MBA program. These steps demand an expanding group of people strongly committed to the course and eager to lead the effort.

From Executives

There have been other indications about the effectiveness of the new program. The executives involved in the Executive Action Teams as executive advisors have been tremendously excited. They offer unsolicited testimonials about their excitement at meetings and approach faculty and the dean in restaurants and cultural or entertainment events outside of school. When the second full year of the new program began, 90 percent of the executive advisors volunteered for another year (and another Executive Action Team). Since then, about 80 percent of the executive advisors continue to volunteer each year.

Design Issues for Management Schools

Ten issues were of concern to faculty at the WSOM and may be to faculty at other schools in developing and implementing courses such as Managerial Assessment and Development. They are: (1) self-assessment alone versus "three voices" of data, (2) feedback alone versus time devoted to interpretation, (3) ad hoc opportunities versus a detailed Learning Plan (that is, a plan for development that is specific, comprehensive, and consistent with learning styles and skills), (4) workshop format versus a "course," (5) intensive experience versus a semester-length course, (6) elective versus required course, (7) pass/fail versus graded course, (8) individual development versus social context (that is, development within a team), (9) connectedness to the school and each other, and (10) lockstep versus individualized curriculum plan.

Self-Assessment Alone Versus Three Voices of Data

The course is designed around the finding that self-assessment is filled with error (Goleman, 1985). Students in our MBA program (average age 26.7 at entry) are usually at a stage in their lives in which their own views of themselves are central. Added to this tendency toward egocentrism is the observation that those attending MBA programs tend to be unusually gregarious or assertive. Although some schools, such as the University of Michigan, are using an analogous course based primarily on self-assessment (Whetton, Windes, May, and Bookstaver, 1991), other schools use an assessment center approach to complement self-assessment. These schools include Central Missouri State University, Alverno College, University of Pittsburgh, Detroit University, Boise State University, Brigham Young University, University of Illinois, and University of Utah (Mullin, Shaffer, and Gelle, 1991). The list is not meant to be comprehensive, but it is indicative of the widespread variation and experimentation. The assessment center approach adds the additional "voice" of exercises and instruments coded by trained observers. In our course, we add a similar voice using the coders trained to a high degree of reliability on the coding system, who then code videotape and audiotape. We also explicitly add the "third voice" of others. The here-and-now benefit of having members of the Executive Action Team confirm, disconfirm, or clarify feedback to students and help them interpret the results is beneficial.

Feedback Alone Versus Time Devoted to Interpretation

Often, using the assessment center approach results in more time being spent on the assessment than on the feedback. In our course, as in other analogous courses (Mullin, Shaffer, and Gelle, 1991), more time than usual is spent on feedback *and* interpretation. Without the time spent on interpretation, students often do not change their prior understanding of concepts such as Self-Confidence, Empathy, or Persuasiveness. For example, in such interpretation discussions, students argue about whether Networking is a useful ability or merely office politicking (and is "bad"). Comparing their experiences at work and examining each other's behavior enable students to further refine their understanding of the concept and arrive at an assessment of their level of the ability and its importance to their future career.

Ad Hoc Opportunities Versus a Detailed Learning Plan

We also believe that to merely offer students the assessment, feedback, and interpretation would not increase their maximum use of the MBA program. Evidence from various studies has suggested that experience does not necessarily equal learning (Boyatzis and Renio, 1989; also see Chapter Five), and that people will not always make the best use of opportunities for development unless they are part of an intentional plan for development (Kolb and Boyatzis, 1970b). The development of the Learning Plan provokes a deeper level of thought regarding the specificity of future career interests early in the program. It also provides a structure for thinking about the best use of time during the MBA program. The Learning Plan should provide a method for lifelong self-directed development. It also functions as a type of learning contract for the student (Knowles, 1986).

A number of schools have explored the use of an abilities development course, often called Leadership Development. Whether in modules, residencies (such as workshops), or special luncheon sessions, these activities typically engage in training or skill-building activities directly, often without assessment or Learning Plan development. Although such courses may reflect an easier adjustment to faculty expectations about the nature of courses, the students may express frustration with the activities. They may report not understanding their relevance or utility or just being bored (possibly because they feel that they already have developed and refined a particular skill).

From our perspective, these courses are not engaging self-directed change and learning to the extent possible. People must change themselves. They must want to change themselves. They must conceptualize how and why they want to change themselves. They must have clear targets or images of desired states to change toward.

Self-directed change and learning also provide a much better use of time than alternatives do. If you think that development of managerial skills must occur through courses or workshops only, you have committed yourself to an awesome delivery schedule! If students discover a discrepancy between their ideal state and current state on a skill, formulate a goal for change, and construct a plan for working toward that goal, they can be using any or all of their experiences: inside and outside of class, in part- or full-time jobs, in projects and internships, in clubs and associations, in leisure activities, in civic and volunteer social service or religious or community activities, or at play.

Workshop Format Versus a Course

Among faculty, the discussion of whether activities such as assessment and developmental planning are a "credible, proper, academic experience" becomes most intense when a number of institutional and pedagogical issues are raised: the status of these activities as courses versus workshops, whether they are semester-long or intensive, their status as required or elective offerings, and whether they are taken on a graded or pass/fail basis. For the same reasons that discussion of these topics becomes so heated, it seems important that the activity be a full-fledged, academic course. Often the search for academic credibility is an integral part of the process by which these activities become an accepted part of the curriculum.

In addition, it becomes difficult to keep students' attention unless the activities are courses. Students' prior socialization as to the nature of education (which makes them want to be "taught" in the course format) is so strong that to alter developmental experiences often ensures low participation rates unless the experiences conform to the academic structure. In these types of courses, the use of experiential learning, which is necessary in skill development, is confusing or possibly threatening to the students. They may even see it as "distracting" them from their "real" academic activities. Developing ways of engaging the student's implicit theories of management, work, learning, and careers seems useful in offsetting the effects of prior socialization. Making their implicit theory or expectations of learning a topic for class discussion seems important, but this is again difficult, especially in a workshop format.

Some schools, like Emory University, are experimenting with a workshop-intensive format. Others, like the University of Michigan, have treated this activity as a course for years.

Intensive Experience Versus a Semester-Length Course

A full semester appears necessary for several reasons. First, students need time to absorb, reflect, and integrate the information. Changing one's self-image does not come easy, and MBA students are no exception to this observation. In addition, since a supportive interpersonal or social environment is important for experimentation and learning of this sort, students need time to build relationships within their Executive Action Teams. Some schools, such as Wharton, are experimenting with intensive "short courses" taken throughout the first year, while others have concluded that at least one semester or two quarters are needed per course (Mullin, Shaffer, and Gelle, 1991; McConnell and Seybolt, 1991).

Elective Versus Required Course

The desirability of having this type of course as a required course versus an elective comes from the observation that the students who volunteer for such developmental assessments are often those that already have many abilities and knowledge areas. The students who lack numerous abilities are typically least likely to be aware of these deficiencies and therefore would not want to do something to improve. For example, engineers who have been technically trained and have worked in a technical environment may not think that interpersonal and communication abilities are important to management. They may not have been exposed to "effective" management at work and so may not have seen any role models. Such students would not utilize one of their elective slots for a developmental assessment elective, especially when they could take an extra computer applications or finance course!

Another reason to make the course required is to encourage all students to recognize their strengths and attend to development of their "flat sides." That is, the course should seek to address abilities and knowledge areas important for effectiveness as a manager, but for which students are currently deficient. Some schools — such as the University of Michigan — have made an analogous course required (Whetton, Windes, May, and Bookstaver, 1991), but others — including Harvard — still offer such courses as electives (Clawson, Kotter, Faux, and McArthur, 1991).

Pass/Fail Versus Graded Course

The granting of grades provides a set of benchmarks during the course to students. Pass/fail does not. Since the course is different from most academic courses in emphasizing self-exploration and the development of the whole person, not just the acquisition of knowledge, students find it useful to have assignments graded during the early and middle parts of the course. The pass/fail approach, unfortunately, is often not viewed as empowering. It signals a lower priority, particularly when students are wrestling with the conflicting time demands of other assignments, such as finance cases, accounting homework, marketing projects, or statistics exams. The use of the grades makes expectations of performance clear. In our course, the grades are based on specificity, clarity, and comprehensiveness of analysis and their logic, not on whether students possess an ability or knowledge area.

Individual Development Versus Social Context

Creating a social structure in which students can explore and learn appears vital to most graduate environments, but it is particularly important in management schools. Models of management in technical and professional fields that supply people for management jobs often emphasize rugged individualism; asking for help is seen as sinful and failure is ignominious. In our course, students are told that the school should be a relatively safe environment in which they can experiment and fail on the path toward learning.

Since all management jobs require working with others, the Executive Action Teams give students an opportunity to begin building perspectives and skills in understanding and working with others. Since they are randomly assigned to these groups, they also must deal with the diversity and heterogeneity of the groups. Hopefully, the diversity becomes a source of insight rather than a source of fear.

The Executive Action Teams are an important learning vehicle in the course. Students use consensual validation as a method of learning about abilities and knowledge they demonstrate.

The utility of small groups to facilitate learning was first noted in Western civilization in ancient Greece, replicated in the tutorial concept at Oxford and Cambridge Universities, and most recently documented by faculty at International Management Center at Buckingham (IMCB) in the United Kingdom (Prideaux and Ford, 1988a, 1988b). For all of these reasons, the social context of learning appears to benefit from establishing Executive Action Teams and using the course structure as a way to help them get started.

Connectedness to the School and Each Other

We believe that students should feel connected to others and the school. Previously, there were too many convenient ways a person could become isolated. The development of relationships within the Executive Action Team during the course begins a set of relationships, and at least a process, that is useful throughout the remainder of their program and later in life. Students in a recent spring semester, who were all part-time students, reported that members of their Executive Action Teams got together outside of class an average of 5.6 times to study together for another course, meet with their executive advisor, have a social event, or engage in some other developmental activity during the semester while taking our course. We hope that most of the members of the Executive Action Team will continue to meet for such activities.

Lockstep Versus Individualized Curriculum Plan

Finally, a lockstep program — one in which all students take the same required courses in the same sequence — would be philosophically inconsistent with the new WSOM MBA program. Therefore, students have the opportunity to individualize their course selection within guidelines established by the faculty of each department.

Conclusion

While faculty exhorts students to challenge "what is known, and go beyond the limits of current understanding," it is difficult to do it ourselves. Years in graduate school are a long socialization period, reinforced through the years of assistant professorships and the journey to tenure. No wonder our assumptions about what and how to provide graduate education are deep rooted and relatively unyielding.

The spirit of the new WSOM MBA program and the Managerial Assessment and Development course is to explore, experiment, and learn better ways to prepare our students for management careers in the future. We have rediscovered an atmosphere of excitement and learning among the faculty arranging creative encounters with other stakeholder groups in our community.

The number of schools exploring methods to develop "the whole student" is growing exponentially each year. A candid exchange of the results and experiences underway is vital to our growth. We offer the story of our experience in this spirit, not as a set of answers we have found, but as a set of discoveries — sometimes frustrating and often exciting.

Each of the twenty-two abilities that are part of the WSOM model of management is defined by the intent of the person using it and the behaviors we would see when the person uses it.

Goal and Action Management Abilities

1. *Efficiency orientation:* The intent is to perceive input/output relationships and includes the concern for increasing the efficiency of action (i.e., maximizing output per unit of input). This will often appear as a concern for doing something better, whether this comparison is with previous personal performance, others' performance, or a standard of excellence. It is indicated when a person:

(a) Assesses inputs and outputs, or costs and benefits, with the expressed intent of maximizing efficiency (i.e., output/input);

(b) Expresses a concern with doing something better or accomplishing something unique;

(c) Seeks to exceed or outperform a standard of excellence, or goal; or

(d) Uses resources (e.g., time, people, money, etc.) to maximize efficient progress toward goals.

2. *Planning:* The intent is to identify and organize future or intended actions with a result or direction. It is indicated when a person:

(a) Sets goals or objectives in measurable terms;

(b) Outlines a series of actions — at least three actions — toward achieving a goal (the link to the goal must be clear, if not explicit) or overcoming a stated obstacle to achievement of a goal;

(c) Organizes materials or activities to accomplish a task or reach a goal;

(d) Takes calculated risks, evident in assessing and moderating risks in a situation prior to taking action; or

(e) Anticipates obstacles to a course of action and describes what to do to overcome them, should they occur (i.e., contingency planning).

3. *Initiative:* The intent is to take action to accomplish something, and to take this action prior to being asked or forced or provoked into it. A person displaying initiative is clearly identified as the initiator of actions in a situation. It is indicated when a person:

(a) Takes action first, not reacting to or being forced by events (e.g., he/she seizes opportunities);

(b) Takes action by seeking information in a nontraditional or unusual way (e.g., utilizes a wide variety of sources of information not typically used); or

(c) Takes action different than anyone else or the expectations of others.

4. *Attention to detail:* The intent is to seek order and predictability by reducing uncertainty. This is often enacted by a person giving careful consideration prior to and taking actions (e.g., making sure that your shoes are shined as well as your clothes pressed prior to a presentation). It is indicated when a person:

(a) Shows consistent attention to detail (e.g., double-checks information or accuracy of own or others' work, summarizes group discussion, etc.); or

(b) Keeps records diligently.

5. *Self-control:* The intent is to inhibit personal needs or desires for the benefit of organizational, family, or group needs. Although it is often not visible (i.e., if a person has self-control you cannot easily see them controlling himself/herself). It is indicated when a person:

(a) Remains calm in stressful settings (e.g., when being attacked);

(b) Explicitly inhibits aggressive outbursts or impulsive behavior that may hurt others or hurt progress toward goals; or

(c) Explicitly denies a personal impulse, need, or desire (i.e., makes a personal sacrifice) for the good of an organizational or group need.

6. *Flexibility:* The intent is to adapt to changing circumstances, or alter one's behavior to better fit the situation. It is often associated with a tolerance for ambiguity and uncertainty. It is indicated when a person:

(a) Changes a plan, behavior, or approach to one that is more appropriate in response to a major change in a situation or changing circumstances; or

(b) Changes a plan, behavior, or approach to a situation to one perceived to be more appropriate when the desired impact is not occurring.

People Management Abilities

7. *Empathy:* The intent is to understand others. It is indicated when a person:

(a) Understands the strengths and limitations of others;

(b) Understands the reasons for others' behavior (i.e., knows what motivates or demotivates specific other individuals);

(c) Accurately reads or interprets the moods, feelings, or nonverbal behavior of others; or

(d) Listens to others by asking questions and waiting for their reply, or taking the time to allow another person to explain or describe something at his/her own pace and manner.

8. *Persuasiveness:* The intent is to convince another person or persons of the merits of, or to adopt, an attitude, opinion, or position (i.e., getting others to do or think what you want them to do or think). It is indicated when a person:

(a) Gives directions or orders based on the rules, procedures, government regulations, authority of their position in the organization, or personal authority without soliciting the input of others;

(b) Explicitly expresses a need or desire to persuade others;

(c) Attempts to convince others by appealing to their interests (i.e., pointing out what each will gain personally);

(d) Attempts to convince others by anticipating how people will react to an argument, appeal, or situation and develops the communication to their level of understanding or emotional condition at that time;

(e) Uses questions or other techniques explicitly intended to result in the audience feeling and accepting ownership of the ideas, projects, or activities; or

(f) Explicitly expresses concern with his/her image and

reputation, the image or reputation of his/her organization, or its products and services.

9. *Networking:* The intent is to build relationships, whether they are one-to-one relations, a coalition, an alliance, or a complex set of relationships among a group of people. It is indicated when a person:

(a) Acts to build a relationship with someone that might be useful in the present or in the future to accomplish a task;

(b) Maintains personal relationships that are or might be work-related; or

(c) Uses a network of informal relationships to get things done.

10. *Negotiating:* The intent is to stimulate individuals or groups toward resolution of a conflict. This ability may be demonstrated in situations in which the person is one of the parties in the conflict or merely a third party. It is indicated when a person:

(a) Involves all parties in openly discussing the conflict with the intent of resolving the conflict;

(b) Identifies areas of mutual interest or benefit, often an objective to which all parties can aspire; or

(c) Determines the concerns or positions of each of the parties and communicates them to all involved as an initial step toward open discussion of the conflict.

11. *Self-confidence:* The intent is to consistently display decisiveness or presence. It is indicated when a person:

(a) Consistently presents himself/herself, verbally or nonverbally, in an assured, forceful, impressive, and unhesitating manner; or

(b) Consistently expresses the belief that he/she is among the best and most capable for a job, and likely to succeed.

12. *Group management:* The intent is to stimulate members of a group to work together effectively. It is indicated when a person:

(a) Creates symbols of group identity, pride, trust, or team effort;

(b) Acts to promote commitment to a team, task, or shared goal through friendly, personal contact;

(c) Involves all parties concerned in openly resolving conflicts within the group as a vehicle toward collaboration among the group members;

(d) Allows the group to take responsibility for certain task accomplishments and does not assume personal responsibility for them; or

(e) Explicitly communicates to others the need for cooperation or teamwork within the group.

13. *Developing others:* The intent is to stimulate someone to develop his/her abilities or improve their performance toward an objective. It is indicated when a person:

(a) Gives someone performance feedback to be used in improving or maintaining effective performance;

(b) Provides others with information, tools, other resources, or opportunities to help them get their job done or to improve their abilities (e.g., giving a promotion as part of their development);

(c) Invites others to discuss performance problems with the explicit purpose of improving their performance; or

(d) Explicitly tells another that he/she can accomplish an objective and provides encouragement and support.

14. *Oral communications:* The intent is to explain, describe, or tell something to others through a personal presentation. Although the overall quality and effectiveness of a presentation to the audience is the ultimate indicator of a person's possession and use of this ability, a number of components contribute to determination of the overall quality and effectiveness. This ability may be demonstrated in presentation to one or more people, in live or electronically reproduced settings. Some material allows this ability to be coded in great detail. When this opportunity occurs, the person is coded on the "degree to which each indicator is shown" through the use of the "0", "1", or "2" levels explained below each indicator. The indicators and their coding are:

(a) Relationship between you and your audience: Expresses feelings and responds to the expression of feelings in others (note: humor can be coded for this indicator);

1 = Does this once (e.g., at the beginning saying, "You must be tired. Stand up and stretch.")

2 = Does this more than once (i.e., clearly relates to and/or expresses the audiences' feelings explicitly)

(b) Structure: Presents well-organized material (i.e., includes an introduction, the message or concepts, and a summary); the message or concepts, if complex, are organized for the audience into a conceptual framework;

1 = Sets up the presentation (i.e., repeats the instructions or role-play instruction), says briefly that they will describe the issue and give a recommendation *and* shows some demarcation during their presentation through pauses or emphasis of when they are making a conceptual transition

2 = Explains the outline of their presentation, and follows it, or refers to it throughout the presentation *and* stays within the ten-minute period (allowing a thirty-second or so grace period—a person does not get a "2" if they run over the ten-minute period)

(c) Presentation of content: Uses examples relevant to the presentation that clarify the message;

1 = Briefly mentions examples

2 = Uses examples repeatedly to emphasize or reinforce the message

(d) Appropriate conventions and style: Uses symbols, nonverbal cues (e.g., gestures, posture, etc.), intonation (e.g., volume, rate of delivery and enunciation), and so forth to reinforce or interpret the meaning of the message;

1 = Gestures or uses enough intonation and nonverbal devices to enhance the presentation

2 = Uses symbols, nonverbal cues, and intonation to explain, interpret, and reinforce the message consistently, or repeatedly

(e) Charts and visual aids: Uses diagrams, exhibits, or other visual aids to explain the message to the audience;

1 = Writes an outline on the board, uses a transparency or handout

2 = Uses many visual aids (i.e., transparencies) or uses one repeatedly to explain the message to the audience

(f) Engaging audience: Speaks clearly and convincingly

to others (i.e., is articulate and persuasive in maintaining the attention of the audience or listener);

> 1 = Speaks articulately (i.e., you can understand their English, not necessarily the message) without interference from excessive "ums" or such
>
> 2 = Speaks articulately, takes a position, and maintains the attention of the audience in convincing or persuading them about their position

Analytic Reasoning Abilities

15. *Use of concepts:* The intent is to apply concepts to interpret or explain situations. The concepts should have been in mind prior to the event or situation being interpreted. It is indicated when a person:

(a) Explains, not just describes, events through the application of a concept, framework, or theory held prior to the event;

(b) Sees similarities between a new situation and a similar past situation and uses a concept, framework, or theory to explain the similarity; or

(c) Identifies discrepancies or variations from what is expected or desired in a situation or plan (i.e., applying a concept in the form of a plan or expectation).

16. *Systems thinking:* The intent is to order multiple causal events. It is indicated when a person:

(a) Describes multiple causal events (i.e., multiple cause-and-effect relationships) in terms of a series, plan of action and events, or flow diagram; or

(b) Establishes priorities among a list of at least three alternative actions reflecting a concept of multiple causality (i.e., A should be done first because it leads to B, which leads to C and we want C to occur).

17. *Pattern recognition:* The intent is to identify a pattern in an assortment of unorganized information or seemingly random data. It is indicated when a person:

(a) Identifies a pattern in events or information not used by others and uses the pattern to explain or interpret the events or information;

(b) Reduces large amounts of information through the use of a concept not previously applied to this situation or information;

(c) Sees similarities of a new situation to aspects of past situations of a different type; or

(d) Uses metaphors or analogies to explain events or information (this should be more than a figure of speech or single phrase).

18. *Theory building:* The intent is to develop, or invent, new theories, models, or frameworks that explain available information and predict future events. It is indicated when a person identifies a theory, model, or framework that explains available information and makes predictions about future events, where the theory, model, or framework is clearly different from those currently available or in use.

19. *Using technology:* The intent is to use computers, robotics, or other forms of advanced technology to perform tasks or functions on the job. It is indicated when a person:

(a) Uses a computer to perform statistical, accounting, or forecasting analysis;

(b) Uses a computer to create a simulation, model, or planning program to represent a system or process;

(c) Designs work requiring the use of advanced technology (e.g., robotics, CAD/CAM, etc.); or

(d) Implements a technological innovation in a system or process.

20. *Quantitative analysis:* The intent is to derive meaning from the use of arithmetic and mathematical symbols, methods, and theories. It is indicated when a person:

(a) Uses statistical models to analyze data and interpret its meaning;

(b) Uses quantitative methods in the diagnosis and operations of various functions of management (e.g., financial analysis, market research, SPC in manufacturing, etc.); or

(c) Identifies a problem in operations through the use of statistical methods.

21. *Social objectivity:* The intent is to perceive another person's beliefs, emotions, and perspectives, particularly when they are different from the observer's own beliefs, emotions, and perspectives. It is indicated when a person:

(a) Perceives multiple perspectives, or views, of the same situation or issue;

(b) Sees merits of differing perspectives, especially when they are different than his/her own; or

(c) Describes another person's thoughts, feelings, or values as unique to the individual in the context of others claiming or making stereotypical generalizations about the person because of a group or category of individuals to which he/she belongs.

22. *Written communication:* The intent is to explain, describe, or tell something to others through a memo, letter, report, or written document. Although the overall quality and effectiveness of a document to the audience is the ultimate indicator of a person's possession and use of this ability, a number of components contribute to determination of the overall quality and effectiveness. Some material allows this ability to be coded on the "degree to which each indicator is shown" through the use of the "1" or "2" levels explained below each indicator. Written Communication is indicated when a person:

(a) Relationship between you and your audience: Uses an engaging style appropriate to the audience (i.e., the audience would see it as easy to read);

    1 = Occasionally uses a quote, metaphor, and/or colorful adjectives, words, or phrases

    2 = Repeated use of quotes, metaphors, and/or colorful adjectives, words, or phrases (may include humor)

(b) Structure: Presents well-organized material (i.e., includes an introduction, the message or concepts, and a summary); the message or concepts, if complex, are organized for the audience into a conceptual framework, with the aid of visual cues (e.g., bullets, highlights, or headings);

    1 = Presents an introduction, message, and summary

    2 = Use of bullets, or list of highlights, or headings to indicate introduction, message, or separate sections

(c) Presentation of content: Uses factual information and/or quantitative data accurately and appropriately for the audience;

    1 = Cites several facts from available sources

    2 = Constructing argument using facts cited from available sources in which causality is clear

(d) Appropriate conventions and style: Presents a document using proper word usage/grammar, spelling, punctuation, and sentence and paragraph structure of the language of the audience (two or more errors would constitute not meeting the specifics below):

.5 = Proper usage/grammar appropriate

.5 = Spelling correct appropriate

.5 = Punctuation appropriate

.5 = Sentence/paragraph structure appropriate

(e) Charts and visual aids: Uses charts, tables, figures, or appendixes to explain or support the message or concepts.

1 = A chart, table, figure is used

2 = Charts, tables, or figures are used to make multiple points

Part Two

OUTCOME ASSESSMENTS
AND RESULTS

Five

PAST ACCOMPLISHMENTS: ESTABLISHING THE IMPACT AND BASELINE OF EARLIER PROGRAMS

Richard E. Boyatzis, Anne Renio-McKee, and Lorraine Thompson

Schools of management and MBA degree programs in the United States have been criticized as contributing to, if not causing, the decline of American industry (Hayes and Abernathy, 1980). They have also been accused of not responding to the needs of prospective employers (Porter and McKibbin, 1988). At the same time, the cost of a college education has increased dramatically, and degree escalation in the workforce continues. These criticisms have led students, parents, prospective employers, and educators to join in a call for accountability from the educational system. *The educational bottom line is: What are the retained learnings of students from an MBA program?*

One response to this call for accountability came in 1979 from the American Assembly of Collegiate Schools of Business (AACSB). As part of numerous efforts to improve the quality of management education, the AACSB began to focus on inno-

This chapter is an integration of a previously published paper, by Boyatzis and Renio, appearing as "The Impact of an MBA Program on Managerial Abilities," *Journal of Management Development*, 1989, *8*(5), 66–77, and an unpublished paper by the three authors. The authors wish to thank Scott Cowen and John Aram for their encouragement during this project.

vative ways of assessing business school programs on the basis of their actual impact on students (American Assembly of Collegiate Schools of Business, 1987). That is, the AACSB sought means of granting accreditation based on a school's performance. The early phases of the Accreditation Research Committee's project resulted in a set of possible standards to which schools may aspire in terms of graduates' knowledge and skills and personal characteristics (Zoffer, 1981). To date, potential measurement problems, political and philosophical differences between educators and administrators at many schools, and the significant cost of any such assessment have precluded full-scale implementation of these standards. Through this process, the concept of "outcome assessment" was introduced into the language of business schools. Changes in federal educational policy and the consequences for accrediting bodies have already brought outcome assessment to the attention of every college, university, and professional school seeking accreditation or up for renewal.

While some undergraduate business programs had embraced outcome assessment in the 1970s, most of the earlier work in this area involved liberal arts programs (Winter, McClelland, and Stewart, 1981; Mentkowski and Strait, 1983; Astin, 1992; Pascarella and Terenzini, 1991). Schools of management are only one type of professional school attempting to use outcome assessment to determine their "effectiveness" and identify areas for improvement. Schools of dentistry have extended the typical "clinical outcomes" often assessed for licensing or certification in health professions into assessing outcomes regarding patient care, interpersonal relationships with patients, communication skills, and so forth (Boyd, Bennett, and Bentley, 1991; Morgenstein, 1990). Schools of Medicine, Nursing, and Law are exploring outcome assessment beyond the former "quality assurance" criteria into areas of patient, or client, relationships.

Early attempts to determine the impact of MBA programs on students assumed that knowledge outcomes—that is, assessing whether or not students knew more information, facts, concepts, and such at graduation than when they entered—were the domain of the faculty, disciplines, and departments (Keys and Wolfe, 1988). The tests administered in courses were considered a relatively adequate measure. Through AACSB efforts, the impact of MBA programs on abilities related to management jobs became the target of early research projects.

Boyatzis and Sokol (1982) and Development Dimensions International (1985) showed a positive impact of MBA programs on students' abilities. But the samples were not random and may have been subject to contamination of volunteer effects. Boyatzis and Sokol (1982) demonstrated that students had significantly increased on 40 percent and 50 percent of the variables assessed in two MBA programs, respectively. They also decreased significantly on 10 percent of the variables. Development Dimensions International (1985) reported that students in the two MBA programs in their sample significantly increased on 44 percent of the variables assessed. Overall, the studies indicate that MBA programs may have a positive impact on abilities and that business schools could respond to the call for accountability with more than merely citing their placement record or the starting salaries of their graduates. At the same time, the Academy of Management Outcome Measurement and Management Education Task Force (Albanese and others, 1990) surveyed deans about their views on outcome measures. It reported that the two statements showing the highest ratings in the survey for each type of program (that is, those mandated to use outcome measurement, those considering using it, and those with no current program) were: (1) "College of business faculty should be encouraged to develop student interpersonal competence in the classroom," and (2) "Colleges of business should make greater use of outcome measures as a means for assessing and improving the quality of the educational process."

An outcome assessment project was initiated to determine the impact of the Weatherhead School of Management (WSOM) MBA experience on students' abilities. In particular, the objective was to measure abilities other than factual knowledge. This area was targeted because various departments and disciplines were addressing the program's impact on factual knowledge in their courses. The purpose of the project was to collect, analyze, and provide data on changes in students' abilities to the stakeholders of WSOM — the faculty, students, administration, employers, alumni, and advisory boards. The results of the study were intended to shed light on areas of strength and areas that could be improved. Another goal was to establish baseline data for a longitudinal study of WSOM graduates.

Abilities that have been shown to relate to effectiveness in management jobs were selected for outcome assessment (Boyatzis, 1982; Kolb, 1984). The time constraints during any test session and the desire to impose as little as possible on graduate students resulted in a multiyear design in which specific abilities would be assessed each year. Beyond the typical methodological concerns of reliability and validity, a key consideration in selecting instruments was to maximize the diversity of assessment methods.

Method

A value-added, cross-sectional design was chosen for the initial years of the outcome assessment project. That is, to determine the impact of the WSOM MBA program on its students, students entering the program and those graduating from it would be assessed on a number of abilities (skills and/or competencies). A value-added design identifies the students' abilities at entrance to the program as the starting point, thereby controlling for admissions standards when considering the abilities of the graduates. The research question is, simply: Have the students' abilities improved since entering the program?

A cross-sectional design was chosen for the first year of the study for a number of reasons. The debate as to the best developmental research design contrasts longitudinal studies with cross-sectional designs. Although each subject's degree of change is noted in longitudinal studies, these studies take a long time and do not always preserve continuity of subjects and researchers. They have a sampling bias resulting from availability and tracking of people once they have left the system. They often suffer from test-retest bias—that is, the test-retest reliability of instruments works against demonstrating any change (since people often remember what they previously answered). Finally, these studies have a potential bias of special historical events occurring that make generalizations inappropriate to eras when such special events did not take place.

A cross-sectional design represents the effects of the program without retesting the same students by comparing all or a sample of the graduating students in a year with all or a sample of the entering students in that specific year. The limitations of a cross-sectional design include sampling bias and special-event bias. To eliminate potential sampling bias, a census sample (that is, the entire population) or a random sample must be used. The special-event bias implies that changes in admissions policies or in the elements of the MBA program during the years that both of the cadres were in the program might result in confusion as to the factors producing particular results.

In this case, it was determined that there was no change in admissions policies or standards or in program design possibly affecting the cadres in these two years of outcome studies. These cadres represented students entering the MBA program in 1987 and 1988 *and* those graduating in 1988 and 1989. These graduating students may have entered the MBA program as early as 1984 (that is, part-time students taking all twenty courses) or as recently as 1988 (that is, full-time students taking twelve to fourteen courses). A random sample was used for three sections of the population studied, and a census sample was used for the other part of the sample.

1987–88 Sample

The WSOM MBA program has a full-time (daytime) and a part-time (evening) program. It was determined that each would have to be sampled separately. Of the entering full-time students, seventy-two were included in the sample (72 percent of the entering class in August 1987). The tests were administered during an orientation meeting students were attending prior to the start of classes. Of the full-time students graduating in May 1988, a random sample of twenty-seven (44 percent of the class) was tested. Three of those in the random sample did not participate because they had relocated, had a new job and were too busy, or for some other reason. Of the part-time students entering in January, June, or August 1988, a random sample of twenty-six (10 percent of the entering class) was tested. Eight of those in the random sample did not participate because they had dropped out of the program by the time of testing, had moved away, had jobs that prevented them from taking the time, or had a similar reason for not participating. Of the part-time students graduating in May 1988, a random sample of twenty-three (51 percent of the class) were tested. Seven in the random sample did not participate for reasons similar to those cited above for the graduating full-time students. Of the students in this study: females were 31 percent of the full-time sample and 33 percent of the part-time sample; nonnative English-speaking students were 20 percent of the full-time sample but none were in the part-time sample.

The sample was checked as to representativeness of the population from which they were drawn. Regarding gender (35 percent female), age (average 26.4), and grade-point average (average 3.1), the sample was similar to the entire classes entering during these two years and the prior year. With regard to GMAT, the sample of entering students was slightly lower than the population. It was concluded that the sampling technique provided a representative sample, with a caution as to differences in GMAT scores. A detailed description and analysis of the sample and comparison to population characteristics is shown in Appendix 5.1.

Tests Administered in the 1987–88 Study

Three tests were administered to the samples in the study. They were: (1) the Thematic Apperception Test (TAT); (2) the Learning Styles Inventory; and (3) an earlier version of the Learning Skills Profile, called the Executive Skills Profile. They were administered in this order and took approximately one hour to complete. The Learning Styles Inventory and Learning Skills Profile are used in the Mangerial Assessment and Development course and are described in Chapter Four.

A six-picture version of the TAT was used. The TAT is a projective test asking respondents to write imaginative stories to a series of pictures. The stories were coded for three motives using established coding schemes: Need for Achievement, Need for Affiliation, and Need for Power (McClelland, 1985). Need for Achievement is a motive concerning the person's desire to do better. Need for Power is a motive concerning the person's desire to have an impact on others. The coder had established interrater reliability with expert coding (Atkinson, 1958; Winter, 1973) on the three motives of .94 to .95. The stories were also scored for a trait called Activity Inhibition (that is, self-control) (McClelland and Boyatzis, 1982).

Protocols varied in length, and the motive scores correlated with the number of words written. To control possible contamination resulting from the length of the protocol, the motive scores were adjusted via the regression coefficient of the number of words on each of the motive variables, respectively (Winter, 1979). The adjusted standardized scores were not found to correlate with the length of the protocol and were used for the analysis reported.

An earlier version of the current Learning Skills Profile, originally called the Executive Skills Profile, was used in these initial outcome studies. Studies have shown both instruments to be similar, if not the same, as to scale (that is, skill) reliability, construct validity, and criterion validity (Boyatzis and Kolb, 1991; Boyatzis and Kolb, in press). The studies reported in this chapter and in Chapter Six used the earlier version. The course and studies reported in Chapters Four and Eight used the current version. Since several of the labels of the scales (or skills) were changed, the new labels are used throughout this book to allow for easier comparison.

All of the tests in these studies required writing or reading English. Since a number of the MBA students, especially in the full-time program, were not native English speakers (for example, some were from Japan or China), all analyses were repeated with the native English-speaking sample as well as with the entire sample of students.

Throughout this chapter, whenever a cross-sectional design is being statistically tested, two separate samples were assessed. Therefore, a nonparametric test—the Mann-Whitney

U test — was used. In longitudinal samples, a matched-pairs sample *t* test was used with test data. In later chapters, such as Chapter Eight, behavioral data (that is, data from behavioral coding of videotapes and audiotapes), even though from the same students, had nonnormal distribution requiring a nonparametric test. In such cases, the Wilcoxon matched-pairs, signed-ranks test was used.

1988–89 Sample

Full-time and part-time WSOM students were sampled separately during 1988 and 1989. Of the entering full-time students, seventy (79 percent) were tested in August 1988. Of the full-time graduating students, a random sample of seventeen (24 percent of the full-time students graduating in 1989) were tested. A random sample of twenty-two part-time students entering in January, June, or August 1988 were tested (8 percent of the class). A random sample of twenty-six part-time students graduating in 1989, representing 36 percent of that group, were tested in April 1989. Comparison of entering and graduating students indicated that the samples were similar to the groups they were selected to represent. Of the students assessed in this study: 31 percent of the full-time students and 48 percent of the part-time students were female; 35 percent of the full-time students and 2 percent of the part-time students were nonnative English-speaking students.

A small longitudinal sample was available. Fifteen of the full-time students graduating in May 1989 were in the August 1987 sample of entering students. This small sample had disproportionately fewer female students (13 percent female versus 32 percent and 37 percent in the two outcome studies), had disproportionately higher nonnative English-speaking students (40 percent versus 14 percent and 23 percent in the two outcome studies), and was older (average entering age was 28.5 versus 26.3 and 26.4 in the two outcome studies). These differences indicate that the results should be examined with caution. Nonetheless, we thought that the sample could provide some interesting observations. The only test used in both studies was the Learning Skills Profile.

Tests Administered in the 1988–89 Study

Four tests were administered to the students in the study. They were (1) the Test of Thematic Analysis, (2) the Future Time Perspective, (3) the Profile of Nonverbal Sensitivity, and (4) the same Learning Skills Profile used in the 1987–88 study. The tests were administered in this order and took about two hours to complete.

The Test of Thematic Analysis (McClelland and Winter, 1978) measures critical thinking abilities. In this test, critical thinking refers to the ability to see and identify similarities and differences among sets of verbal material. Once identified, the person is asked to articulate themes observed in the similarities and differences. In this manner, the text assesses the ability called Pattern Recognition in the WSOM model (see Appendix 4.1). Respondents were asked to read two groups of stories and then to describe the similarities and differences they noticed. After reading the coder training materials, the tests were scored for Direct Compound Comparisons, Exceptions-Qualifications, Examples, Analytic Hierarchy, Redefinition, and Subsuming Alternatives, Apples and Oranges, Affect and Subjective Reaction.

The Future Time Perspective Scale (Bird and Jordan, 1987) is a respondent measure of a person's attitude toward time. The thirty statements are rated on a Likert scale and are scored for the variables Density, Intent, Pace, Optimism, and Pessimism and summed for an overall Future Time Perspective score.

The Profile of Nonverbal Sensitivity measures an individual's ability to decipher nonverbal messages (Rosenthal and others, 1979). Respondents view and/or listen to a video consisting of 220 ten-second clips of a woman's face, body, voice only, or a combination of these. After each segment, participants must choose one of two statements that most accurately represents the message the woman was trying to convey. The test is scored for accuracy in the categories Tone Only, Random Spliced Voice, Content Filtered Voice, Face, Body, Figure, and Video Only. In addition, measures of interpretation of affective messages are obtained through the categories Positive and Submissive, Positive and Dominant, Negative and Submissive, and Negative and Dominant.

Results

In the 1987–88 study, examination of the Learning Skills Profile showed graduating students significantly higher than the entering students on Information Gathering, Information Analysis, Theory, Quantitative, Technology Skills, Action, and Initiative Skills. The graduating students were higher than the entering students at a near-significant level on Sense-Making Skills. When the nonnative English-speaking students were removed from the analysis, graduating students were significantly higher than entering students on Information Analysis, Theory, Quantitative, Technology, and Action Skills, and higher on Initiative Skills at a near-significant level. Statistical details are shown in Table 1 of Appendix 5.2.

In the 1988–89 study, examination of the Learning Skills Profile showed that graduating students were significantly higher than the entering students on Information Analysis, Theory, Quantitative, and Technology Skills; they were also higher in Information Gathering Skills at a near-significant level. When the nonnative English-speaking students were removed from the analysis, the graduating students were significantly higher than the entering students on Information Analysis, Theory, and Quantitative Skills, and higher in Technology Skills at a near-significant level. Statistical details are shown in Table 2 of Appendix 5.2. Profiles of the entering and graduating samples are shown in Figure 5.1.

Although the requirements and courses for the full-time and part-time programs are identical, the different length of time students take to graduate may have had an effect on the development of their abilities. Full-time students graduate within two years of entering the program. Part-time students graduate an average of four years after entering the program.

The full-time graduating students showed higher scores than the full-time entering students, through the Learning Skills Profile, on Sense-Making, Information Gathering, Information Analysis, Theory, Quantitative, Technology, Initiative, and near significant Action Skills for the native English-speaking and entire 1987–88 sample. The full-time graduating students, in the 1988–89 sample,

Figure 5.1. Profile of Graduating Versus Entering
Students' Mean Scores on the Learning Skills Profile Scales.

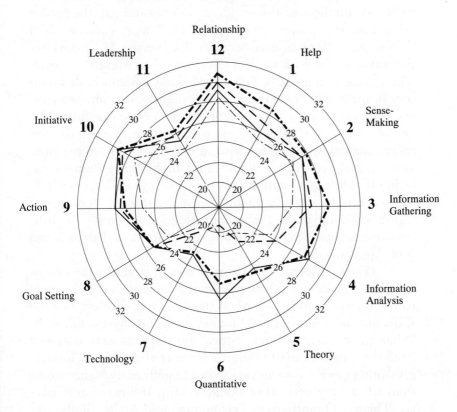

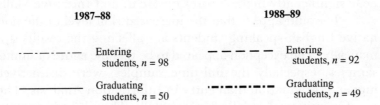

showed higher scores than the entering full-time students on Information Analysis, Theory, Quantitative, and Technology Skills. When the part-time students were examined, the graduating students showed higher scores on Theory (average 24.9 versus 22.7), Quantitative (average 26.0 versus 23.7), and Action (average 28.4 versus 26.7) Skills at a near-significant level. There were no nonnative English-speaking students in this sample. In the 1988–89 sample, the graduating part-time students showed significantly higher scores on Theory (average 25.5 versus 22.0), which declined to near significance when the one nonnative English-speaking student was dropped from the analysis. They showed a near significantly higher score than the entering students on Quantitative Skills (average 24.7 versus 21.8) for the entire and native English-speaking sample, and a near-significant decrease in Technology Skill for the native English-speaking sample. Statistical details are shown in Tables 3 and 4 of Appendix 5.2.

When the longitudinal sample is examined with the Learning Skills Profile, the fifteen graduating students showed significantly higher scores than when they entered on eleven of the skills and near significantly higher score on the twelfth skill. When the nonnative English-speaking students were removed from the sample, the significance drops considerably. The nine remaining graduating students showed significantly higher scores than when they entered on Relationship, Information Analysis, Theory, Quantitative, Technology, and Action Skills, and near significantly higher scores on Help, and Initiative Skills.

It would appear that the increased skill level of the nonnative English-speaking students are affecting the results dramatically. The exception appeared to be that the entire or limited samples, especially the full-time samples, were distinctively higher at graduation than entry in Information Analysis, Theory, Quantitative, and Technology Skills. These have been called Assimilative learning skills (Kolb, 1984). Statistical details are shown in Table 5 of Appendix 5.2.

In the 1987–88 sample, no significant differences were found between graduating and entering students with the entire sample or the native English-speaking students as to the dimensions of Learning Styles (Active Experimentation minus Reflective Observation, Abstract Conceptualization minus Concrete Experience) or motives (Needs for Achievement, Affiliation, and Power). When only the full-time students were examined, the Need for Achievement motive appears to increase at a near-significant level (average entering 47.5, graduating 51.0, Mann-Whitney U test $z = -1.74$, $p < .10$). This finding holds with the native English-speaking sample as well. No other differences even approached significance. No significant differences were found for the part-time students.

In the 1988–89 sample, the graduating students showed significantly higher scores on the PONS measure (that is, the measure of nonverbal sensitivity) for Content-Filtered audio, Face video, Figure video, Positive Submissive, and Positive Dominant, and with Tone audio at a near significant level. When only the native English-speaking students were examined, all of the findings dropped to nonsignificance except the Content filtered audio measure. When only the full-time students were examined, the Content Filtered audio, Figure video, and Positive Dominant measures were significantly higher for graduating students than entering students, but all drop to nonsignificance when the nonnative English-speaking students are removed from the analysis. Nothing is statistically significant for the part-time students with the PONS. It appeared that, on the whole, the significant findings can be explained by nonnative English-speaking students learning to "encode" and interpret American audio and video communications. Statistical details are shown in Table 6 of Appendix 5.2.

Two other measures were assessed in the 1988–89 sample. No statistically significant results were found with the Future Time Perspective measure for the entire sample, the full-time students, the part-time students, and the native English-speaking subsamples of each sample.

The surprising, and somewhat alarming, finding was that graduating students showed a significant decrease in critical thinking ability on the verbal material presented in the Test of Thematic Analysis. This was defined as Pattern Recognition in later studies described in this book. This significant decrease was also found for the native English-speaking subsample of the entire sample and the entire sample of full-time students, as shown in Table 6 of Appendix 5.2. No statistically significant difference was found regarding this measure of critical thinking with the native English-speaking full-time students nor any of the samples of the part-time students.

Discussion

Attending an MBA program, at least in this case, adds some value to students. Results have shown that they increase their skills in some areas. The MBA program had a strong, positive impact on the students' development of four of the twelve skills assessed in the Learning Skills Profile, namely, Information Analysis, Theory, Quantitative, and Technology Skills, as shown in Table 5.1.

The MBA program had some positive impact on the students' development of two of the skills addressed in the Learning Skills Profile, namely, Action and Initiative Skills. It also had some positive impact on students' development of the motive,

Table 5.1. Summary of Findings on the Impact of the MBA Program.

Strong evidence increased	Some evidence increased	Questions about increase	No evidence of change	Some evidence of decrease
Information Analysis Skills Theory Skills Quantitative Skills Technology Skills	Action Skills Initiative Skills Need for Achievement Content-Filtered Audio Score	Relationship Skills Help Skills Sense-Making Skills Information Gathering Skills	Leadership Skills Goal Setting Skills Need for Affiliation Need for Power Learning Styles Future Time Perspective Other Nonverbal Sensitivity Measures	Pattern Recognition (verbal)

Need for Achievement as measured from the Thematic Apperception Test, and the Content-Filtered Score of nonverbal sensitivity from the audio portion of the PONS. Similarly, some statistical evidence for students' decrease in capability was found in Pattern Recognition or critical thinking skills using verbal information (in contrast to quantitative information).

"Strong evidence" was defined as mostly statistically significant, with occasional near-significant, findings from two outcome studies, confirmed in the longitudinal study, and with regard to the entire sample as well as the native English-speaking sample of students. "Some evidence" was defined as mostly statistically significant, with occasional near-significant, findings from one outcome study, confirmed in the longitudinal study with the Learning Skills Profile only (that is, other measures were only used in one outcome study and, therefore, were not a part of the longitudinal study), and with regard to the entire sample as well as the native English-speaking sample of students.

Furthermore, there were questions about possible added value with regard to Relationship, Help, Sense-Making, and Information Gathering Skills from the Learning Skills Profile. Significant findings were noted in one of the outcome studies or in the longitudinal study but not confirmed in the others. No significant results were found for the entire sample and the native English-speaking sample with regard to Leadership and Goal Setting Skills, the Need for Power and Need for Affiliation motives, learning styles, time orientation, and ten other, nonverbal communications abilities assessed in the PONS.

In terms of MBA programs assessed in earlier studies, the WSOM program appeared to have about the same degree of impact. Graduating students had more of about 40 to 50 percent of the characteristics assessed in these studies than entering students. They decreased on one ability, and showed no value added on the others assessed in the studies.

A number of other statistically significant increases in students' capability were found for the entire sample, but when the subsample of native English-speaking students was examined, the results dropped from significance. These findings suggested that the nonnative English-speaking students were also changing (that is, experiencing value added) on a number of characteristics, but these were probably related to "being in America and in a university program" rather than solely in the MBA program. If one of their personal objectives in attending the program, or one of the objectives of the company or government that sponsored them in attending the program, was to understand and acculturate to U.S. society, these results suggest strong accomplishment of this objective.

Most, if not all, of the findings reported can be attributed to the changes in the full-time students. The part-time students showed statistically significant change for the native English-speaking subsample in none of the variables examined in these two outcome studies! An analysis of the near-significant results reveals a hint of the assimilative learning pattern mentioned earlier — that is, improvements in Theory and Quantitative Skills.

What Are We Doing in Professional Education?

The findings in this study are consistent with the criticism often made of MBA programs regarding their lack of impact on people management and interpersonal abilities (Porter and McKibbin, 1988). In contrast, this MBA program appeared to be having a significant positive impact on abilities involved in two other criticisms often cited about MBA programs: (1) not preparing people for technical, computer, and information technologies, and (2) not preparing people in implementation and entrepreneurial abilities (Porter and McKibbin, 1988).

Professional education within a number of fields appears to have an impact similar to the MBA program. Kolb (1984) reported a number of studies showing that formal professional education for engineers and social workers accentuated their Assimilative skills — those ranging from Sense-Making to Technology in Figure 5.1 (Kolb, 1984). That is, professional education enhances a person's ability to adapt, collect, and analyze information, develop and use quantitative models, plan for the use of this information, and use technology. In a similar vein, Friedman (1989) reported that female middle-level managers with master's degrees had significantly higher levels of the Information Analysis, Theory, and Quantitative Skills than their less educated colleagues. These represent the Information Analysis through Quantitative Skills, as shown in Figure 5.1.

The skill findings may be interpreted as reflecting only a change in the students' self-image, or perceptions of their abilities, rather than a change in their skills. A number of criterion validation and construct validation studies suggest that the Learning Skills Profile scales do represent actual changes in abilities (Boyatzis and Kolb, 1991; Boyatzis and Kolb, in press).

The lack of findings concerning changes in learning styles might be the result of the varying learning approaches used by the various disciplines represented in the WSOM curriculum. A student taking the required courses and a variety of electives and also being involved in the noncourse development activities such as workshops, internships, and projects would be exposed to faculty and disciplines using all of the learning modes (Kolb, 1984). As a result, no particular mode or style would be emphasized to the degree necessary to effect a change.

The increase in achievement motivation is probably associated with the heavy orientation of the MBA program toward measurement. Quantitative analysis and measurement of anything allows and encourages ongoing assessment of progress. Achievement motivation reflects a persistent concern for doing better. The person seeks measures of performance to assess progress. This attitude also typically reflects an emphasis on individualism rather than a group orientation.

The increase in sensitivity to Content-Filtered, audio, nonverbal communication is somewhat of an anomaly in the context of the other results. This sensitivity to audio messages whose high and low signals have been truncated (that is, high-pitch and low-pitch signals have been eliminated from the recording of the sound) suggests greater attunement to the "music" or rhythm of a person's communication. At the same time, other measures of interpersonal sensitivity (for example, LSP Relationship Skills or TAT Need for Affiliation) showed no change. The lack of clear and consistent evidence as to sensitivity to others in these studies with the other variables can only be explained if the development of this skill is a precursor to, or foundation for, the more advanced and sophisticated interpersonal skills.

The most alarming finding, the decrease in Pattern Recognition or critical thinking skill, seems inconsistent with the strong evidence of improvement in the Information Analysis and Theory Skills. The Test of Thematic Analysis presents verbal information about people's thoughts and asks the respondent to compare and contrast two sets of three stories. Critical thinking applied to verbal information is different than when applied to quantitative information (Kurfiss, 1988; Briars, 1983; Pellegrino and Goldman, 1983; Crooks, Campbell, and Rock, 1979). It is possibly also different when applied to people rather than systems, organizations, or markets. These distinctions would suggest that the MBA program, while enhancing quantitative critical thinking and probably enhancing critical thinking about organizations, is not enhancing students' critical thinking about people.

The differences found between the full-time and part-time students may be a function of the type of person that chooses to engage in a graduate program while working full time. Such a schedule requires a great deal of determination and energy to attend classes, write papers, conduct fieldwork projects, and take tests in the evening after a full day at work.

It is surprising that the part-time students did not increase on a greater number of abilities and that they did not increase more than the full-time students. The part-time students and full-time students enter the program at about the same age: twenty-six to twenty-seven. The part-time students have twice the number of years of work experience than the full-time students by graduation. They are at work every day, where they can apply their newly acquired knowledge and skills. But the part-time students do not appear to be benefiting from these supposed advantages. One interpretation is that they are not developing any additional abilities at work during these years, especially those assessed in this study. Another interpretation is that the stimulation and reinforcement they are experiencing at work overwhelm and extinguish any learning from school. Their organizational environments and managers may be denying them the opportunity to experiment with new ideas and behaviors. To the extent that work environments seek to maintain conformity to established procedures and practices, innovation may not be possible.

On the other hand, the full-time students have a significantly greater number of contact hours with faculty, other students, and staff at the school. They also participate in various activities — such as clubs and informal seminars — more extensively. It would appear that the complete experience of the MBA program for the full-time students, including but not limited to the courses they take, is the source of the increased abilities they show by graduation.

Conclusion

While it appears that an MBA program can help a person develop some of the abilities needed to be an effective manager or staff analyst, many abilities needed to be an effective manager or leader do not appear to be developed as easily in MBA programs, especially the interpersonal abilities. Since the number of people participating in graduate management education on a part-time basis has been increasing, programs should seek ways to involve and engage the part-time students as fully as they do the full-time students. For this or any MBA program achieving the same results, the challenge is to discover ways to help people learn about and improve on the abilities necessary for working effectively with others.

The results of these studies were presented to various faculty, alumni, student, and employer groups in the early years of the curriculum change effort. For employers and alumni, it typically confirmed what they had been experiencing in organizations: MBA graduates — even from the WSOM program — had some strengths but many gaps in their skills. Alumni or employers had to seek alternative training programs to address these needs, or watch others get the promotions and best job opportunities. They felt the results would be the same for MBA graduates of any of the "better" schools, and probably were stronger than for MBA graduates from other schools.

The results were presented to faculty as some information about our program's impact that was not perfect, or conclusive, but suggestive. Faculty reactions were divided. Some faculty had their fears confirmed by the results. They had suspected that we were not providing as complete a developmental experience as desired. Other faculty, often remembering specific students, criticized our methods, measures, and conclusions. The discussions evolved as certain faculty, in addressing their reluctant colleagues, said, "Look, even if the results are somewhat questionable, do we doubt that, overall, our students are graduating with fewer skills and fewer strengths than we would hope?" Allowing time in faculty committees to discuss the results and the interpretation became a high priority.

As faculty, we enjoyed the intellectual debate and the excitement of "dueling data." But the data from the studies provided a focal point for discussions. As a consensus on specific conclusions, or "distinct possibilities" as some called them, emerged about our current impact on the MBA student, a sense of dissatisfaction with the current program took shape.

Appendix 5.1. Sample Characteristics and
Comparison to Population Characteristics.

In the 1987–88 sample, females constituted 34 percent of the entering students and 28 percent of the graduating students in the 1987–88 sample and 36 percent of the entering and 39 percent of the graduating students in the 1988–89 sample, as compared to 34 percent of the entire entering classes of 1986 through 1988. The average age of the sample of entering students was 26.3 for the 1987–88 sample and 26.4 for the 1988–89 sample, as compared to the average age of the entire entering classes of 1986 through 1988 of 26. The graduating students were significantly older than the entering students (1987–88 study: 28.2 years old versus 26.3 years old, $df = 1,146$, $F = 5.48$, $p = .02$; and 29.6 versus 26.4 in the 1988–89 sample)!

The average grade-point average of the sample of entering classes was 3.0, as compared to an average grade-point average of 3.1 of the entire entering classes of 1986 through 1988. No significant difference was found in comparing the entering and graduating students (3.00 versus 3.03, $df = 1,127$, $F = .06$, $p = $ n.s.). The average GMAT of the sample of entering classes was 540, as compared to an average GMAT score of 571 of entire entering classes from 1986 through 1988. The graduating students showed significantly higher GMAT scores than the entering students (571 versus 540, $df = 1,143$, $F = 4.61$, $p = .03$). Since these represent GMAT scores taken before entrance into the MBA program, the difference may be the result of a change in admissions standards during the several years elapsing between the admission of the graduating classes and the entering classes. But the director of admissions indicated that no changes had occurred in admissions policies or standards during the entire period. The average GMAT scores of the population of the entering classes during the two years of data collection and for the year prior to the start of this study were reported earlier as 571, the same as the average for the graduating students. The director of admissions reported that the published figure of average GMAT scores was for those students "fully matriculated" (that is, were not on probation for lack of an undergraduate transcript or some other aspect of the admissions procedure). The samples for the study were drawn from the population of students entering the program and included a number of students who were not classified as "fully matriculated" by the admissions office. Some of these students later became "fully matriculated," once their applications were complete or a particular admissions criterion was fulfilled.

Students who had higher GMAT scores on entering may have had a greater tendency to stay in the program until graduation. The number of withdrawals from the full-time program is low, at about 5 percent. The number of withdrawals from the part-time program is higher, at about 25 percent, resulting from people relocating or changing careers.

Appendix 5.2. Studies of Program Impact.

Table 1. 1987–88 Study of Program Impact with the Learning Skills Profile.

Skills	All students			Native English-speaking		
	Entering (n = 98)	Graduating (n = 50)	z	Entering (n = 82)	Graduating (n = 46)	z
Leadership	24.3	25.2	-.60	24.6	25.3	-.18
Relationship	28.4	29.1	-1.01	28.9	29.0	-.22
Help	25.6	26.2	-.79	25.9	26.2	-.40
Sense-Making	26.2	27.8	-1.58+	26.4	27.8	-1.22
Information Gathering	25.1	26.3	-1.99*	25.6	26.2	-1.12
Information Analysis	23.9	28.1	-4.13***	24.7	28.3	-3.38***
Theory	20.7	24.8	-4.01***	21.0	24.6	-3.21***
Quantitative	20.3	26.4	-5.12***	20.7	26.0	-4.30***
Technology	19.5	22.8	-2.83**	20.2	22.4	-1.87*
Goal Setting	23.9	25.0	-.75	24.0	25.1	-.55
Action	25.9	28.1	-2.85**	26.2	28.0	-2.12*
Initiative	27.6	29.7	-2.23**	28.3	29.6	-1.52+
Total	291	320	-3.96***	297	318	-3.08***

Note: Significance levels reported are for Wilcoxon matched-pairs, signed-ranks tests as one-tailed tests ($^+p < .10$; $^*p < .05$; $^{**}p < .01$; $^{***}p < .001$). Means are shown for visual comparison.

Table 2. 1988–89 Study of Program Impact with the Learning Skills Profile.

Skills	All students			Native English-speaking		
	Entering (n = 92)	Graduating (n = 49)	z	Entering (n = 66)	Graduating (n = 41)	z
Leadership	25.7	26.2	-.50	26.0	26.1	-.05
Relationship	30.0	30.9	-1.23	30.8	31.0	-.61
Help	27.4	28.6	-.97	28.2	28.4	-.01
Sense-Making	27.5	27.9	-.58	28.5	28.2	-.16
Information Gathering	27.1	28.7	-1.43+	27.7	28.9	-.90
Information Analysis	24.2	27.8	-3.43***	24.7	28.1	-2.83**
Theory	21.6	25.3	-3.54***	21.6	25.5	-3.15***
Quantitative	19.2	25.0	-4.33***	18.9	24.9	-3.96***
Technology	20.3	22.9	-1.91*	20.8	23.1	-1.42+
Goal Setting	25.2	25.2	-.07	25.2	25.3	-.05
Action	27.8	27.4	-.42	28.0	27.5	-.26
Initiative	29.3	29.8	-.52	30.1	30.1	-.00
Total	305	326	-2.30**	310	327	-1.54+

Note: Significance levels reported are for Wilcoxon matched-pairs, signed-ranks tests as one-tailed tests ($^+p < .10$; $^*p < .05$; $^{**}p < .01$; $^{***}p < .001$). Means are shown for visual comparison.

Table 3. 1987–88 Study of Program Impact for
Full-Time Students Only with the Learning Skills Profile.

Skills	All students			Native English-speaking		
	Entering (n = 72)	Graduating (n = 27)	z	Entering (n = 56)	Graduating (n = 23)	z
Leadership	23.8	24.7	−.45	24.1	25.0	−.05
Relationship	28.3	29.7	−1.44+	29.0	29.5	−.46
Help	25.8	26.4	−.61	26.2	26.3	−.11
Sense-Making	25.9	28.4	−1.86*	26.1	28.5	−1.61*
Information Gathering	24.5	27.5	−3.49***	25.0	27.5	−2.65**
Information Analysis	22.9	28.6	−4.20***	23.9	29.0	−3.54***
Theory	19.9	24.7	−3.70***	20.2	24.2	−2.83**
Quantitative	19.1	26.7	−4.99***	19.4	25.9	−4.10***
Technology	18.0	23.0	−3.79***	18.7	22.4	−2.27**
Goal Setting	23.8	25.2	−.65	24.0	25.4	−.47
Action	25.6	27.9	−2.37**	25.9	27.5	−1.50+
Initiative	27.3	30.1	−2.37**	28.1	30.0	−1.62*
Total	285	323	−4.05***	291	321	−3.14***

Note: Significance levels reported are for Wilcoxon matched-pairs, signed-ranks tests as one-tailed tests ($+p < .10$; $*p < .05$; $**p < .01$; $***p < .001$). Means are shown for visual comparison.

Table 4. 1988–89 Study of Program Impact on
Full-Time Students Only with the Learning Skills Profile.

Skills	All students			Native English-speaking		
	Entering (n = 70)	Graduating (n = 23)	z	Entering (n = 45)	Graduating (n = 15)	z
Leadership	25.7	26.0	−.50	26.2	25.5	−.45
Relationship	29.8	31.6	−1.23	30.8	32.3	−1.16
Help	27.4	29.1	−.97	28.3	29.0	−.04
Sense-Making	27.2	27.6	−.58	28.6	28.1	−.08
Information Gathering	27.2	28.5	−1.43+	27.9	29.0	−.75
Information Analysis	23.5	27.9	−3.43***	23.8	28.7	−2.62**
Theory	21.5	25.1	−3.54***	21.4	25.5	−2.55**
Quantitative	18.4	25.5	−4.33***	17.7	25.2	−3.43***
Technology	18.6	22.9	−1.91*	18.4	23.3	−2.31**
Goal Setting	25.1	25.4	−.07	24.9	26.0	−.38
Action	28.0	27.6	−.42	28.2	28.2	−.05
Initiative	29.1	29.7	−.52	29.9	30.3	−.15
Total	302	327	−2.30**	306	331	−1.66*

Note: Significance levels reported are for Wilcoxon matched-pairs, signed-ranks tests as one-tailed tests ($+p < .10$; $*p < .05$; $**p < .01$; $***p < .001$). Means are shown for visual comparison.

Table 5. 1987–89 Longitudinal Study of Program Impact
on Full-Time Students Only with the Learning Skills Profile.

Skills	All students			Native English-speaking		
	Entering (n = 15)	Graduating (n = 15)	t	Entering (n = 9)	Graduating (n = 9)	t
Leadership	22.4	25.7	-2.63**	23.8	25.2	-1.11
Relationship	26.3	30.6	-2.92**	28.1	31.3	-1.99*
Help	24.0	28.3	-3.37**	25.8	28.0	-1.64+
Sense-Making	25.1	27.9	-1.84*	26.6	28.7	-1.06
Information Gathering	25.2	27.6	-1.73*	26.8	27.7	-.59
Information Analysis	22.6	29.1	-4.48***	25.7	29.7	-2.27*
Theory	20.3	25.6	-4.15***	22.0	26.2	-2.70**
Quantitative	19.6	28.2	-7.56***	20.7	28.3	-5.73***
Technology	19.2	24.6	-3.71***	21.1	25.0	-3.42**
Goal Setting	22.6	24.7	-1.33+	24.1	25.4	-.87
Action	24.7	28.76	-2.85**	26.2	29.7	-1.91*
Initiative	25.9	29.7	-2.27*	28.2	31.1	-1.42+
Total	278	331	-3.88***	299	336	-2.57*

Note: Significance levels are for matched-pairs sample t tests as one-tailed tests ($+p < .10$; $*p < .05$; $**p < .01$; $***p < .001$).

Table 6. 1988–89 Comparison of Impact on
Nonverbal Communication, Time Orientation, and Critical Thinking Skills.

Skills	All students			Native English-speaking		
	Entering (n = 92)	Graduating (n = 49)	z	Entering (n = 66)	Graduating (n = 41)	z
PONS: Tone	25.5	26.5	-1.52+	26.3	26.8	-.61
Random Spliced	63.9	64.8	-.59	65.3	64.7	-1.10
Content Filtered	61.5	63.6	-3.05***	63.1	64.2	-2.11*
Face	50.8	51.7	-1.67*	51.6	52.0	-.96
Body	46.3	46.9	-.53	47.7	47.2	-.86
Figure	50.9	52.3	-1.93*	52.4	52.5	-.22
Video	48.1	49.1	-1.17	49.5	49.6	-.05
Positive Submissive	39.7	41.0	-2.21**	40.9	41.5	-1.23
Positive Dominant	41.0	42.1	-1.73*	42.2	42.3	-.19
Negative Submissive	43.6	44.3	-.75	44.6	44.6	-.05
Negative Dominant	48.6	49.4	-1.01	49.5	49.6	-.34
Future Time Perspective	148.9	149.3	-.60	149.6	149.8	-.76
Test of Thematic Analysis Score	2.19	1.50	-2.70**	2.34	1.73	-2.17*

Note: Significance levels for Wilcoxon matched-pairs, signed-ranks tests as one-tailed tests, with the exception of the test reported for the Test of Thematic Analysis, which is two-tailed ($+p < .1$; $*p < .05$; $**p < .01$; $***p < .001$).

Six

GATEKEEPERS
OF THE ENTERPRISE:
ASSESSING FACULTY INTENT
AND THE STUDENT OUTCOME

Richard E. Boyatzis

Because much of the pressure for educational change has recently come from stakeholders other than faculty, it is easy to forget that curriculum innovation is the primary responsibility of the faculty. The process of curriculum change must start with significant faculty involvement, or it will not get far.

Discussing vision and strategy with faculty is essential (see Chapter Two), but discussing desired outcomes is impossible without faculty participation. Therefore, the process of curriculum change requires faculty to consider what their goals are for students. The study reported in this chapter was conducted early in the Weatherhead School of Management (WSOM) efforts as a way to establish the faculty's objectives and to give the faculty an opportunity to examine whether or not we wished to change our objectives.

Faculty in graduate schools are the first gatekeepers of the occupations and professions they represent. Accrediting and

An earlier version of this chapter appeared in J. D. Bigelow (ed.), *Managerial Skills: Explorations in Practical Knowledge,* Newbury Park, CA: Sage, 1991, pp. 90–102. I wish to thank John Aram, David Bowers, David Kolb, Eric Neilsen, Jack Ruhl, Tojo Thachankery, and Xiaoping Tian for assisting in the collection and analysis of the information reported in this study, as well as Anne Renio-McKee and Lorraine Thompson for assistance in data analysis.

licensing bodies and professional associations can be viewed as the second and third gatekeepers, respectively. Knowledge, appropriate norms of conduct, and values are transmitted to graduate students as they are socialized into a field or profession. Faculty are not the only influence on students in graduate school. Other students, internships, projects, clubs, professional associations, and community activities also have an impact, but none command more attention, time, or engagement than faculty. Therefore, examining the effectiveness of professional education with respect to its two main objectives of adding value to students and evaluating their competence to enter a profession can be turned into an examination of the effectiveness of faculty.

Before faculty effectiveness can be assessed, the overall impact of MBA programs on students must be documented. Confusion exists concerning the nature and degree of the impact of MBA programs. Student-change outcome studies of students' abilities have shown statistically significant positive increases in various abilities — though in surprisingly few abilities (see Chapter Five for a discussion of these studies).

Effective transmission of knowledge by faculty in schools of management has been assumed (Keys and Wolfe, 1988). As a result, discussion of effectiveness has often focused on the relevance of various bodies of knowledge. The almost exclusive focus of this type of discussion on knowledge acquired has also contributed to ignoring the impact of faculty and programs on students' abilities. At the same time, abilities have been shown to have greater impact on job performance than only possession of knowledge in various professions (McClelland, 1973) and management (Crooks, Campbell, and Rock, 1979).

Even with regard to abilities, the relevance and appropriateness of what is taught must be examined prior to assessing the effectiveness of the teaching. These studies can be called job competency outcome studies. Employers and faculty could be studied to determine which abilities graduates will need in management or other jobs to perform effectively. Various competency studies have been conducted and are available in the literature (Boyatzis, 1982; Howard and Bray, 1988; Kotter, 1988; Campbell, Dunnette, Lawler, and Weick, 1970; Luthans, Hodgetts, and Rosenkrantz, 1988; Spencer and Spencer, 1993; Mentkowski, McEachern, O'Brien, and Fowler, 1982).

Similarly, faculty can be surveyed as to what they believe to be the relevant and appropriate abilities. Porter and McKibbin (1988) collected information from various stakeholders regarding their views of the impact of MBA programs. The study included interviews and questionnaires given to 2,055 faculty and 1,835 MBA students from the 620 schools in the American Assembly of Collegiate Schools of Business (AACSB) regarding skills and personal characteristics. They found that faculty and students agreed as to where the current emphasis was placed in MBA programs. Analytic and decision-making skills were seen as "emphasized very much" by more than half of the students and more than a third of the faculty. With the exception of computer skills, the rank order of the skills—based on the percentage of responses saying it was "emphasized very much"—is identical from the faculty and students. Both students and faculty felt that the order of emphasis was: analytic (62 and 38 percent, respectively), decision making (51 and 32 percent), planning and organizing (51 and 18 percent), written communication (42 and 15 percent), oral communication (28 and 14 percent), leadership and interpersonal (26 and 14 percent), initiative (21 and 11 percent), and risk-taking skills (8 and 5 percent). Computer skills ranked eighth in the view of students and fourth in the view of faculty (14 and 15 percent). In summary, the faculty and students' views of the emphasis of MBA programs on particular abilities appear consistent with employer observations that students with MBA degrees enter the workforce with a great deal of analytic and quantitative ability and less interpersonal, communications, and entrepreneurial ability than desired (Porter and McKibbin, 1988; Byrne, Norman, and Miles, 1988).

While providing a great deal of useful information, Porter and McKibbin's (1988) survey may have suffered from distortion. They asked faculty and students for their overall view of program emphasis. This method often elicits faculty and students' views as to what they wish or hope for. These views may not reflect what actually occurs (Argyris, 1985). A study focused on classroom behavior and outcome would provide further information relevant to the assessment of faculty effectiveness.

The present study attempted to compare faculty intent and student outcome on various abilities related to effectiveness in management and occupations of graduating MBAs. The intentions of faculty would include their learning objectives, determination of relevant topics, and organization of material in the design and delivery of their courses. This study was completed prior to the design and development of the new WSOM MBA program. The results reported are from the old WSOM MBA program and were used in the discussions among faculty, students, and other stakeholders.

Method

In the spring and summer of 1988, WSOM faculty were interviewed by a special senior faculty committee about specific courses each had recently taught in the MBA program. Forty-two of the forty-seven full-time faculty who taught in the MBA program during the prior year were interviewed. Twenty-nine faculty were interviewed regarding the required courses. At least two faculty were interviewed regarding each of the thirteen required courses. Economics was also a required course but was taught by the economics department, which was, at the time of this study, not in the WSOM. Of the thirty-eight elective courses taught during the same year, twenty-one faculty were interviewed regarding twenty-nine (76 percent) of the elective courses. Some faculty were interviewed about required and elective courses, but in such cases the interview protocol was completed concerning each course separately.

The interview involved three questions and administration of one instrument. Questions were asked about each specific course: (1) In general, what are you trying to teach in this course? What are your overall objectives? (2) What topics do you see as important to cover in the course? (3) What other objectives, besides course topics, are you trying to cover in this course? Following the second question, the syllabus was reviewed and discussed.

After these questions were answered, the faculty member was asked to repeat the answer to the third question in a way that could facilitate analysis across courses by means of an adaptation of the Learning Skills Profile (LSP) (described in Chapter Four). The Executive Skills Profile used in this study was an earlier form of the LSP currently used in the Managerial Assessment and Development course and the current outcome studies. (See Chapters Four and Eight.) Both versions have demonstrated similar, if not the same, pattern of reliability, construct validity, and criterion validity.

In this case, the instructions were modified and the faculty member was asked to describe the specific course being discussed by placing each of the seventy-two cards into one of the following five categories: (5) "skills that are of primary importance to me in designing and conducting my class," (4) "skills that are important but not primary in designing and conducting my class," (3) "skills that are less clearly addressed or 'implicit' in designing and conducting my class," (2) "skills that are mentioned or addressed only once or twice in designing and conducting my class," and (1) "skills that are not addressed and/or not applicable in designing and conducting my class." The faculty member was then asked to review each stack to ensure appropriate placement of the cards.

The numeric value assigned to each statement (that is, each card) corresponded to the number of the stack into which the faculty member placed the card. Scale scores were computed as a total of the items in each scale.

The full response of faculty members to all questions for each course was written and reviewed with the faculty members, including a list of all the LSP items they rated as a level 5 for the course. Any changes desired by the faculty members were made, and the resulting written documents and the complete LSP scores were used in the analysis. Only the analysis regarding the abilities assessed with the LSP are reported in this study. For each course in which several faculty provided information, an average score per item in the LSP was calculated. The resulting scores for the forty-two courses (that is, thirteen required and twenty-nine elective courses) were used for the analysis.

Student outcome data used was from the first year (1987–88) of the student-change outcome studies of the MBA program at the WSOM (Boyatzis and Renio, 1989; also see Chapter Five). The study assessed a random sample of twenty-six entering part-time students (10 percent of the population), seventy-two of the entering full-time students during the orientation program (72 percent), a random sample of twenty-seven graduating full-time students (44 percent), and a random sample of twenty-three graduating part-time students (51 percent). The LSP was one of the instruments used in the study.

Results

Analysis of LSP scores for all courses indicated that faculty intent was to emphasize Sense-Making Skills above all, then Theory Skills, followed by Information Analysis Skills, Initiative Skills, Goal Setting Skills, Quantitative Skills, and Information Gathering Skills (details are shown in Appendix 6.1). Other skills were relatively less important in terms of faculty intent. They were, in order of decreasing importance: Technology Skills, Leadership Skills, Action Skills, Relationship Skills, and Help Skills.

Comparison of the graduating and entering students' scores on the LSP revealed that students changed the most on skills emphasized by the faculty in their courses. A visual comparison of the entering students' scores, the graduating students' scores, and the faculty's intent scores are shown in Figure 6.1.

To help clarify faculty intent, the six items with the highest mean score and the six items with the lowest mean score are shown in Table 6.1. The items with the highest overall mean score, indicating that they were considered "primary" and "important but not primary" in the design and teaching of courses, concerned conceptual, analytic, and planning skills. The items with the lowest mean score, showing that they were "not addressed at all," "implicit," or "mentioned only once or twice," concerned managing people, interpersonal relationships, and self-awareness.

A transformation of the LSP data was required to compare faculty intent and student outcome in more detail. The

Figure 6.1. Profile Comparison of Faculty Intent, Entering MBA Students,
and Graduating MBA Students on the Learning Skills Profile Scales.

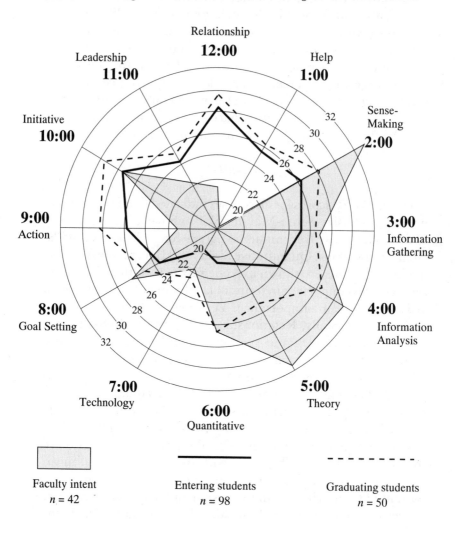

Table 6.1. Faculty Intent on Learning Skills Profile Items Showing Highest and Lowest Mean Scores Over All Forty-Two Courses.

Item	Mean score
Identifying and defining problems	4.62
Building conceptual models/conceptual thinking	4.48
Seeing how things fit in the big picture	4.38
Making decisions under conditions of risk and uncertainty	4.17
Innovating/developing new solutions to problems	4.10
Adapting to changing circumstances	4.07
Establishing trusting, dependable relationships with co-workers	2.14
Establishing relationships with co-workers in which honest feedback is given and received	2.07
Helping others gain opportunities to develop their abilities	2.07
Directing and supervising the work of others	2.05
Understanding and being influenced by the feelings of others—empathy	2.05
Being aware of and understanding yourself, assessing yourself accurately	2.02

Note: The specific wording of these items is from the earlier version of the Learning Skills Profile known as the Executive Skills Profile.

percentage that each scale score represented of the total score of all scales was computed to adjust for the difference between a seven-point and a five-point scale. The adjusted score indicates relative emphasis of a skill within each set of data.

A comparison of the entering MBA students' skills with the faculty emphasis using the adjusted scores is shown in Table 6.2. The entering students had significantly greater relative strength on Leadership Skills, Relationship Skills, Help Skills, Action Skills, and Initiative Skills than the faculty did in their courses. The faculty placed significantly more relative emphasis on Sense-Making Skills, Information Analysis Skills, Theory Skills, Quantitative Skills, and near significant Goal Setting and Technology Skills than the entering students did.

A summary of the comparisons is shown in Table 6.3. The graduates improved, as compared to entering students, on all four skills for which the relative emphasis of faculty was significantly greater than entering students' relative abilities. These skills included Sense-Making Skills, Information Analysis Skills, Theory Skills, and Quantitative Skills. On the two skills where

Table 6.2. A Comparison of the
Relative Priority of Faculty Intent and Entering Students' Skills.

| | Percentage of total skills score | | |
| | Entering students | Faculty intent | |
Skill	(n = 98)	(n = 42)	t
Leadership	8.30	7.04	4.00***
Relationship	9.79	6.87	7.76***
Help	8.80	5.70	7.69***
Sense-Making	9.03	10.80	−5.46***
Information Gathering	8.63	8.40	1.04
Information Analysis	8.21	10.16	−5.43***
Theory	7.04	10.44	−10.03***
Quantitative	6.98	8.86	−3.32**
Technology	6.63	7.35	−1.76+
Goal Setting	8.18	8.68	−1.63+
Action	8.91	6.86	7.75***
Initiative	9.51	8.86	2.30*

Note: $+p < .10$; $*p < .05$; $**p < .01$; $***p < .001$

faculty emphasis was greater than entering students' relative abilities at a near-significant level, there was significant change on Technology Skills but no change on Goal Setting Skills. On three of the six skills on which there was no difference between faculty emphasis and entering students' relative abilities or the entering students had relatively more ability than the faculty emphasis, students showed no improvement between entering and graduating from the MBA program. These skills were Leadership Skills, Relationship Skills, and Help Skills. On Action Skills and Initiative Skills, entering students had relatively more ability than faculty emphasis, and yet graduates improved as compared to entering students. On Information Gathering Skills, students changed but no difference was found in faculty intent.

Discussion

The way the faculty design and conduct their classes has a significant impact on how students change during an MBA program. Students improve on eight skills and remain about the same on four skills, and it appears that faculty drive the change in the direction they desire. Student improvement is seen in areas

Table 6.3. Summary Comparison of Faculty Intent
and Entering Students' Skills with Outcome.

Skill	Faculty intent vs. entering MBA students	Student outcome
Sense-Making	Faculty >> students	Graduates > entering
Information Analysis	Faculty >> students	Graduates >> entering
Theory	Faculty >> students	Graduates >> entering
Quantitative	Faculty >> students	Graduates >> entering
Technology	Faculty > students	Graduates >> entering
Goal Setting	Faculty > students	ns
Information Gathering	ns	Graduates >> entering
Leadership	Students >> faculty	ns
Relationship	Students >> faculty	ns
Help	Students >> faculty	ns
Action	Students >> faculty	Graduates >> entering
Initiative	Students >> faculty	Graduates >> entering

Note: ">" means near significant, $p < .10$; ">>" means significant, $p < .05$

where faculty intent is high—specifically on Information Analysis Skills, Theory Skills, Quantitative Skills, Initiative Skills, and Sense-Making Skills. In areas where faculty intent is low, little change occurs in students, specifically on Leadership Skills, Relationship Skills, and Help Skills. One exception involves Goal Setting Skills. Relatively high faculty intent does not appear to affect student change on Goal Setting Skills. With Information Gathering Skills the absolute numbers are somewhat related.

At the same time, although faculty placed a relatively low priority on these skills, students did significantly improve on Technology Skills and Action Skills. The positive impact could be attributed to effects of the school, program, faculty contact outside of courses, or community activities. Using a median to split the scales into High Faculty Intent and Low Faculty Intent, it appears that students improve, significantly or near significantly, on five of the High Faculty Intent scales (83 percent), and do not improve or change on four of the Low Faculty Intent scales (67 percent).

A similar pattern of student change was found in the second year of the student-change outcome studies (1988–89). This included a small longitudinal sample of fifteen students. Both the sample from the second study and the small longitudinal sample showed significant improvement in students' Information Analysis, Theory, Quantitative, and Technology Skills.

The number of items in each scale for which students showed significant or near-significant improvement further illustrated the impact of faculty intent. The number of items on which students showed improvement for the five scales on which faculty intent was greater than entering students' skills was 4.0 per scale (see Table 6.3). For the two scales on which faculty intent and entering students showed no or near significant differences, the number of items that showed improvement was 1.0 per scale. For the five scales on which entering students were significantly greater than faculty intent, the number of items that showed improvement was 1.4 per scale.

An alternative explanation would be that students compensate for their skill levels at point of entry into the MBA program. They might seek to improve on their relatively weak skills and not pay attention to their relatively strong skills. This effect should work regardless of faculty intent. The concept of compensating development worked on seven of the twelve skill areas. A median split on entering students' skill levels revealed that students improved on four of the six skills with which they entered the program relatively low (67 percent) and showed little or no change on three of the skills with which they entered the program relatively high (50 percent). Four of the five skills on which the student-change data did not confirm the compensating effect are involved in implementation and are the most action-oriented skills assessed in the LSP. It appears that students change the most on abilities on which they are relatively weak and do not change much on abilities on which they are relatively strong.

Despite the impact of the compensating development effect on students' learning, faculty intent seems to have a profound effect on students' learning. The good news is that when faculty intend a change, the students improve. The bad news is that when faculty do not intend a change, the students do not improve.

Although this study provides a more rigorous assessment of faculty intent than the study by Porter and McKibbin (1988), both studies show strong faculty emphasis on similar skills, with the exception of this program's significant impact on Action Skills, Initiative Skills, and Technology Skills. Does this suggest that much of the relationship between faculty intent and student outcome found in this study would also be characteristic of other management programs? Until MBA programs assess this relationship, it will be difficult to determine how similar or dissimilar these findings are to the faculty intent and student changes in other programs.

The relationship between faculty intent and student outcome observed in this program may also be similar to the impact of graduate professional education in other fields. A number of studies of alumni of graduate engineering and social work programs showed increased Information Analysis, Information Gathering, Theory, and Quantitative Skills attributed to their graduate education. In a similar vein, Friedman (1989) reported that female middle-level managers with master's degrees had significantly higher levels of the Information Analysis, Theory, and Quantitative Skills than their less educated colleagues. Faculty intent in those graduate programs was not known, so it is difficult to conclude that student change was a function of faculty priorities in the various graduate programs.

These findings suggest that graduate professional education increases students' abilities in the areas of information collection and analysis, theory building, and quantitative analysis. But interpersonal and self-awareness abilities do not seem to be affected.

It could be argued that the faculty intent shown here and in other graduate professional education programs is, in part, a result of the student impact. That is, over the years, faculty come to realize that students only improve, or add value, on these information collection and analysis abilities. Therefore, the faculty focus their intent only on those abilities they believe can be changed during graduate education.

While the influence of past impact on students cannot be eliminated as a contributor to the socialization of faculty — thereby affecting faculty expectations and intent — the evidence seems to suggest that faculty try to influence students in broader arenas. Some faculty have expressed doubt in faculty meetings about the efficacy of influencing a person's interpersonal ability,

ability to work with others in groups, or action and implementation abilities. At the same time, many faculty do feel that they have a positive impact on a student's maturation and improvement on a broad range of skills. Because management is an applied field, it has been said that faculty in schools of management should have even greater impact than we have had in many of these other areas, such as interpersonal, leadership, and action skills (Porter and McKibbin, 1988).

The belief that education should shape a broad range of student abilities has a long history. The apprenticeship and tutorial aspects of advanced, professional education first popularized by Socrates, Plato, and Aristotle have continued to have advocates down to the present day. The "affective education" movement of the 1960s, the "experiential learning" movement of the 1970s, the "competency-based education" movement of the 1980s, and the efforts of professional schools to mirror the priorities and work environments of their graduates reveal this commitment to developing the whole student. Against this background, it is difficult to embrace the notion that faculty have limited their intent to only those information collection and analytic abilities on which students have been shown to change in the past.

Conclusion

Faculty intent appears to affect the degree of graduate student learning in terms of abilities. Other aspects of the program assessed may also have a positive impact on students in facilitating change, but on the whole, if faculty do not view a skill as a key item on which to focus, students will not change during their graduate program. Student outcomes indicate that faculty are effective in their teaching of abilities.

Unfortunately, the abilities on which faculty focus may be too limited for the intended and desired occupations of their graduates. If the criticisms reported in Porter and McKibbin (1988) and gaps in substantive progress in terms of innovation in management education (Keys and Wolfe, 1988) are taken seriously, faculty must change their focus within courses or change other aspects of the graduate program. Faculty could change their focus on skills without changing the content of their courses by changing the way they teach the courses and the type of interaction they expect from students. Other program elements, such as learning teams, can also be introduced into a curriculum to bolster attention to those skill areas not thoroughly addressed in courses (Caie, 1987; Prideaux and Ford, 1988a, b).

Whether the desire for curriculum change and for a different impact on students comes from employers, students, parents, or administrators, the faculty must be directly involved. The faculty already have certain goals for their courses that address content topics and abilities. To stimulate a change effort, the faculty must buy into the effort.

Once a deficiency in a curriculum is noted, the standard academic response is to add a course on the topic. The findings of this study suggest that merely adding another course to the curriculum would not have the desired effect. For example, adding a course on leadership or a course on ethics will not significantly alter the overall impact of the courses and program on students as to leadership abilities or ethical behavior. The influence of one course on students is minuscule compared to the combined effects of all courses, faculty, and the entire program. This study suggests that a greater faculty emphasis on abilities will most likely result in more impact on students, more value added, and greater retained learning than is currently the case. While a shared sense of purpose and focus on the part of the faculty may be difficult to achieve, it is an essential first step in the direction of increased positive impact on students' abilities.

As mentioned in Chapter Three, the results of this study became a focal point for numerous faculty meetings. The raw data were presented and became a playground for faculty. From the intellectual discussions, assorted methods of statistical analysis, and voluminous graphic portrayals of the data, a shared interpretation of the information emerged: "This reflects our current objectives, and our current impact on students. But it is not what we wish our impact to be." Starting with the affirmation of what we had been doing, the faculty were able to agree that it was time to change our objectives. We realized that it was time to challenge our assumptions and design a curriculum appropriate to the 1990s.

Appendix 6.1. Comparison of Faculty Intent and Student Change.

Skill	Faculty intent (n = 42) Courses	Student change: graduates (n = 50) as compared to entering students (n = 98)
Sense-Making	23.40	1.6+
Theory	22.55	4.1***
Information Analysis	22.00	4.2***
Initiative	19.52	2.1*
Goal Setting	19.19	1.1
Quantitative	19.10	6.1***
Information Gathering	18.62	1.2*
Technology	15.98	3.3**
Leadership	15.67	0.9
Action	15.42	2.2**
Relationship	15.33	0.7
Help	12.83	0.6

Note: $^+p < .10$; $^*p < .05$; $^{**}p < .01$; $^{***}p < .001$
Source: Table 1 in Appendix 5.2 of this book.

Seven

GENDER DIFFERENCES IN STUDENT DEVELOPMENT: EXAMINING LIFE STORIES, CAREER HISTORIES, AND LEARNING PLANS

Susan S. Case and Lorraine Thompson

Traditionally, business schools have drawn applicants from the same population that businesses have drawn white-collar employees from: a relatively homogeneous pool of white American males. The curricula of business schools have been designed to meet the needs of these students.

However, the composition of the American workforce has changed dramatically over the last thirty years. In 1980, 43 percent of the total workforce was women. Throughout the 1990s, 85 percent of the net growth in the American labor pool will consist of white women, people of color, and immigrants, with a projection that by the year 2000, these groups will comprise approximately 50 percent of the total workforce (Johnston and Packer, 1987). This shift in the demographics of the labor force is not reflected in the nation's top business schools. These schools

Susan Schick Case wishes to acknowledge the financial support of the National Center on Adult Learning and of a Case Western Reserve University Research Initiation Grant in the preparation of this manuscript. The authors also wish to thank Richard Boyatzis, Scott Cowen, Melinda Forthofer, Mike Hitt, David Kolb, Laurie Larwood, Bob Mason, Eric Neilsen, and Don Wolfe for commenting on earlier versions of this paper.

have experienced a decline of 25 percent or more in female enrollment since 1990, when women received 34 percent of all MBAs awarded in this country, while male enrollment is slightly up. The proportion of women in incoming classes in 1992 ranged from 16 to 30 percent (Cowan, 1992; Fuchsberg, 1992). The authors' own university's MBA population increased its female representation from 24 to 40 percent over a period of eight years, a phenomenon that until recently had been repeated at universities across the country.

This increasing trend in the diversity of the workforce has important implications for managerial education. Gallos (1993) found that traditional methods of teaching such as transmitting facts and knowledge, introducing theories and models, developing reasoning skills, discussing frameworks, and assigning cases and readings were not sufficient for the needs of her female students. She found that "the women had clear expectations that all of their learning would touch the core of their central identities" (p. 9). They expected their education to play an important role in their search for self-knowledge and personal development as well as increasing their technical knowledge and skills. Other researchers have similarly indicated that women are developmentally different from men (Belenky, Clinchy, Goldberger, and Tarule, 1986; French, 1985; Gallos, 1990; Gilligan, 1977; Kohlberg, 1976; Miller, 1986; Schaef, 1981). All of the research surrounding developmental differences between men and women has a similar theme. Women's conceptions of themselves, their lives, and the world around them are constructed differently from those of men.

For graduate programs to be effective for all participants, it is important to identify and address potentially significant differences across groups in how they might approach their own managerial development. Although the desires for equal opportunity and equal treatment of men and women may be laudable, the results of such good intentions may be detrimental to all students, particularly those in graduate programs, when they lead to the neglect of differences in how men and women develop. Gender, therefore, has become a factor that business schools cannot ignore.

Relevant Literature

Traditional theories of career and personal development focus on the centrality of work to identity and the need for separation and individuation in the search for maturity and personal empowerment (Erikson, 1968; Gallos, 1990; Levinson, 1978). Adult development has typically meant increased autonomy and separation from others as a means of strengthening identity, empowering the self, and charting a life course (Gallos, 1990).

It has already been established that attachment to significant other people is an important source of identity, maturity, and personal power for women (Bardwick, 1980; Bateson, 1989; Eichenbaum and Orbach, 1988; Gilligan, 1982; Josselson, 1987; McClelland, 1975). The central role that attachments and relationships play in women's identity formation and in their conceptions of mature adult selves is incongruent with traditional theories of career and personal development.

In earlier studies (Erikson, 1968; Kohlberg, 1981; Kohlberg and Kramer, 1969) women's focus on intimacy, intense attachments, concern for relationships, and context-based decisions were cited as deficient behaviors with respect to developing as an adult. Barnett and Baruch (1980) have reframed these perspectives, not as deficiencies but as differences, and have noted the importance to women of stressing both relationships and personal achievement over the course of a lifetime.

Researchers have begun to question the applicability of theories about career and personal development that have been derived from studies that used all-male samples and then applied those findings to women. Several studies (Gilligan, 1982; Harvard Assessment Project, 1990; Josselson, 1987; Miller, 1986; Roberts and Newton, 1986; Velsor and Hughes, 1990) have focused on the ongoing impact of others on women's development and on the notion that women may develop their skills and abilities in different ways than men. In particular, Gilligan (1982) discussed women's definitions of themselves in a context of human relationships that demonstrate a capacity to care. Miller (1986) called for a new psychology of women that recognizes the different starting point for women's development. She pointed out that women stay with, build on, and develop in a context of attachment and affiliation with others.

The Harvard Assessment Project (1990) found that female students focused on the importance of a personal relationship with an advisor to enhance their learning experience, whereas male students focused on the instrumental value of an advisor to "know the facts" or "how to get them." Thus, it seems that women's sense of self becomes organized around being able to make, and then to manage, affiliation and relationships. Roberts and Newton (1986) concluded from their examination of women's biographies that women's images of their lives focused on the relational significance of finding a special partner and maintaining the relationship. In contrast, men had images of themselves in a particular occupational role. Similarly, Josselson (1987) described a process of relational anchoring that took place for women through their family of origin, partner/children, and career and/or friends that was critical to their identity formation, providing an anchor for personal growth, change, and new life directions. Thus, it seems that women's sense of self becomes organized around being able to develop and manage affiliations and relationships.

In contrast to men's development, which focuses on the primacy of the occupational role, development for women is tied to understanding and strengthening the self in relationship to others. Attachments and relationships color how women see themselves, their lives, their careers, and their ongoing responsibilities to those around them (Bardwick, 1980; Bettelheim, 1965; Bloch, 1977; Chodorow, 1974; Douvan and Adelson, 1966; Gilligan, 1980; McClelland, 1975). Berzoff (1985) found that valued female friendships promoted self-definition, catalyzed change, and provided experiences of self-continuity over time. A similar recurring theme in Hancock's (1989) study of women's life stories was growth and development within the context of relationships. Tannen's (1990) discussion of how boys and girls learn to handle complexity describes boys as learning in terms of complex rules and activities and girls as learning in terms of complex networks of relationships.

Thus, interdependence and a combining of attachment

and accomplishment seem key to women's life content and phases. But in addition to playing an important role in the development of women's identities, relationships with others have been found to impact professional development. Stewart and Gudykunst (1982) showed that women perceived both the help of friends and spending a lot of time communicating with their supervisors to be important to their career success. They also found that the perceived importance of skills in obtaining promotions was much greater for men than for women. Similarly, Gallos (1993) noted that support, encouragement, and acceptance from others were critical for women's learning. In their study of how women managers learn from experience, Velsor and Hughes (1990, p. 37) said that "although a manager's tendency to learn from work assignments and hardships does not appear to be gender-related, the capacity of the women to learn from other people is remarkable." Roberts (1991) found that women's self-evaluations were more responsive to the evaluative feedback they received than were those of men in achievement settings.

The lessons women learned after feedback from reflecting on their own behavior helped them perceive themselves as more competent (Valliere, 1986; Velsor and Hughes, 1990). Men, on the other hand, "were more responsive to evaluations of their ability when interacting with those who were clearly superiors, such as coaches or advisors" (Roberts, 1991, p. 305).

This suggests that there may be gender-specific ways in which women and men develop some of their abilities. Studies done on the impact of relationships on women's career development have shown that women's career gains and professional accomplishments are complements, rather than substitutes, for strong interdependent relationships (Abramson and Franklin, 1986; Baruch, Barnett, and Rivers, 1983; Bateson, 1989; Gallese, 1985; Gallos, 1993; Hardesty and Jacobs, 1986; Keele, 1986; Roberts and Newton, 1986).

Building on the notion that the centrality of others for women affects their definitions of achievement, other studies (Astin and Leland, 1991; Case, 1987, 1988; Hegelson, 1990; Rosener, 1990; Velsor and Hughes, 1990) have suggested that women bring different skills and abilities to the work environment that include concern for, and attachment to, others. In her description of managerial language, Case (1988) identified themes of responsibility, affiliation, fairness, understanding, and commitment to a group that were used predominantly by the women she studied but not the men. The "talk" of females seemed to attempt to manage relations with others and was collaborative in drawing out other speakers. She suggested that women have different value systems and different expectations than do white males as a result of their socialization. Feelings about past experiences, group memberships, and self-concept may be involved in what women experience, how it is interpreted, and how these observations and interpretations affect their behavior. These differences lead to a set of different skills and abilities displayed in the workplace (Case, 1993).

Rosener (1990, p. 120) suggested that women draw on "the skills and abilities they developed from their shared experience as women." She characterized women's leadership style as interactive leadership, observing that "these women actively work to make their interactions with subordinates positive for everyone involved." Women in her study tended to exhibit concern for the relationship established with employees.

As the literature has shown, women's orientation toward others and their desire to balance personal and professional development greatly impact the nature of women's contributions to their work environments.

Independence, self-sufficiency, and an emphasis on a work career underpin life phases for men, whereas interdependence and a struggle to combine attachment and accomplishment are keys to explaining women's life content and phases. Biological factors related to the different roles men and women play in the reproductive process would be expected to affect career development outcomes and to interact with socially constituted elements of gender roles. Research has already shown us that women's development is not as sequential and predictable as men's, nor is it as singularly focused on work and career (Abramson and Franklin, 1986; Baruch, Barnett, and Rivers, 1983; Bateson, 1989; Case and Thompson, 1994; Gallese, 1985;

Gallos, 1990; Giele, 1982; Hardesty and Jacobs, 1986; Hennig and Jardin, 1978; Josselson, 1987; Powell and Mainiero, 1992; Roberts and Newton, 1986). As a result, women consider all aspects of their lives as providing valuable insight into their personal development.

The task achievements that occur at work are stressed in the broader context of life achievement to benefit personal development as well as career development. The major means by which task achievements are stressed in the broader context of life is through self-reflection. Bateson (1989) found that women have been particularly interested in the notion of reflexivity, of looking inward as well as outward as a means for personal development. In their study of the development of managers, Velsor and Hughes (1990) found that men tended to focus on achieving skill mastery without feedback or self-reflection, whereas women both sought out feedback and reflected on it. Men acknowledged the importance of individuality and emphasized workplace accomplishments, whereas women made "little distinction between professional learning and personal development. . . . The women had clear expectations that all of their learning would touch the core of their central identities" (Gallos, 1993, p. 9). Real learning for women implied personal growth.

White and Gruber (1985) found similar patterns by gender in choice of leisure activities. Interactions and relationships with others were important elements in leisure activities for women, who rated the following attributes as salient: feeling satisfied, cooperating with other people, and significantly affecting the lives and well-being of others. Men, on the other hand, rated feeling secure and seeing the results of their own efforts as more salient in their leisure activities.

Researchers (Eccles, 1987; Veroff and Feld, 1970) have emphasized the importance of giving women the flexibility to develop their own conceptions of achievements. Eccles (1987) stressed the importance of societal influence on definitions of achievement and its assignment of differential worth to various forms of activities. She said that "too often scientists adopt a male standard of ideal achievement when judging the value of female accomplishments; they seek to understand why women do not 'achieve' like men without considering the possibility that not engaging in some activity may reflect the choice of an alternate activity rather than avoidance. . . . As a consequence, very little systematic information has been gathered regarding the more typical female achievement domains, such as the academic accomplishments of one's offspring and/or one's pupils, satisfaction of one's clients, or one's contribution to local organizations" (p. 136).

Similarly, Veroff and Feld (1970) have also noted differences in how men and women choose to express their achievement motivation, suggesting that gender-role definitions may play a major role in these choices, with relational components prevalent in women's achievements.

Work is the major source of male identity in our culture. Thus men place importance on career achievements as a major responsibility in their lives, adjusting other obligations like marriage and family to fit around their careers (Sekaran, 1986). Objective variables that emphasize getting ahead in an organization have been associated with a traditionally male definition of success (Powell and Mainiero, 1992).

Although work is important to women, it does not necessarily provide their source of identity. Women tend to focus on the multi-arenas of responsibility and obligations in their lives, juggling and prioritizing, committed to doing everything well. In attempting to strike a balance between their relationships with others and their personal achievements at work, women seek levels of personal satisfaction in both areas. Women primarily handle family responsibilities in dual-career marriages (Gutek, Repetti, and Silver, 1988; Hochschild, 1989; Piotrkowski, Rapoport, and Rapoport, 1987; Sekaran, 1986). As a result, the ability to shift from one arena to another, to divide one's attention, to improvise in new circumstances, has always been important to women.

Gallos (1990) argued that women take a more holistic approach to their lives than men and that images of balance between work and relationships affect career decisions and choices. Roberts and Newton (1986) found that women's dreams were equally concerned with marriage, motherhood, and a profession, whereas men's dreams focused on occupational achievement. Lee (1993) found that women who were juggling paid employment and young children at home achieved a sense of mastery from the daily balancing act that was required. Women appear to compose lives that honor all their commitments and still enable them to express all their potentials.

Hypotheses

Review of past research resulted in identifying four conceptual topics as hypotheses regarding Personal Development, Centrality of Others, Role Development, and Arenas of Responsibility. In each of these topics, it was believed that women and men would construct and write about their lives, work, and development differently. To operationalize these hypotheses, a thematic analysis was conducted to develop a code that could differentiate the women from the men. Since both the Life Story and Career History are about a person's past, one code was developed from them. The Learning Plan looks to the future, so another code was developed from it. The code development process is described in the section of this chapter on methodology. We present the full hypotheses here in logical order, even if this approach does not reflect the chronology of the actual research process.

Personal Development

Women focus more on personal development within the context of their careers than men do. From the Life Story and Career History, Personal Development was defined as task achievement in the broader context of life. Three dimensions were examined: self-reflection, personal learnings, and self-confidence. Self-reflection was coded when individuals described how particular events affected them personally and what they learned from these events. Personal learnings was coded when people wrote about lessons they learned about themselves within a work context with applicability to all aspects of their lives. Self-confidence was coded when individuals described an awareness of their level of self-confidence by writing about feeling confident, lacking confidence, or needing to develop confidence. Self-confidence is a recurring theme in the literature, with women reporting lower self-confidence than men, even when given positive feedback (McCarty, 1986).

From the Learning Plan, Personal Development was defined in the same way, with the exception that we dropped the Personal Learnings theme from the analysis of the Learning Plans.

Centrality of Others

The centrality of relationships with others is more important to the learning process as related to women's career development than it is in the case of men's career development. The ongoing importance of other people to women's development has been continually noted. From the Life Story and Career History, Centrality of Others included three dimensions: achievement through involvement of others, impact of another individual, and family and friends. Achievement through involvement of others was coded when subjects focused on lessons that they had learned that required interactions with other people. Lessons learned about others were also included here. Impact of another individual was coded when individuals wrote about the impact a particular individual, such as a mentor, had on their life at a specific time. Family and friends was coded when individuals focused on the importance of family members and friends at particular points in their life.

From the Learning Plan, four dimensions of Centrality of Others were: learning from interactions, caring for well-being of others, development of responsibility, and seeking feedback. Learning from interactions focused on statements in which individuals sought out others in order to learn through interaction. Caring for well-being of others involved statements in which people wrote about the emotional well-being of individuals before, during, or after an interaction with them. This dimension also encompassed statements in which a concern for the understanding and interest of another person was expressed. Development of responsibility concerned written statements in which accepting others, or being given or giving responsibility, was mentioned. Letting others assume responsibility for their own work was included in this theme. Seeking feedback statements were those in which people described requesting feedback from others.

Role Development

Women develop their career roles from both work assignments and inter-actions with others, while men rely more heavily on task assignments for learning their career roles. From the Life Story and Career History, the Role Development concept stresses task achievements in the work context and deals with two dimensions: achievement through self and tasks involving people. Achievement through self was coded when individuals wrote of developing skills by themselves. Tasks involving people was coded when individuals either explicitly referred to the development of skills by involving others or suggested implicitly that learning could not have been accomplished without others.

From the Learning Plan, the Role Development concept dealt with three dimensions: task achievements, observing others, and formal feedback. Task achievements at work are one way in which women develop skills and abilities, but such achievements are stressed in the broader context of life achievement to benefit both personal development and career development. In contrast, task achievements are the way men develop skills and abilities. Since their work provides them with the main source of their identity, we expected men's statements to focus on task achievements within their careers as a means of role development. Statements of task achievement were coded when individuals wrote about engaging in tasks that they could accomplish alone. We expected that the frequency of such statements for men and women would be similar, since both were concerned with achieving in their careers.

Observing others concerned those situations in which an individual focused on watching another individual in order to learn. We expected that men would make more statements in which they focused on observing others to learn, since development for men has typically meant increased autonomy, the importance of individuality, empowering the self, and an emphasis on workplace accomplishments. In contrast, since women derived many of their learnings from reflecting on their own behavior after interacting with others and seeking out feedback (Case and Thompson, 1994), we expected women to make fewer such statements.

Formal feedback concerned statements in which people expected to rely on feedback given through channels built into the infrastructure of the system in which they were located. Examples of such formal feedback would be annual performance reviews, test grades, and work evaluations. The giver of this feedback was usually reported as the superior of the recipient. Following Roberts's (1991) suggestion that men are more responsive to evaluations when given by superiors, we expected that men would make a greater number of statements concerning the use of formal feedback.

Arenas of Responsibility

Women stress both personal achievements and relationships throughout their career, while men focus primarily on personal achievements as their main arena of responsibility. Work is important for women to do yet is not all-encompassing. Women focus on the multi-arenas of responsibility and obligations in their lives — constantly juggling, prioritizing, and balancing. Dale Spender (personal communication, April 1991) has suggested that the concept of multi-arenas of responsibility implies commitment to all areas for which a woman is responsible, in contrast to "balance," which implies a lessening commitment to work. On the other hand, work is the major source of adult male identity in our culture. Since men put prime importance on their career achievements as their major responsibility and adjust most obligations to fit around their career, we expected women to make frequent mention of maintaining a high level of responsibility to multiple arenas in their lives (for example, work, parenthood, extended family, marriage, volunteer activities), and we expected men to focus on their work-related responsibilities as their primary obligations. This theme was appropriate to the Life Story and Career History but not the Learning Plan, so it was only coded for the first two instruments.

Methodology

This section provides an overview of our methodology.

Sample

The initial population for this study consisted of 126 part-time students and 105 full-time students who entered an MBA program at the Weatherhead School of Management (WSOM) in the fall of 1990. All students entering the MBA program were required to take a fourteen-week course titled Managerial Assessment and Development (Boyatzis, 1994a; also see Chapter Four) their first semester. Excluded from the sample were twenty-six students who denied permission to use their data for research and those from other cultures (identified by scores on the TOEFL exam), since we assumed that cultural differences in non-English-speaking countries would be too great for comparison across gender. We divided the remaining students by part-time or full-time status, as well as by gender, thus creating four groups to be compared and contrasted. The mean age of the students entering both the part-time and the full-time MBA programs was twenty-seven. The mean grade-point average and GMAT percentile scores for part-time students were 3.13 and 75 percent, respectively, and for full-time students, 3.14 and 80 percent.

Since there were only thirty-two full-time English-speaking males available for the sample, we used a random number table to randomly select thirty-two subjects from each of the three remaining groups. Previous studies that used a random number table for sample selection of the same population found that their sample was representative of the population from which it was extracted (Boyatzis and Renio, 1989; also see Chapter Five). Since the resulting sample of 128 students that was randomly obtained in this study constituted 55 percent of the population of entering MBA students, we assumed it to be representative of the entering MBA student population. The Learning Plans of three students could not be used in this study: two were unavailable and one was so different that it could not be coded with the codes we had developed.

Life Stories and Career Histories

Two of the assessment instruments used by students during the Managerial Assessment and Development course (Boyatzis, 1994a; also see Chapter Four) were the Career History and the Life Story (Dreyfus, 1991). In writing their Career History, students were given the following instructions: "Begin with your current job and list the jobs going backward in time. Indicate the dates, the name of the organization, the title of the job, the primary responsibilities or duties of the job, and what, if anything, you learned while you had that job. Use additional pages if necessary. Please include all jobs, full-time and part-time, since you began working."

In the first part of the Life Story exercise, students were asked to do the following: "Think of your life as if it were a book. Most books are divided into chapters. Each chapter tells a kind of story; that is, it has a plot. Think about this, then divide your life into chapters, give each chapter a name and for each provide a short plot summary in two to four sentences. Try to think about the major events in your life as 'turning points' leading from one chapter to the next." A second part of the exercise required the students to write about a peak and a nadir experience in their lives.

Development of the Life Story and Career History Code

A preliminary code was developed after a thematic analysis of both the Career Histories and Life Stories. To develop this code, a sample of these written instruments was taken from four men and women not in this sample, but from the same fall 1990 entering MBA class. In the Career History, the analysis was performed on the section titled "What I Learned." A content analysis of the complete Life Story was performed. This preliminary analysis led to the development of a specific coding scheme for both the Life Story and the Career History. The detailed code is available from the authors on request. Every occurrence of codable themes, words, and actions was counted.

To obtain reliability, the Career Histories and Life Stories of sixteen students from the fall 1989 Managerial Assessment and Development course were coded by two independent coders. An initial interrater reliability of 86 percent was obtained between the two coders for both documents for all sixteen students. After a discussion between the two coders about where the differences in coding had occurred, an additional sample of four histories was coded with 100 percent reliability. Based on these results, one coder then coded all of the Career Histories and Life Stories in the sample of 128 students. Any reference to the subjects' names, genders, or program status had been eliminated by the course administrative assistant from both documents used in this study before they were coded. Thus, all coding was performed with the coder blind to the gender and program status of the subjects.

In the analysis of the data, Personal Development was defined by instances of the variables described as self-reflection, personal learnings, and self-confidence. Centrality of Others was calculated by adding achievement through involvement of others, impact of another individual, and family and friends. Role Development was calculated by adding the variables achievement through self and tasks involving people. Arenas of Responsibility was represented by adding statements regarding performing multiple tasks simultaneously or balancing a variety of roles.

Learning Plans

The final product of the Managerial Assessment and Development course was an individualized written Learning Plan. The students' Learning Plans were to take into account peer feedback on their skills and abilities as well as the results of several assessment instruments and self-assessment exercises that the students had completed over the course of the semester. The students were instructed in writing their Learning Plan to include as a prologue a two- to five-year career vision statement, followed by learning goals and action steps that would enable them to achieve their career vision within the next five years. Each overall goal was to be drawn from one or a combination of the twenty-two managerial abilities assessed in this course (Boyatzis, 1982). The action steps were to be activities that students would carry out that would move them closer to achieving the respective learning goal. Students were then to describe evidence of how they would know their goal was achieved and how others would know if they had achieved their goals. Students were instructed to make each goal, action step, and evidence both specific and personal.

Development of the Learning Plans Code

The code development of the Learning Plans involved the learning goals, the action steps, and the evidence sections. A preliminary thematic analysis of the Learning Plans written by four men and four women was carried out. We then examined the Learning Plans of an additional four men and four women in order to refine the code. This code was used in examining the 125 Learning Plans in our sample. The detailed code is available from the authors on request.

To obtain reliability on the code, four Learning Plans (not from the sample) were coded by two independent coders. An interrater reliability of 85 percent was achieved. After a discussion about where the differences had occurred, an additional Learning Plan was coded at 90 percent reliability. One coder then coded all the Learning Plans in the sample chosen for this study. All coding was performed with the coder blind to gender and program status.

In the analysis of the data, Centrality of Others was calculated by adding the number of times the variables identified as learning from interactions, caring for well-being of others, development of responsibility, and seeking feedback were coded in the Learning Plans. Personal Development was calculated by adding the number of times self-reflection and self-confidence were coded in the Learning Plans. Role Development was calculated by adding the number of times the variables referred to as task achievements, observing others, and formal feedback were coded in the Learning Plans.

Verbal Fluency

An initial methodological concern was that men and women might write Career Histories, Life Stories, and Learning Plans of different lengths and that these differences would spuriously affect the results. Using a random number table, a random selection of ten individuals from each of the four 32-student groups was taken to simplify counting of the number of words written by the members of each group. Separate word counts were done on the Career Histories, the Life Stories, and the Learning Plans for each of the forty individuals.

No significant differences were found between men and women. The average length of the Life Stories for men was 744 words and for women was 725 words. The average length of the Career History for men was 137 words and for women was 139 words. The average length of the Learning Plans for men was 3,001 words and for women was 3,326 words. All of these analyses were nonsignificant on t tests and Mann-Whitney U tests.

No significant differences were found when comparing part-time and full-time students. The average length of the Life Stories for part-time students was 784 words and for full-time students was 685 words. The average length of the Career History for part-time students was 132 words and for full-time students was 144 words. The average length of the Learning Plans for part-time students was 3,077 words and for full-time students was 3,249 words. All of these analyses were nonsignificant on t tests and Mann-Whitney U tests.

Results: Life Stories and Career Histories

We note the key results in this section.

Personal Development

In Life Stories and Career Histories, women made Personal Development statements significantly more frequently than men.

Of the three component variables (that is, self-reflection, personal learnings, and self-confidence), women showed significantly more self-reflection than men. No other significant differences were found. Statistical details are shown in Table 1 of Appendix 7.1.

Centrality of Others

Although no significant differences were found between men and women as to the total Centrality of Others score in the Life Stories and Career Histories, women were coded more frequently than men for achievement through involvement of others as well as for impact of another at near-significant levels.

Role Development

In Life Stories and Career Histories, no significant differences were found between the number of times that men and women wrote statements concerning Role Development. This finding demonstrates that both men and women were concerned with the development of their career roles.

Arenas of Responsibilities

In Life Stories and Career Histories, women made more statements concerning Arenas of Responsibilities than men. Women appeared to focus on multi-arenas of responsibility far more frequently than men did and at the same time tried to be responsible in all of the arenas. Men appeared to be less likely to refer to concerns about doing multiple tasks or balancing a variety of roles.

Results: Learning Plans

For the following analyses, full-time and part-time students were combined. No significant differences as to main effects were noted with regard to full-time and part-time students. Three interactions between gender and full-time or part-time program were found to be statistically significant.

Personal Development

In Learning Plans, women mentioned Personal Development significantly more frequently than men. Of the component variables, only self-reflection showed a greater number of statements for women than men. Statistical details are shown in Table 2 of Appendix 7.1.

Centrality of Others

In Learning Plans, women made significantly more statements about the Centrality of Others to their career development than men did. Examination of the component variables showed that only Seeking Feedback revealed a significant difference: women made more statements about Seeking Feedback than men. Significant two-way interaction effects of gender and type of program were found for learning from interactions and caring for well-being of others. Part-time female students made substantially more statements about learning from interactions and caring for the well-being of others than men or full-time female students did. Again, statistical details are shown in Tables 3 and 4 of Appendix 7.1.

Role Development

In Learning Plans, women and men wrote comparable statements concerning Role Development. The only component of Role Development to show differences was Formal Feedback, in which women made more statements than men at a near-significant level. A significant two-way interaction effect of gender and type of program was found for task achievements. Part-time female students made many more statements about task achievements than men or full-time female students did.

Variance of Variances

As scholars explore degrees of homogeneity of males and females, it may be useful to note that the female sample showed significantly greater variances than the male sample on twelve of the eighteen themes examined in the Life Stories, Career Histories, and Learning Plans. Of the eighteen themes constituting the four topics, females showed greater variances on fifteen themes and males showed greater variances on only three themes.

Discussion

The findings supported three of the hypotheses as presented. First, women appear to make more statements than men with a focus on Personal Development within the context of their careers, in Life Stories, Career Histories, and Learning Plans. Second, Centrality of Others is more important to women than men, as evident in their Life Stories, Career Histories, and Learning Plans. Third, women stress personal achievements and relationships (that is, multiple Arenas of Responsibility) more often than men in Life Stories and Career Histories. The fourth hypothesis — concerning women focusing on Role Development from both work and interactions with others versus men focusing only on tasks for their Role Development — was not supported as predicted. No differentiation was found from the analysis of the Life Stories and Career Histories, but women appeared more likely to engage in task-oriented Role Development (that is, through formal feedback and task achievement) than men in their Learning Plans.

Personal Development

The hypothesis that women would engage in more frequent self-reflection than men was confirmed. In contrast, men focused on achieving skill mastery without reflection. This suggests that, for women, reflecting on their own actions provides a more accurate depiction of their role in events that occurred. Self-reflection serves as an important mode of understanding life experiences.

Our findings indicated that, contrary to our earlier expectations, women did not mention the need to develop more self-confidence any more frequently than men. Both were equally concerned with its increased development for career success, yet women mentioned the importance of personal development in the context of their career role development significantly more frequently than men.

A possible explanation for the absence of gender differences in developing more self-confidence centered around the entrance requirements of the MBA program. Given this program's reputation, it may be that only those with high levels of self-confidence applied for admission. Those with less confidence in their abilities may have applied to other less competitive programs in the area, of which there are five.

Centrality of Others

Given that relationships have been found to play an important role in women's development (Gallos, 1990; Gilligan, 1982), we had hypothesized that women would make more statements than men about engaging in interactions with others to learn, being concerned with the emotional well-being of others, achievement through involvement of others, and impact of others, and that they would also be concerned with helping others take responsibility. In contrast, we had expected that men, whose development focuses on separation and individuation (Kohlberg, 1976), would make more statements indicating that they intended to learn from their observations of the actions of others, where no interactions were necessary. Our results revealed a complex picture of Centrality of Others — in some cases confirming our hypotheses and other cases not, and in some cases confirming expected patterns from the literature and in some cases disconfirming expected patterns from the literature.

Our findings did not reflect the stereotyped image of women as nurturing and men as nonnurturing and competitive that has been suggested by others (Bakan, 1966; Eisler, 1988; Erikson, 1968). It may be, as with the variable learning from interactions, that these findings are an artifact of the setting in which the study took place. Dialogue with peers played an important role in the course's design, and students were encouraged to learn from one another and to be respectful of each other's well-being.

Our findings did not support those of Velsor and Hughes's (1990) study, in which women were found to be more likely than men to learn from others. This may be an artifact of the environment in which this study took place. The men and women in this sample were first-year MBA students in their first semester of the program. They had just spent the major part of ten weeks giving and receiving feedback in a group of twelve people. Furthermore, they were strongly encouraged by the groups' facilitators and the course's instructors to use one another as resources for information. Additionally, seven of the twenty-two managerial abilities, many of which the students were trying to develop, were clearly interaction oriented. These were empathy, persuasiveness, networking, negotiating, group management, development of others, and oral communications. It may be that in looking for ways to develop skills that clearly involve other people, men as well as women in this sample turned to other people. This may have carried over to the goal and action management abilities (such as planning and efficiency orientation) and the analytic reasoning abilities (such as systems thinking and pattern recognition), which the students also selected to develop.

The results confirmed our hypothesis that women seek out feedback more frequently than men do as one way to develop their skills and abilities, seek achievement through involvement of others, and are interested in the impact of others. Men relied primarily on formal channels of feedback like yearly reviews, but women still relied on this type of feedback more frequently than men did, demonstrating the importance to women of feedback from others. Our hypothesis that women engage in self-reflection about their actions and their consequences more frequently than men do was also verified. In contrast, men focused on achieving skill mastery without reflection and without soliciting feedback. Women took the opportunity to incorporate solicited feedback into their reflections on their own actions, enabling them, after reflection, to get a more accurate depiction of their role in events that had occurred. Because of the importance of feedback to women, the Centrality of Others to their development was significant.

Roberts and Nolen-Hoeksema's (1989) work on gender differences in the responsiveness to others' evaluations suggests that women perceive others' evaluations to be more informative about their true abilities than men do. The women were very interested in the information they could get about their own performance from others. A concern for the lack of constructive criticism, except at annual performance reviews, may be why women find it necessary to go to others and request feedback. Our findings supported the hypothesis that women would make a greater number of statements requesting feedback from others for the development of their skills and abilities than men would.

Given that attachment to other people is an important source of identity and personal power for women, it is not surprising that they would ask others for information about their own development. Women could use a request for feedback as both a means for self-learning about their abilities and to reach out and establish contact with others. Hence, it is not just the feedback that is important, but also the establishment of contact with another. Because it appeared to be an acceptable way to make contact, women asked for feedback in both their academic and work environments.

Within the Centrality of Others, we found two revealing interaction effects. Noticeably high scores of part-time female students were found as compared to the other three groups in Learning from Interactions, Caring for Well-Being of Others, and Task Achievements. We attribute this to a combination of differences between part-time and full-time students and differences between men and women around career development. The experience of part-time students who are working full time on their careers while taking classes to enhance career mobility is much more similar to the career experiences of professionals in general than to the experience of full-time graduate students involved primarily in classroom learning. In fact, the experience of the part-time woman MBA student closely parallels that of professional women's desire to "do it all," juggling multi-arenas of responsibility as well as combining their personal development with career development. This observation provides additional explanation for the hypothesis supported about Arenas of Responsibility. For these women, personal identity was enmeshed in being the best one could be at work, with MBA classes primarily a means to gain status through increased knowledge, skills, and abilities on the job. These women appeared highly career motivated and were interested in devoting their energies to activities that would enhance their positions. The contrast in learning from interactions between part-time women and part-time men, who also work full time with career enhancement the focus of their MBA education, adds further evidence that there are developmental differences between men and women in the Centrality of Others to their managerial development and the ways in which they respectively go about developing their careers.

Full-time students, in contrast, derive most of their personal identity from being students rather than from their future careers. Since so much of full-time coursework is done through group projects, study groups, and Executive Action Teams, and since feedback is a regular part of the educational process, it may be that learning from interactions with others happens for full-time women without their having to seek it out. Thus, they do not have to create the opportunity for learning from interactions in the same way that part-time women do.

Role Development

Our hypothesis that women focus on task achievements as a means of skill development as often as men do was confirmed. A closer examination of the data showed that women in the part-time program engaged in task achievements significantly more than the men (both full-time and part-time). We suspect that one factor that may account for this finding is that part-time women have learned that they must outdo their male colleagues at work to obtain recognition, whereas an academic classroom setting is more merit based.

Both men and women focused on task achievements as a major part of their career role development. Maccoby and Jacklin's (1974) classic study of gender differences found no evidence in their research that boys would be more interested in task achievement than girls. Because women are concerned with personal development and maintaining relationships, an erroneous assumption is that their task achievements are fewer. It was evident that this component variable was largely responsible for the mean frequency of the overall role development category. Also, as expected, our findings confirmed that men engaged in task achievements without reflection, which was in accordance with findings of Velsor and Hughes (1990) and Case and Thompson (1994).

These results bring into question studies that suggest that women define achievements differently than men (Eccles, 1987; Veroff and Feld, 1970). Our overall results suggest that women's definitions for achievement encompass not only traditional ones such as high task performance but also include more relationship-oriented definitions such as enabling co-workers to feel satisfied and accomplished on the job.

The lack of a clear gender split in these findings may also be a reflection of changing societal norms. An increasing number of men are rebelling against the stereotype of what it means to be a man in America. Stoltenberg's *Refusing to Be a Man* (1990) is almost unprecedented in its outright rejection of domination masculinity. Brod (1987, p. 1), one of the pioneers of the men's studies movement, calls for nothing less than a fundamental "deconstruction and reconstruction of masculinity." Other men propose new ways of defining masculinity that are more stereotypically "feminine" (Coltrane, 1988; McGill, 1985). Not all men expect, nor do they always desire, to be stoic individuals, marching to work everyday and competing with the rest of the world on a hero's journey concerned at all costs with being "independent"—as Bly would suggest in his popular book, *Iron John* (1990). Men are turning down promotions that involve relocating in order to accommodate their spouse's careers and/or to prevent the disruption of their children's lives. These trends all reflect a different form of concern for others that has not traditionally been part of the male gender role.

While a number of studies (Roberts, 1991; Valliere, 1986; Velsor and Hughes, 1990) have shown that women seek out feedback about their abilities, our findings about the formal feedback variable indicate that women also value formal channels of feedback for information about their abilities as well as the feedback that they have solicited.

The results of this study suggested, too, that in their development of skills and abilities, women rely on feedback from structured channels as often as men do. We expected to find that men would utilize formal feedback more frequently than women did. This finding, combined with results that indicated that women request feedback more frequently, supports Roberts's (1991, p. 303) suggestion that "women perceive others' evaluations to be more informative about their abilities than do men." Further studies of the students' self-assessment of their abilities before and after receiving feedback from a variety of sources may support the idea that women pay closer attention to evaluative feedback than men do. Theoretically, the women's self-evaluations after the feedback should take into account the feedback they received more frequently than the men's.

There were two factors that we could not ignore in examining the results of our research: the setting in which this study took place and the instructions on the format of the Learning Plan assignment. An academic setting is structured so that formal feedback such as grades and comments on written assignments and presentations is given on a regular basis. In the instructions on the format of the Learning Plans, students were told that they had to include an evidence section on how others would know they had accomplished the corresponding learning goal. One easy way to do this was through the formal channels of feedback, such as grades and performance reviews, which were easily accessible. It may be that if this section had not been included in the instructions of the structure of the Learning Plans, this variable of formal feedback would have been coded a lot less frequently. Further examination is needed to determine whether the mean frequencies of occurrence would continue to differ for men and women if statements coded for formal feedback in the evidence section were eliminated.

Arenas of Responsibility

As hypothesized, women seemed to consider their careers to be one component of their lives, rather than their sole focus. Women tended to discuss their lives as comprised of many complementary parts, including their careers, which they continually balanced with the rest of their activities and which together form a whole. Women spoke of their multi-arenas of responsibility not as competing responsibilities that could be traded off and on in turn, but as areas in which they were constantly responsible and engaged. In contrast, men did not discuss a need to similarly balance areas other than work and school. The hypothesis that women would focus on career task achievement as well as on personal development was also supported. Women tended to think about task achievement on the job as often as men did. This finding, coupled with the finding that women tended to be responsible in multi-arenas of their lives, is important in that it shows that although women are very concerned with balancing the many components of their lives, their concern does not interfere with task achievements. Finally, the expectation that women would make more statements regarding personal development than men was supported. It seems that men focus primarily on role development through skill mastery, whereas women's development occurs as an interaction between self-reflection and expression of feelings on the one hand and skill mastery and task achievements on the other.

While studies of managers have revealed that for many managers, personal and family time was sharply curtailed and that personal identity was indistinguishable from work (Halper, 1988; Mintzberg, 1973), managers suggested that such sacrifices were costs they were willing to pay for career achievement (Halper, 1988). More recently, Hegelson (1990) found that women were more likely than men to view their jobs as just one element of who they were and were not willing to sacrifice themselves to their careers. Providing evidence that there is a need to broaden the definition of career development to include women's experiences of professional accomplishments as well as other arenas of responsibility, our findings confirm those of Hegelson. Powell and Mainiero (1992) take this notion of complementarity one step further and suggest that in balancing the multiple arenas of work and personal lives, women tend to seek some desired level of satisfaction with both realms. They argue that this satisfaction with their multiple arenas of responsibility may make women better equipped for coping with the trials and tribulations of management than those who focus on more objective measures of career success. That is, managerial success in this ever-changing business climate may be becoming dependent on the ability to measure career success subjectively and flexibly rather than in harshly objective terms.

Conclusion

Although we found significant overall differences between men and women in several developmental areas, it is crucial that these findings be viewed in an appropriate context. Women are not a homogeneous mass in which each member is identical to the others. Indeed, we found wide ranges in the female subsample when compared to the male subsample in this study. Schein's (1982) life-style anchor, Derr's (1986) getting-balanced careerist, and Larwood and Gutek's (1987) theory of women's career development are steps in acknowledging that career can no longer be limited to occupational choice while ignoring life-style issues. Further, Fraser and Nicholson (1990) and Ely (1991) have stressed the need to examine differences among groups of women as well as between men and women. While we have presented data that show some differences between men and women, we expect that, as we continue to examine the data by generational cohorts, both historical circumstances and the positioning of women in their reproductive life cycles may have important implications for understanding the developmental differences both within and between groups of men and women. Our finding of significant two-way interactions of gender and type of program (full-time or part-time) provides further support for this notion.

Understanding the developmental differences both confirmed and suggested in this study is also important for business schools in designing their curricula and delivering their instruction. Schools need to recognize differences in developmental needs of women and men MBA students as the need to maximize all employees' productivity continues to be an important issue. Business schools are now faced with the demands of a student population that includes larger proportions of women than ever and, as we found, women rely on assessment both by themselves and by others and seek feedback and dialogue with others as conscious elements of the learning experience. MBA education must take the developmental needs of female students into account in order to effectively prepare business students for their responsibilities as managers. Not only must students themselves be provided with substantial and frequent feedback, but they also must be taught to recognize the importance of providing opportunities for such feedback and corresponding dialogue when they are in positions of authority.

The result of the discovery of developmental differences between men and women is that not only must MBA programs be designed to meet the needs of their female students, but male and female students alike must be prepared for managing, while at the same time encouraging, such differences in the workplace. Currently, most MBA programs focus on providing students with functional reasoning skills (that is, learning how to achieve their goals). However, in many instances, managers do not actually spend that much time using functional reasoning skills; they spend more time using substantive reasoning to manage the various components of their lives (that is, choosing priorities, determining why it is important to do something, integrating multiple tasks). Ethical questions arise at intersections of professional and private lives; thus, instruction in critical thinking — which management programs seek to provide — must address these intersections if it is to influence behavior (Kurfiss, 1988). Although conversations about ethical questions necessitate skills that many are not accustomed to using in the classroom, deliberations on such matters give purpose to learning. It would then seem that women, with their tendency to focus simultaneously on issues of personal development and career development, may be particularly well suited to addressing and resolving ethical questions. Consequently, since integrating several tasks at once and balancing multiple priorities are skills that are critical to managerial success, women's tendency to use substantive reasoning in balancing personal and professional development should be encouraged by MBA education. Programs can be designed that allow students who have not developed such skills to learn from those who have.

We also need ways to design and describe professional work that incorporate professional and nurturing roles over time, including simultaneous high achievement and high relations for both men and women. Insights such as these are useful for managing a diverse workforce of the 1990s, which will include a large number of women. Implicit in understanding individual career motivation are strategies for effective supervising and maximizing productivity. Such strategies include the importance of more frequent feedback from others for self-reflection, flexibility in job design, recognition of balance needs, and assignment of important task responsibilities to women, since women learn through task accomplishment just as men do.

Not only is the nature of work changing, but the nature of people who work is changing, too. They are concerned with growth opportunities and happiness at work. They do not want inhumane and stifling jobs. Managers are called on to appreciate the legitimate differences that exist in how individuals develop both personally and professionally and to devise organizational structures that encourage and nurture human growth. Through this approach, people can be made to feel that they are bringing something of value to their organizations and that they are being judged, as they should be, on their organizational contributions.

Appendix 7.1. Gender Differences in
Life Stories, Career Histories, and Learning Plans.

Table 1. Female and Male Differences in Life Stories and Career Histories.

| Theme | Average number of statements | | | | | Homogeneity of variance |
	Female (n = 64)	SD	Male (n = 64)	SD	t	F
Personal Development	10.49	5.63	8.41	5.28	2.12*	1.13
Self-Reflection	5.33	3.57	3.72	2.84	2.78***	1.58*
Self-Confidence	0.59	0.82	0.59	0.90	−.02	1.22
Personal Learnings	4.57	3.97	4.10	3.44	0.71	1.33
Centrality of Others	14.83	11.96	12.57	7.94	1.24	2.27***
Achievement Through Others	2.74	3.05	2.11	2.17	1.32+	1.98***
Impact of Another	0.56	1.15	0.33	0.57	1.39+	4.06***
Family/Friends	11.52	10.53	10.13	7.26	0.85	2.11***
Role Development	11.19	8.96	9.63	6.90	1.09	1.69*
Achievement Through Self	7.38	6.31	6.38	5.36	0.96	1.39
Tasks Involving People	3.81	3.58	3.25	2.75	.98	1.69*
Arenas of Responsibility	0.78	0.92	0.34	0.63	3.04***	2.15***

Note: For one-tailed t tests and F tests of homogeneity of variance: $+p < .10$; $*p < .05$; $**p < .01$; $***p < .005$. Personal Development, Centrality of Others, and Arenas of Responsibility were coded from the Life Stories and Career Histories. Role Development was coded from the Career History.

Table 2. Female and Male Differences in Learning Plans.

| Theme | Average number of statements | | | | | Homogeneity of variance |
	Female (n = 64)	SD	Male (n = 61)	SD	t	F
Personal Development	3.55	2.89	2.72	2.39	1.74*	1.46+
Self-Reflection	0.61	1.16	0.16	0.42	2.88***	7.83*
Self-Confidence	2.93	2.40	2.56	2.35	0.90	1.04
Centrality of Others	6.03	4.31	4.69	3.40	1.94*	1.61*
Learning from Interactions	1.80	2.42	1.66	1.73	0.38	1.95**
Caring for Well-Being of Others	2.06	1.75	1.70	1.86	1.11	1.13
Development of Responsibility	0.28	0.95	0.15	0.44	1.02	4.65***
Seeking Feedback	1.89	2.82	1.18	1.50	1.77*	3.53***

165

Table 2. Female and Male Differences in Learning Plans, Cont'd.

| | Average number of statements | | | | | Homogeneity of variance |
| | Female (n = 64) | SD | Male (n = 61) | SD | t | |
Theme						F
Role Development	47.32	19.56	44.03	15.90	1.03	1.51
Task Achievements	42.17	17.40	39.46	15.00	0.93	1.34
Observing Others	1.94	2.26	2.43	2.76	−1.09	1.49+
Formal Feedback	3.20	4.54	2.15	2.99	1.54+	2.30***

Note: For one-tailed t tests and F tests of homogeneity of variance: $+p < .10$; $*p < .05$; $**p < .01$; $***p < .005$.

Table 3. Means of Statements in Learning Plans
with Interaction Effects of Program Status and Gender.

| | Female | | Male | |
| | Full-time (n = 32) | Part-time (n = 32) | Full-time (n = 30) | Part-time (n = 31) |
Variables				
Learning from Interactions	1.09	2.50	1.73	1.58
Caring for Well-Being of Others	1.47	2.66	1.87	1.55
Task Achievements	38.00	46.34	41.10	37.87

Table 4. Analysis of Interactions Between Program and Gender.

Effect	Sum of squares	df	Mean square	F
Learning from Interactions				
Gender	.67	1	.67	.16
Full-time/part-time	13.02	1	13.02	3.05+
Gender × FTPT	18.97	1	18.97	4.45*
Caring for Well-Being of Others				
Gender	4.08	1	4.08	1.32
Full-time/part-time	6.41	1	6.41	2.07
Gender × FTPT	17.70	1	17.70	5.72*
Task Achievements				
Gender	233.60	1	233.60	.90
Full-time/part-time	227.28	1	227.28	.88
Gender × FTPT	1045.58	1	1045.58	4.04*

Note: Significance levels for two-tailed tests: $+p < .10$; $*p < .05$.

Eight

WILL IT MAKE A DIFFERENCE?: ASSESSING A VALUE-ADDED, OUTCOME-ORIENTED, COMPETENCY-BASED PROFESSIONAL PROGRAM

*Richard E. Boyatzis, Ann Baker,
David Leonard, Kenneth Rhee, and
Lorraine Thompson*

Outcome studies are critical during a time of major transition, such as the current era in graduate management education. These studies provide systematic feedback necessary for continuous improvements. They also provide a test of our assumptions about education and our traditions, as well as a means of testing new ideas and methods. Another rationale for conducting outcome studies is that the American Assembly of Collegiate Schools of Business (AACSB) has changed its accrediting guidelines to include self-study as a major component of the accreditation review process, and outcome studies are recommended as a desirable form of self-study (American Assembly of Collegiate Schools of Business, 1989).

Only a few schools have conducted student-change outcome studies — one of the five types of outcome assessment studies described in the Preface — comparing their graduates to their

We wish to thank Deborah Griest and Louella Hein for their essential contributions in the design, data collection, and data analysis of this project.

students at the time of entry into the program (Albanese and others, 1990). But many schools have conducted other types of outcome studies, such as studies of their alumni, studies with the people who hire their students, and studies with business executives. Some schools have examined the student-change impact of specific courses (Bigelow, 1991).

While outcome studies have been a focus of attention in undergraduate programs, less attention has been paid to the effects of graduate programs (Astin, 1992; Banta, 1988; Banta and Associates, 1993; Pascarella and Terenzini, 1991; Melchiori, 1988; Mentkowski and Strait, 1983; Mentkowski and others, 1991; Winter, McClelland, and Stewart, 1981). This may be a function of the professions in which the faculty and other "experts" believe themselves to be the best agents to regulate and evaluate the products of their professional schools.

Prior outcome studies of MBA programs have shown significant improvement of students with regard to some abilities, as mentioned in Chapter Five. However, the improvement has been less than desired or expected. Students showed gains on about 50 percent of the abilities assessed in any particular study (Boyatzis and Sokol, 1982; Development Dimensions International, 1985; American Assembly of Collegiate Schools of Business, 1987). In these selected MBA programs, graduates were shown to have significantly more of *several* of the following abilities: Planning, Decision Making, Resistance to Stress, Inner Work Standards, Tolerance for Uncertainty, Analytic Thinking, Perception of Threshold Cues (Empathy), Information Gathering/Problem Analysis, Written Communication, and Leadership. The specific abilities enhanced and the number of abilities enhanced varied by institution. In these studies, graduates of some of the programs were shown to have significantly less than entering students of: Social Objectivity, Perception of Threshold Cues (Empathy), and Planning. Given the common criticisms of MBA graduates, it is difficult to believe that many MBA programs were attaining even these modest gains.

The Weatherhead School of Management (WSOM) developed a new value-added, outcome-oriented, competency-based MBA program to address the criticisms and issues facing graduate management education (Boyatzis, Cowen, and Kolb, 1991; also see Chapter Three). As part of a fifty-year longitudinal study of the development and careers of the WSOM MBA graduates, seven cohorts of students are being assessed as they enter the program, as they graduate from the program, and in intervals of five to seven years until they retire. The first and second cohorts of students who graduated from the new MBA program were the focus of this study. In particular, the study focused on changes in their abilities.

Method

This section summarizes methodological details.

Sample for the 1990–1992 Study

In the fall of 1990, the new MBA program was implemented for all entering students. One hundred and five students entered the short and long (that is, the one-year and two-year) full-time program in August 1990; 19 additional students entered the full-time one-year program in June 1991. Of those, 108 (87 percent) gave their permission for their information to be used in continuing research. Those not giving permission to use their personal information in future research were compared to those giving their permission on a number of demographic variables. There was no difference in age, years of work experience, GMAT scores, undergraduate grade-point average, and native language (that is, native English-speaking versus nonnative English-speaking). A higher percentage of women than men denied permission to use their information in future research.

Of the 108, 96 (89 percent) graduated in January or May 1992. Ten of the students not graduating were in joint degree programs, such as the joint MBA/JD, which take an additional two years. Two converted to the part-time program due to job pressure; none left the program. Students entering the new part-time MBA program in the fall of 1990 were not included in the study since they would not be graduating until 1994 or 1995.

The 96 students were contacted by letter in February 1992

and asked to participate in a two- to two-and-a-half-hour session examining their reactions to the program and some assessment activities. Before the students were contacted, 33 were randomly assigned to assessment condition A, 33 were randomly assigned to assessment condition B, and 30 were randomly assigned to assessment condition C.

Overall, 74 percent of the population (that is, 71 of the 96) participated in the study: 73 percent in condition A, 58 percent in condition B, and 87 percent in condition C. Of those who did not participate in the study, 53 percent had scheduling difficulties, 31 percent could not be contacted by telephone or did not respond to the letters, and 16 percent refused to participate.

The sample in the study appears comparable to the population of entering students. The 71 students in the study were the same age at entry (average age of 26.5, range from 21 to 41) as the entering sample of 108 who gave permission to use their information in the research (average age of 26.4, range from 20 to 45). Fifteen percent of each sample were nonnative English speakers. Thirty-seven percent of the 71 students in the study sample were female, and 43 percent of the 108 entering students giving their permission were female.

In an attempt to provide a comparison group of graduates from the old MBA program, two samples of part-time graduating students were identified. They had not gone through the new MBA program, although they were taking electives along with full-time students during two years of the implementation of the new program. It was not, therefore, a true comparison to the old program but could provide some information. Forty-three graduating part-time students were randomly assigned to condition A, and forty-five were assigned to condition B. It was difficult to get part-time students to participate. Thirty-five percent of the students contacted for condition A participated, but only 22 percent of the students contacted for condition B participated. Since the ten students in this condition were considered too small for any behavioral comparison, an additional sample of twenty students were contacted and resulted in nine more students in this condition.

Sample for the 1991–1993 Study

In the summer of 1991, 32 students entered the full-time MBA program. In the fall of 1991, 73 students entered the full-time program. Of the 105 students, 83 (79 percent) gave their permission for their information to be used in continuing research. Of the 83, 71 (86 percent) graduated in January or May 1993. Two of the students not graduating were in the joint MBA/JD program, which takes an additional two years. Two converted to the part-time program, eight decided to extend their program by one semester, and none left the program. Seven additional students were graduating in 1993 and eligible to participate in the study: 3 had entered in the fall of 1990 and extended their program and 4 had switched from the part-time to the full-time program.

The 89 students were contacted by letter in January 1993 and asked to participate in a two- to two-and-a-half-hour session examining their reactions to the program and some assessment activities. Since 11 were not going to graduate, they were eliminated from the study. Before the students were contacted, 26 were randomly assigned to assessment condition A, 31 were randomly assigned to assessment condition B, and 32 were randomly assigned to assessment condition C.

Overall, 74 percent of the population (that is, 58 of the 78) participated in the study: 64 percent in condition A, 78 percent in condition B, and 81 percent in condition C. Of those who did not participate in the study, 52 percent had scheduling difficulties or refused to participate, 16 percent could not be contacted by telephone or did not respond to the letters, 29 percent were not graduating, and 3 percent switched from the full-time to the part-time program.

The sample in the study appears comparable to the population of entering students. The 58 students in the study were the same age at entry (average age of 26.5, range from 20 to 34) as the entering sample of 83 who gave permission to use their information in the research (average age of 26.6, range from 20 to 37). Seventeen percent of the students in the study sample and 18 percent of the students giving their permission were nonnative English speakers. Thirty percent of the students in the study sample were female, and 32 percent of the 83 entering students giving their permission were female.

Data Collection at Entry

As mentioned previously, all entering MBA students are required to take a course called Managerial Assessment and Development (Boyatzis, 1994a; also see Chapter Four). During the course, the students complete, among other instruments, exercises and tests, the Learning Skills Profile, the Adaptive Style Inventory, the Presentation Exercise, the Group Discussion Exercise, and the Individual Interview (that is, a critical incident interview) (see Chapter Four for detailed descriptions of each instrument and exercise).

The Learning Styles Inventory was not used in these outcome studies because it was not predicted or expected that any consistent change would occur in the students' learning-style preferences. Changes in people's learning style are expected as they become socialized into certain fields or specializations. The students in the MBA program are expected to enter all of the fields and specializations available in the WSOM. Although no consistent shift in learning-style preferences was expected, it was thought that exposure to diverse learning situations may result in increased learning flexibilities, as assessed with the Adaptive Style Inventory.

In addition, during this outcome study only, the coder of the Presentation Exercise assessed the Enthusiasm shown by each presenter after the presentation and question-and-answer period were over by placing a mark along a continuum from "Puts me to sleep" to "Keeps me at the edge of my seat." A grid was later superimposed on the continuous line and a score of 1 to 7 was assigned, 7 indicating an exciting and enthusiastic presentation.

Some of the abilities are relatively infrequently coded in the Group Discussion Exercise. Flexibility, Negotiating, Quantitative Analysis, and Social Objectivity did not appear during the first study (in 1990–1992). That is, these abilities were not coded in any of the Group Discussion Exercises for the graduating students in the study or in their entering exercises. Similarly, Flexibility, Group Management, and Quantitative Analysis did not appear during the second study (in 1991–1993).

The individual interview conducted in the first study was an in-depth review of the student's reactions to the program with the sole intention of obtaining program feedback. It was not coded for any abilities.

Graduating Assessment Conditions

The three sets of assessment conditions are outlined below.

Condition A. Students completed the Learning Skills Profile (the same one used in the course at entry), the MBA Career Progress Study Questionnaire, the Presentation Exercise (the same exercise used in the course at entry), and the Adaptive Style Inventory in the 1991–1993 Study. Each person randomly selected one of the eight topics for presentation; the topic could not be the same one used for the presentation made during the course. It was videotaped. The MBA Career Progress Study Questionnaire asks each student for their reactions to aspects of the program and to activities they have participated in.

Condition B. Students completed the Learning Skills Profile, the MBA Career Progress Study Questionnaire, the Group Discussion Exercise (the same one used in the course at entry, but with different business cases presented), and the Adaptive Style Inventory in the 1991–1993 study. The Group Discussion Exercise was videotaped.

Condition C. Students completed the Learning Skills Profile, the MBA Career Progress Study Questionnaire, a taped In-Depth Interview, and the Adaptive Style Inventory in the 1991–1993 study. In the first study, the interviewer asked the student to recall high and low points during the program. In the second study, a critical incident interview was given.

Coding

The Presentation Exercise and Group Discussion Exercise videotapes and Individual Interview audiotapes were coded by advanced doctoral students and faculty trained in the coding system. After several weeks of training, the prospective coders took a reliability test. Only those demonstrating 70 percent or better reliability with the experts — that is, professionals using the code in validation studies — became coders. To minimize code bias during this study, all videotapes of the graduating students were mixed among the videotapes from the same students' entering exercises and coded in random order. Videotapes for the graduating part-time students were also mixed among the data.

The entering tapes were recoded to control for possible coding shifts — gradual shifts in coding conventions that may occur over time. The original and the new coding of Oral Communication ability from the Presentation Exercise videotapes at the time of entry were highly correlated ($r = .715$, $n = 24$, $p < .001$). Of the nine abilities coded once or more in the Group Discussion Exercise videotapes from the graduating students and their entering exercises (that is, Efficiency Orientation, Planning, Initiative, Attention to Detail, Persuasiveness, Self-Confidence, Group Management, Systems Thinking, and Pattern Recognition), the correlation of the new coding and the original coding at the time of entry was highly significant. The average correlation was .643 ($n = 19$, $p < .001$), the median was .674, and the range was .261 to 1.00. This showed significant correlation between the original and recoding, but the range of association supported the necessity of recoding all tapes to maximize coding consistency.

Because they contain a number of students and are complex to code, the Group Discussion Exercise videotapes were coded for the research studies by a pair of the trained coders and then by another member of the research team independently. All differences between the pair and the third coder were discussed and reconciled to their mutual satisfaction. The Individual Interview audiotapes were coded by two independent coders; all differences between the pair of coders were reconciled.

Analysis of the results will be reported for the entire sample and then reported for the sample with nonnative English-speaking students removed. Whether nonnative English-speaking students come from China, Japan, India, Korea, Brazil, or Greece, the assessment activities at entry into the program may reflect their degree of comfort with English and with cultural norms during their first two or three weeks in the United States. Although many of the abilities assessed have been validated as relating to managerial performance in many countries and cultures around the world (Boyatzis, 1982; Thornton and Byham, 1982; Spencer and Spencer, 1993), lack of English proficiency may result in artificially low coding. That is, students may not demonstrate abilities they have because the use of English does not come easily to them while under pressure during the exercises.

Results

Two basic questions need to be addressed.

Did Students Change in the 1990–1992 Study?

The graduating students showed statistically significant increases on eight of the twelve skills measured by the Learning Skills Profile and the Total Score. Those skills were: Help, Sense-Making, Information Gathering, Information Analysis, Theory, Quantitative, Technology, and Goal Setting. The students did not show significant change in the areas of Leadership, Relationship, Action, and Initiative. When the nonnative English-speaking students were removed from the sample, only one result changed in significance: the Sense-Making skill showed no improvement. Statistical details are shown in Table 1 of Appendix 8.1.

The graduating students showed significant increases in Oral Communication and Enthusiasm, as measured from the Presentation Exercise (the graduating students' average was 6.25 and the entering students' average was 4.25; $t = 5.54$, $n = 19$, $p < .001$). Statistical details are shown in Table 2 of Appendix 8.1.

Graduating students showed significant increases in Efficiency Orientation, Empathy, Networking, Self-Confidence, and Pattern Recognition from the Group Discussion Exercise (details are shown in Table 3 of Appendix 8.1). In the same exercise, they showed near-significant increases in Planning, Initiative, and Group Management. Also, graduating students showed significant increases in the total score of abilities, reflected in the sum of their scores on all abilities from this exercise. The graduating students showed significant increases in the number of different abilities for which they were coded in the Group Discussion Exercise. The only abilities coded in this exercise that did not show a significant increase were Attention to Detail, Persuasiveness, Developing Others, and Systems Thinking. Again, no significant change was noted for Flexibility, Negotiating, Quantitative Analysis, or Social Objectivity; these abilities could not be analyzed because no one was coded as showing them in either the entering or graduating exercises. When the sample of native English-speaking students was analyzed, the only change from the above results was that Initiative dropped from near significance to nonsignificance.

Did Students Change in the 1991–1993 Study?

The graduating students showed statistically significant increases on ten of the twelve skills measured by the Learning Skills Profile and the Total score. Those skills were: Leadership, Relationship, Sense-Making, Information Gathering, Information Analysis, Theory, Quantitative, Technology, Goal Setting, and Initiative skills. The students did not show significant change in the Action and Help skills. When the nonnative English-speaking students were removed from the sample, only one result changed in significance: the Initiative skill showed no improvement. A graphic representation of the overall scores from the Learning Skills Profile for the 1990–1992 and 1991–1993 entering versus graduating students is included in Figure 8.1. Statistical details are shown in Table 4 of Appendix 8.1.

The graduating students showed significant increases in Oral Communication and Enthusiasm, as measured on the Presentation Exercise (details are shown in Table 5 of Appendix 8.1).

Figure 8.1. Profile of Graduating Versus Entering
Students' Mean Scores on the Learning Skills Profile.

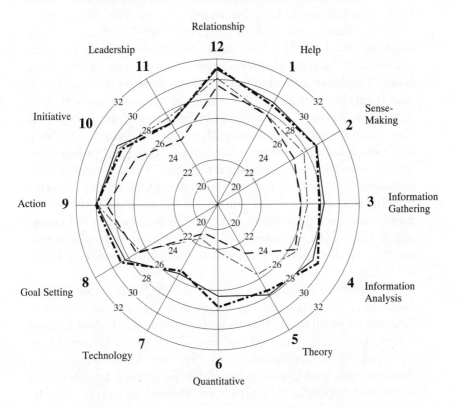

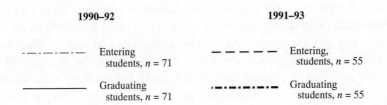

Graduating students showed significant increases in Efficiency Orientation, Planning, and Pattern Recognition from the Group Discussion Exercise. In the same exercise, they showed near-significant increases in Empathy, Self-Confidence, Networking, Systems Thinking, and Quantitative Analysis. Also, graduating students showed significant increases in the Total score of abilities, reflected in the sum of their scores on all abilities from this exercise. The graduating students demonstrated significant increases in the number of different abilities for which they were coded in the Group Discussion Exercise. The only abilities coded in this exercise and not showing a significant increase were Initiative, Attention to Detail, Persuasiveness, Negotiating, Developing Others, and Social Objectivity. No significant change was noted (and could not be analyzed because no one was coded as showing these abilities in either the entering or graduating exercises) for Flexibility, Group Management, and Use of Technology. Statistical details are shown in Table 6 of Appendix 8.1.

Graduating students showed significant increases in the Individual Interview (that is, the critical incident interview) in Efficiency Orientation, Planning, Initiative, Self-Control, Flexibility, Empathy, Networking, Self-Confidence, Group Management, Oral Communications, Systems Thinking, Pattern Recognition, and Quantitative Analysis (details are shown in Table 7 of Appendix 8.1). Graduates showed more Use of Technology and Social Objectivity than when they entered at a near-significant level. Graduates also showed significant increases in the total of all abilities and the number of different abilities during the events described in the interview. When nonnative English-speaking students were removed from the sample, the only findings to change were that Use of Technology went from near significant to significant and Social Objectivity went from significant to nonsignificant. No change was found in the interview with Attention to Detail, Persuasiveness, Negotiating, and Developing Others.

When learning flexibility was examined, the only significant change found was that graduating students appeared to have less flexibility with regard to Active Experimentation situations than entering students (Active Experimentation Flexibility for graduating students was 1.18 versus 1.69 for entering students, $n = 50$, $t = 3.06$, $p < .01$, with comparable results for the native English-speaking sample of $n = 41$). All other forms of learning flexibility showed nonsignificant results.

Discussion

It appears that the new MBA program is having a positive impact in helping students improve their abilities between the time of entry and graduation. The graduating students present themselves orally as more capable than when they entered (as reflected in the Oral Communication score from the Presentation Exercise), demonstrate more capability when interacting with others than when they entered (as shown by the sum score and number of abilities scored in the Group Discussion Exercise and the Individual Interview), and view themselves as more capable than when they entered (indicated by the improvement in the Total score from the Learning Skills Profile).

The results from the three exercises and one test over the three years and two cadres or cohorts of students suggest that the graduating students showed significant improvement on thirteen abilities, as shown in Table 8.1 and summarized in Table 8.2. These included Efficiency Orientation, Planning, Self-Control, Empathy, Networking, Self-Confidence, Oral Communication, Use of Concepts, Systems Thinking, Pattern Recognition, Quantitative Analysis, Use of Technology, and Written Communication. When considering the information from all of the exercises on the following five abilities, the graduating students showed some significant improvement with some positive and some neutral results: Initiative, Flexibility, Group Management, Developing Others, and Social Objectivity. A lack of improvement in graduating students (that is, they were similar when graduating to when they entered) is suggested in three abilities: Attention to Detail, Persuasiveness, and Negotiating.

Table 8.1. Summary of Results: 1990–1992 and 1991–1993 Studies.

Ability	Individual Interview 1993	Group Discussion Exercise 1992	1993	Learning Skills Profile 1992	1993		Presentation Exercise 1992	1993
Efficiency Orientation	+	+	+	0	0	[9:]	na	
Planning	+	+	+	+	+	[8:]	na	
Initiative	+	~	0	0	~	[10:]	na	
Attention to Detail	0	0	0	na			na	
Self-Control	+	na		na			na	
Flexibility	+	?	?	0	0	[2:40]	na	
Empathy	+	+	+	0	+	[12:]	na	
Persuasiveness	0	0	0	0	+	[11:]	na	
Networking	+	+	+	+	+	[12:& 3:]	na	
Negotiating	0	?	0	0	0	[11:40]	na	
Self-Confidence	+	+	+	+	+	[Total]	na	
Group Management	+	+	?	0	0	[11:50]	na	
Developing Others	0	0	0	+	~	[1: & 8:]	na	
Oral Communication	+	na		0	+	[11:10]	+	
Use of Concepts	na	na		+	+	[4:]	na	
Systems Thinking	+	0	+	+	+	[5:]	na	
Pattern Recognition	+	+	+	~	+	[2:]	na	
Quantitative Analysis	+	?	+	+	+	[6:]	na	
Use of Technology	+	na		+	+	[7:]	na	
Social Objectivity	~	?	0	~	+	[3:00]	na	
Written Communication	na	na		~	+	[4:10]	na	

Notes

- Theory Building was not assessed in any of the four instruments used in this outcome study; therefore, no comment can be made about it.
- "+" refers to statistical support for improvement; "~" refers to statistical support for improvement but only when the entire sample is considered, not when the native English-speaking students are considered by themselves; "na" refers to Not Assessed from this instrument; "?" indicates abilities for which no one was coded once in any of the entering or graduating videotapes (it is feasible to be coded, but since no one was coded here and they are infrequently coded in general, the implications for the summary were considered questionable).
- The numbers in brackets refer to scales or specific items within scales from the Learning Skills Profile; they are labeled by a clock position.
- Graduating students showed significant improvement in Written Communication assessed in item 4:10 in the Learning Skills Profile: in the 1991–1993 study, the average entering score was 4.60 versus a graduating score of 5.04, $n = 55$, $t = -2.74$, p (one-tailed) < .004; native English-speaking students only, entering average score 4.70 versus average graduating score 5.08, $n = 46$, $t = 2.21$, p (one-tailed) < .02; in the 1990–1992 study, the average entering score was 4.56 versus a graduating score of 4.92, $n = 71$, $t = -2.61$, p (one-tailed) < .01; native English-speaking students only, entering average score 4.87 versus average graduating score 5.12, $n = 60$, $t = -1.37$, p (one-tailed) < .10).

Table 8.2. Summary of Impact: 1990–1993.

Strong evidence	Some evidence	No evidence
Efficiency Orientation	Initiative	Attention to Detail
Planning	Flexibility	Persuasiveness
Self-Control	Group Management	Negotiating
Empathy	Developing Others	
Networking	Social Objectivity	
Self-Confidence		
Oral Communication		
Use of Concepts		
Systems Thinking		
Pattern Recognition		
Quantitative Analysis		
Use of Technology		
Written Communication		

One ability in the model was not assessed in any of the exercises or tests used in this study: Theory Building.

Some improvement was shown in 86 percent (eighteen out of twenty-one) of the abilities assessed in this study. Strong evidence appeared for improvement in 62 percent (thirteen out of twenty-one) of the abilities assessed. Results showing improvement on some exercises and neutral impact in other exercises was found on 24 percent (five out of twenty-one) of the abilities assessed in this study. It is important to note that a statistically significant decrease was not found in any of the abilities assessed.

Is This Impact Different from That of the Old Program?

There is anecdotal evidence of the positive changes and differences in the students during and following the new MBA program as compared to the old program (Boyatzis, Cowen, and Kolb, 1992; also see Chapter Nine), and the two sources of data allowing some comparison in this study suggest that the new program is responsible for significant increases in students' abilities. Although not a perfect comparison, a sample of part-time graduating students who went through the old MBA program were assessed in the Presentation Exercise. The students graduating from the old program showed similar Oral Communication ability and Enthusiasm to the entering students in the new program, and significantly less of these abilities than the students graduating from the new program. Statistical details are shown in Table 8 of Appendix 8.1.

When a sample of students graduating in 1992 from the old, part-time program was compared to the 1990–1992 sample of graduates from the new program with the Group Discussion Exercise, the graduates of the new program showed significantly more Networking and Self-Confidence than their peers graduating from the old program (details are shown in Table 9 of Appendix 8.1). In addition, the graduates of the new program showed more Attention to Detail, Group Management, Total of all abilities, and number of abilities than the graduates of the old program at a near-significant level. When the nonnative English speakers were excluded from the analysis, the same pattern of significant results emerged. In addition, the graduates of the new program showed more Efficiency Orientation than did their counterparts from the old program at a near-significant level.

A similar comparison of the graduating part-time students from the old program to the graduating full-time students from the new program was made using the Learning Skills Profile. It indicated that, on the whole, the students graduating from the old and new programs saw themselves as similar on these skills. The exceptions were that students graduating from the new program assessed themselves as significantly higher on Action Skills than students graduating from the old program. This was true both for the entire sample and for the native English-speaking sample only (average for the new program graduates 30.3, for the entire sample $n = 71$, and 30.4, for the native English-speaking sample $n = 60$, respectively, average for the old program 28.3, for the entire sample $n = 32$, and 28.3, for the native English-speaking sample $n = 32$, respectively, one-tailed Mann-Whitney U test $z = -1.53$ and $z = -1.64$, $p = .06$ and .05, respectively). The students graduating from the new program were higher at a near-significant level than the students graduating from the old program, for the native English-speaking sample only, on Help Skills and Technology Skills.

A time-series comparison can be made of the impact of the new versus the old MBA program regarding full-time students, because the Executive Skills Profile (an earlier form of the Learning Skills Profile) was used in the 1987–88 and 1988–89 outcome studies at the WSOM (Boyatzis and Renio, 1989; Boyatzis, Renio, and Thompson, 1990; also see Chapter Five). Both versions of this instrument are card sort instruments, with the same underlying conceptual framework and mostly the same items. Some items were reworded for clarity. The skill scales demonstrated remarkable similarity in various reliability and validity studies (Boyatzis and Kolb, 1991; Boyatzis and Kolb, in press). In 1987–88 and again in 1988–89, a cross-sectional design was used with census data collection of full-time students at entry (that is, all of the entering students completed the instruments) and random sampling of the graduating students. In the 1987–88 outcome study, seventy-two entering full-time students and a random sample of twenty-seven graduating full-time students were assessed. In the 1988–89 outcome study, seventy entering full-time students and a random sample of twenty-three graduating full-time students were assessed. The average age of the entering students of all three outcome studies was similar: 26.4 in 1987–88, with a range of 21 to 41; 26.3 in 1988–89, with a range of 19 to 41; 26.5 in 1990–1992, with a range of 21 to 40; and 26.5 in 1991–1993, with a range of 20 to 34. The gender distribution was similar in all three studies but showed some changes, from 31 percent female in 1987–88 to 34 percent female in 1988–89, to 37 percent female in 1990–1992, to 30 percent female in 1991–1993. Fifteen of the students who entered in 1987 were also in the 1989 sample of graduating full-time students. This constituted a small longitudinal sample useful for exploration purposes but different from the other samples in that students were older with distinctly fewer females.

The comparison of these studies with the Learning Skills Profile suggests that the new program is having a greater impact on developing students' abilities than the old full-time MBA program, as shown in Table 8.3. The new program is having a similar positive impact on the four skills on which the old

Table 8.3. Comparison of 1987–88 and 1988–89 Outcome Studies
with the 1990–1992 and 1991–1993 Outcome Studies: Full-Time Students.

Skill scale	1987–88 Study (a)	1988–89 Study (b)	1987–89 Study (c)	1990–92 Study (d)	1991–93 Study (e)
Leadership	ns	ns	ALL	ns	ALL, E
Relationship	ns	ns	ALL, E	ns	ALL, E
Help	ns	ns	ALL	ALL, E	ns
Sense-Making	ALL, E	ns	ALL	ALL	ALL, E
Information Gathering	ALL, E	ns	ALL	ALL, E	ALL, E
Information Analysis	ALL, E	ALL, E	ALL, E	ALL, E	ALL, E
Theory	ALL, E	ALL, E	ALL, E	ALL, E	ALL, E
Quantitative	ALL, E	ALL, E	ALL, E	ALL, E	ALL, E
Technology	ALL, E	ALL, E	ALL, E	ALL, E	ALL, E
Goal Setting	ns	ns	ns	ALL, E	ALL, E
Action	ALL	ns	ALL, E	ns	ns
Initiative	ALL, E	ns	ALL	ns	ALL
Total	ALL, E	ALL, E	ALL, E	ALL, E	ALL, E
Average age	26.4	26.3	28.5	26.5	26.5
Range of age	21–41	19–41	22–36	21–40	20–34
Percent female	31%	34%	13%	37%	30%

Notes
- For the 1987–88 sample: entering sample = 72; graduating sample = 27; native English-speaking entering sample = 56, graduating sample = 23.
- For the 1988–89 sample: entering sample = 70; graduating sample = 23. Native English-speaking entering sample = 45, graduating sample = 15.
- The 1987–1989 longitudinal sample, composed of students who entered in 1987 and graduated in 1989, all full-time, was 15, of which native English speakers were 9.
- The 1990–1992 sample was 71, of which native English speakers were 60.
- The 1991–1993 sample was 55, of which native English speakers were 46.
- ALL = results for the whole sample were statistically significant with one-tailed tests; E = results for the native English-speaking sample only were statistically significant with one-tailed tests; ns = results for none of the samples were statistically significant.
- Age was calculated at entry into the program.

program showed a consistent, statistically significant impact: Information Analysis, Theory, Quantitative, and Technology. In addition, significant positive impact is shown by the new program on three skills not consistently showing improvement in the old program (that is, there was positive impact in one study but not in the other study or not in the native English-speaking samples): Relationship, Sense-Making, and Information Gathering. The new program showed significant positive impact on three skills never having shown positive impact in earlier 1987–88 and 1988–89 studies, when considering the full sample and native English-speaking sample: Leadership, Help, and Goal Setting.

A number of findings in the series of outcome studies do not appear consistent. First, in either the 1987–88 study or the small longitudinal study, the entire sample showed significant increases in Leadership, Help, Action, and Initiative Skills. The native English-speaking samples of students did not show these results, except in the longitudinal sample regarding Action Skills, and in the 1987–88 sample regarding Initiative Skills. These results may have been primarily a result of "Americanizing" non-English-speaking students. The changes may have reflected foreign students adjusting to American cultural norms. This was an observation made by these students, especially those from Asian cultures.

Second, two findings appeared inconsistent between the 1990–1992 and 1991–1993 studies. The addition of Leadership and Relationship Skills appeared to be more a function of the lower level of these skills on the part of students who entered in 1991 as compared to those entering in 1990. Both cadres seemed to have similar levels at the time of graduation. The absence of significant change in Help Skills in the 1991–1993 study, though the change was significant in the 1990–1992 study, appeared to represent a slight decline in improvement. The means and differences of means are similar but do not reach the same levels of statistical significance.

Consistency with Student Course Evaluations

Positive impact on certain abilities has been shown to result from particular courses, in particular those focused on communication skills (McConnell and Seybolt, 1991; Mullin, Shaffer, and Gelle, 1991). In outcome studies of undergraduates, courses have been shown to have impact, but noncourse activity has also been demonstrated to have impact (Pascarella and Terenzini, 1991; Winter, McClelland, and Stewart, 1981; Astin, 1992; Mentkowski and Strait, 1983).

As part of the continuing improvements in the MBA program, the faculty of the WSOM implemented a new course evaluation form in 1991. The new form included the list of twenty-two abilities and seven value themes and asked each student, while evaluating the course on all of the usual types of items, to indicate abilities and value themes that were "enhanced or developed" during the course. As faculty members, we would like to believe that one course can have substantial impact on a student.

A rough estimate of students' perceptions of the impact of courses on abilities could be obtained from the new evaluation form as used in the first two semesters. We decided that one-third or more of the students in a particular course had to check the ability to consider it "enhanced or developed" in the course. Then, to determine total impact of courses in aggregate (any finer analysis is beyond the scope of this study), the percentage of courses offered in each semester having one-third or more students indicating each ability as enhanced or developed was calculated. The average percentage of the number of courses from the two semesters (that is, 105 courses in the fall term and 75 courses in the spring term), in students' perceptions, that enhanced or developed each of the abilities addressed in this outcome study are shown in Tables 8.4 and 8.5.

The abilities with the highest percentage of courses enhancing or developing them were Use of Concepts (66 percent), Attention to Detail (41 percent), Written Communication (40 percent), Systems Thinking (33 percent), Group Management (33 percent), Planning (32 percent), Oral Communication (30 percent), and Quantitative Analysis (30 percent). They were followed by Use of Technology (18 percent), Pattern Recognition (14 percent), Persuasiveness (12 percent), Social Objectivity (12 percent), and Self-Confidence (10 percent).

We could conjecture that the positive image shown in the outcome study was attributable to the impact of courses on Planning, Oral Communication, Use of Concepts, Systems Thinking, Quantitative Analysis, and Written Communication. Courses might be said to help in the observed improvement in Self-Confidence, Pattern Recognition, Use of Technology, and Social Objectivity. It is more likely that activities and experiences outside of courses are contributing to the improvement on these abilities. It would appear that activities outside of courses *must*

Table 8.4. 1990–1992 Comparison of Outcome Impact
from Exercises and Questionnaire, Their Learning Goals/Plans,
and Student Reaction to the Impact of Courses in 1991–92.

Ability	Outcome impact: exercises and tests	Percent noting outcome impact: in questionnaire	Percent having it in learning goals and plans	Percent of courses enhancing or developing: student reactions in 1991–92
Efficiency Orientation	~	20	45	8
Planning	+	42	61	32
Initiative	~	31	56	9
Attention to Detail	0	23	49	41
Self-Control	na	21	30	0
Flexibility	0	25	56	7
Empathy	~	23	49	8
Persuasiveness	0	25	59	12
Networking	+	39	82	7
Negotiating	0	34	76	8
Self-Confidence	+	39	59	10
Group Management	~	56	73	33
Developing Others	~	18	59	5
Oral Communication	+	52	83	30
Use of Concepts	+	21	20	66
Systems Thinking	~	20	32	33
Pattern Recognition	+	20	41	14
Quantitative Analysis	+	28	41	30
Theory Building	na	14	21	18
Use of Technology	+	41	53	18
Social Objectivity	~	21	44	12
Written Communication	~	51	69	40
Accounting		19	9	
Banking and Finance		53	24	
Economics		19	7	
Labor/Human Resource Policy		30	11	
Marketing		61	28	
Management Information Decision Systems		27	17	
Operations Research		30	4	
Operations Management		6	6	
Organizational Behavior		24	14	
Policy		54	14	
Managerial Statistics		27	6	

Note: See Notes at the end of Table 8.5.

Table 8.5. 1991–1993 Comparison of Outcome Impact
from Exercises and Questionnaire, Their Learning Goals/Plans,
and Student Reaction to the Impact of Courses in 1991–92.

Ability	Impact: exercises and tests	Percent noting impact in questionnaire	Percent in Learning Plans	Percent of courses enhancing or developing
Efficiency Orientation	+	37	53	8
Planning	+	49	65	32
Initiative	~	33	65	9
Attention to Detail	0	30	35	41
Self-Control	+	21	49	0
Flexibility	~	33	63	7
Empathy	+	19	51	8
Persuasiveness	~	28	53	12
Networking	+	40	83	7
Negotiating	0	32	65	8
Self-Confidence	+	37	60	10
Group Management	~	49	79	33
Developing Others	0	26	63	5
Oral Communication	+	56	88	30
Use of Concepts	+	19	0	66
Systems Thinking	+	14	33	33
Pattern Recognition	+	18	47	14
Quantitative Analysis	+	40	35	30
Theory Building	na	11	9	18
Use of Technology	+	35	53	18
Social Objectivity	~	33	65	12
Written Communication	+	42	58	40
Accounting		47	25	
Banking and Finance		65	33	
Economics		26	11	
Labor/Human Resource Policy		37	14	
Marketing		58	30	
Management Information Decision Systems		39	23	
Operations Research		30	5	
Operations Management		16	21	
Organizational Behavior		32	18	
Policy		46	14	
Managerial Statistics		33	12	
Economic Value		44		
Intellectual Value		40		
Human Value		46		
Managing in a complex, diverse . . .		56		
Stimulating professionalism . . .		42		
Innovating in use of information . . .		33		
Developing as team leader/member . . .		49		

Table 8.5. 1991–1993 Comparison of Outcome Impact
from Exercises and Questionnaire, Their Learning Goals/Plans,
and Student Reaction to the Impact of Courses in 1991–92, Cont'd.

Notes

- Self-Control and Theory Building were not assessed in any of the instruments in the Outcome Study.
- Percentages regarding the Outcome Study Questionnaire were the students' perceptions.
- Percentages regarding Learning Goals and Learning Plans were taken from a review of the Learning Plans.
- Percentages regarding courses represent the average from the two semesters.
- In summarizing the results from the 1990–1992 study, the following legend was used: "+" means all possible exercises showed positive results. For abilities coded in two or more exercises, "~" means one exercise showed positive results and the other showed 0s or ?'s. In summarizing the results from the 1991–1993 study, the following legend was used: "+" means all possible exercises showed positive results or if three or more exercises were coded, at least two showed positive results and the other 0. For abilities coded in two or more exercises, "~" means one exercise showed positive results and the other/s showed 0s or ?'s.

be contributing to the improvement of students on Efficiency Orientation, Initiative, Empathy, Networking, and Developing Others. It is possible that involvement with their mentors (for example, managers in local organizations), developmental workshops, internships, clubs, projects, part-time work, and other activities account for a student's improvement on these abilities. Certainly the relationships with mentors, executive advisors, and visiting executives, and among the students through the Executive Action Team, clubs, course projects, and other activities, provide a fertile ground for building Networking ability. Questions arise from this information about the durability of students' perceptions of the work in courses on Group Management. Of course, this level of analysis is speculative, since we are not claiming that the students in this outcome study were taking these particular courses, and the students' perceptions were an aggregate of all MBA students.

Various Measures of Change

Students were asked in the questionnaire administered during the outcome study to indicate which, if any, abilities were significantly enhanced or developed during the program, and which, if any, knowledge areas were significantly enhanced or developed during the program. Their open-ended responses were compared to the results from the exercises in this study and are shown in Tables 8.4 and 8.5. The open-ended response in the questionnaire reflects a perception by the student of "significant enhancement or development" and therefore is expected to be somewhat different from their demonstrated behavior. On the whole, within each of the clusters of abilities (that is, the Goal and Action Management cluster, the People Management cluster, and the Analytic Reasoning cluster), the abilities in which the highest percentage of students thought they had changed as described in the questionnaire were ones in which students demonstrated the most change in the exercises and instrument.

Intentional Change: The Impact of Learning Goals and Plans

The new program is based on the assumption that students can direct their own learning. They will find ways to learn various abilities, whether or not these abilities are addressed in courses. The Learning Goals and Learning Plans of students were reviewed to determine the degree to which their change was "intentional." The percentage of students having a learning goal related to each ability and knowledge area was calculated. The results are shown in Tables 8.4 and 8.5.

It appears that having learning goals is related to the degree of change. The percentage of students having a learning goal regarding an ability and the percentage of students indicating significant enhancement or development regarding that ability (that is, who mentioned the ability in the open-ended question in the questionnaire during the outcome study) were significantly correlated (1990–1992 study: $r = .78$, $n = 22$ abilities, $p < .01$; 1991–1993 study: $r = .72$, $n = 22$ abilities, $p < .01$). The same pattern of results was found with regard to the knowledge areas. The percentage of students with a learning goal was highly correlated with their view of significant enhancement or development of that knowledge area (1990–1992 study: $r = .79$,

$n = 11$ knowledge areas, $p < .01$; 1991–1993 study: $r = .74$, $n = 11$ knowledge areas, $p < .01$).

Effects of Gender and Age on Change

To explore possible effects of gender and age, the 1992 and 1993 samples had to be combined to attain sufficient sample size. As a result of cohort differences and program differences between the early classes in the new program and those that followed, this exploration of the data must be considered with caution; it is more speculative than other analyses. But preliminary results suggest that there were no pronounced differences in the effect of the program on people by gender or age.

The sample included forty-three women and eighty-three men. The analysis for age compared a younger group (students who were 25 years old or younger when they entered the MBA program, representing 48 percent of the students) and those who were 26 or older at entry. While there were no notable demographic differences between the women and men on entering, more of the older students were married than the younger students. The mean age for the younger group was 23.36 years, with 2.09 years of work experience, while the older group had a mean age of 29.53 and 5.83 years of work experience.

Comparison of the entering and graduating means on the Learning Skills Profile, the Individual Interviews, the Group Discussion Exercise, and the Presentation Exercise showed comparable development of both women and men on all of the skills except two in the GDE. There were no statistically significant difference scores (that is, graduating scores minus entering scores) for women and men.

The women show significantly higher mean scores than men for Relationship Skills and Help Skills at both entry and graduation. The men show significantly higher mean scores than women for Theory Skills and Quantitative Skills at both entry and graduation. These findings are consistent with gender socialization patterns. While the program resulted in increased skills from entry to graduation, there were no statistically significant differences in improvement by gender. Astin (1992) reported similar gender-related findings with undergraduate samples; college seemed to have no impact on reducing gender differences of the students at entry. But while he reported that the gaps between the females and males widened over the college years, these findings showed no such dynamic.

As students entered the MBA program at Case Western Reserve University, some gender differences existed in their perceived levels of competency, as measured on the Learning Skills Profile. As Chapter Seven notes, Case and Thompson identified several differences between the types of learning plans women and men created to guide their professional and personal development. For example, women planned to use interaction with others as actions toward the development of key abilities more often than men. The individualized learning program offered at the WSOM allows students to follow personal preferences and develop in ways of their choice. These choices may reflect individual differences but may also reinforce gender-related socialization patterns.

On the fourteen abilities assessed in the Group Discussion Exercise (GDE), eighteen abilities assessed in the Individual Interview (II), and one ability assessed in the Presentation Exercise (PE), only two significant gender differences were found: Networking and Self-Confidence in the Group Discussion Exercise. In the GDE, women showed a greater increase in Networking ability than men (the female average improvement score was .28, $n = 18$, versus the male average improvement score of .00, $n = 26$, Mann Whitney U test $z = -2.82$, $p = .005$). Meanwhile, men showed greater increase in Self-Confidence than women (the male average improvement score was .27, $n = 26$, versus the female average improvement score of $-.06$, Mann-Whitney U test $z = -2.01$, $p = .05$).

No significant differences existed between older and younger students at the time of entry, but the older students showed higher scores for Leadership, Help, Sense-Making, Information Gathering, Goal Setting, and Initiative, and for the Total Score than younger students at the point of graduation. Regarding Help and Goal Setting Skills, the older students showed greater increases than the younger students between entry and graduation. From the Individual Interview and the Group Discussion Exercise, there was a significant difference on only one ability. In the events drawn from the Individual Interview, the older students demonstrated significantly more Group Management ability at graduation than at entry (using a difference score) than did the younger students (the older students' average difference score was .31, $n = 61$, versus .00 for the younger students, $n = 55$, Mann-Whitney U test $z = -2.25$, $p = .02$).

Possible Sources of Error

The findings reported are suggestive and require continued study for confirmation. Multiple cohorts will be important to avoid the claim that these results were a unique event in the history of the program and will expand the sample size. Another possible source of error in the results from the Presentation Exercise, the Group Discussion Exercise, and the Individual Interview may have been unconscious bias on the part of the coders. Although the videos and audios were sorted randomly when coded, or recoded, and they were coded by reliable "judges," it was difficult for a coder not to notice the dates stamped on the videotapes. They did not report this as something they were consciously aware of, but nonetheless, it was impossible to mask the entering or graduating status of the students in the videos. This would not affect the analysis from the Learning Skills Profile.

Another criticism might be that we have observed short-term demonstration of these abilities. Students learned the "code" as part of their Managerial Assessment and Development course and may have merely parroted the codable behaviors to us. Of course, if they can imitate the codable behaviors, these behaviors have become available to the students as part of their behavioral repertoire. That is, if the students could demonstrate the behavior at will, we are hopeful that they could demonstrate them at work when appropriate. The stronger test will be the durability of the improvements. This requires the longitudinal analysis of the students in the years following graduation, which is part of the long-term design but not possible in this report.

Conclusion

Students in two successive cadres—entering and graduating groups—were followed from entry to graduation in the new MBA program. Given the outcome model and value-added intention of the program, these groups of students were studied to determine the degree of development of the specific abilities related to effectiveness in management. The measurement at the time of entry into and graduation from the program included two videotaped exercises, one small-group business problem-solving session, and one session making a presentation to a group of people; one audiotaped critical incident interview; and a card sort test describing their own learning skills. Students also were asked to complete an in-depth questionnaire about the program near the time of graduation.

Considering all of the measures and both years' studies, the results showed significant improvement in thirteen abilities on multiple measures: Efficiency Orientation, Planning, Self-Control, Empathy, Networking, Self-Confidence, Oral Communication, Use of Concepts, Systems Thinking, Pattern Recognition, Quantitative Analysis, Use of Technology, and Written Communications. The results also showed some significantly positive and some neutral results on various measures of five abilities: Initiative, Flexibility, Group Management, Developing Others, and Social Objectivity. No change was found for three abilities: Attention to Detail, Persuasiveness, and Negotiating.

The students graduating from the new MBA program have significantly greater capability than they did when they entered. They have greater capability both in their own eyes and as seen by others observing them. They are able to use these abilities in managerial and work situations. In addition, the total of all abilities tested in each exercise, like the number of different abilities used in each exercise, was shown to be significantly greater for graduating students than for entering students on three different measures in each of the two studies. The results are stronger than shown in other outcome studies of MBA programs.

When these results are compared with earlier outcome studies from the same institution before the new program was implemented and with results for part-time students graduating from the old program, the graduates of the new program demonstrate many of the abilities to a significantly greater degree than do the students graduating from the old program. (See Table 8.6.)

Students' learning goals and Learning Plans appear to be significantly related to their changes. Developing a learning goal reflecting a specific intention to change appears related to significant change demonstrated over the one to two years of the program.

Although men and women students differ when entering the program and establish different types of learning goals and plans, it appears that they change to a comparable degree. The structure of the new program, with its emphasis on individualized Learning Plans, in-context learning, experiential learning, and a social context for learning, provides opportunities for students with different needs and wants to advance and benefit from value added. Analysis of the experiences of older students (with an average age of thirty at entry) shows that they change slightly more than the younger students (those with an average age of twenty-three at entry).

To assist in the institutional change effort, the results from these studies have been presented to faculty and staff in various faculty committees, to students in classes, and—in special "brown bag" luncheon sessions—to employers and alumni. These presentations and discussions have occurred each year as the results were available. The discussions have resulted in (1) an increased sense of pride in the WSOM—our curriculum changes are having a desirable impact on students, and (2) guidance for improvements needed to continue the effort and extend the impact of the program. The discussions have led to a revitalized commitment to the assumptions shaping the new program and have also stimulated a new level of creativity about learning among faculty and staff.

Table 8.6. Comparison of Value Added to Students from the Old Versus the New MBA Program.

Evidence of value added	Old program			New program		
	Goal and Action Management	People Management	Analytic Reasoning	Goal and Action Management	People Management	Analytic Reasoning
Strong evidence		Self-Confidence	Use of Concepts, Systems Thinking, Quantitative Analysis, Use of Technology, Written Communication	Efficiency Orientation, Planning, Self-Control	Empathy, Self-Confidence, Networking, Oral Communication	Use of Concepts, Systems Thinking, Pattern Recognition, Quantitative Analysis, Use of Technology, Written Communication
Some evidence	Efficiency Orientation, Initiative	Empathy		Initiative, Flexibility	Group Management, Developing Others	Social Objectivity
No evidence	Planning, Flexibility, Attention to Detail (Self-Control was not coded)	Persuasiveness, Networking, Negotiating, Group Management, Developing Others, Oral Communication	Social Objectivity	Attention to Detail	Persuasiveness, Negotiating	
Negative evidence			Pattern Recognition (verbal)			

Appendix 8.1. Comparisons of Entering and Graduating Students.

Table 1. 1990–1992 Comparison of Entering and Graduating Students with the Learning Skills Profile.

Skill scale	All students (n = 71)			Native English-speaking students (n = 60)		
	Entering	Graduating	t	Entering	Graduating	t
Leadership	27.7	27.2	.69	28.8	28.1	.76
Relationship	30.0	30.4	−.69	30.6	30.7	−.16
Help	27.7	28.9	−1.72*	28.2	29.5	−1.73*
Sense-Making	27.5	28.7	−1.79*	28.0	28.8	−1.09
Information Gathering	26.7	28.3	−2.81**	27.3	28.6	−2.12**
Information Analysis	26.7	28.6	−3.25***	27.2	29.0	−3.01**
Theory	25.2	27.4	−3.42***	25.4	27.1	−2.71**
Quantitative	22.1	26.3	−4.82***	22.3	26.0	−3.98***
Technology	21.5	25.5	−4.00***	21.7	25.1	−3.34***
Goal Setting	26.8	28.4	−2.65**	27.4	28.6	−1.88*
Action	30.3	30.3	.09	30.6	30.4	.32
Initiative	29.4	29.8	−.62	30.2	30.7	−.75
Total	322	340	−3.33***	328	342	−2.55**

Note: Significance levels reported are for paired-sample t tests as one-tailed tests (*p < .05; **p < .01; ***p < .001).

Table 2. 1990–1992 Comparison of Entering and Graduating Students with the Presentation Exercise on Oral Communication (Total Score) and Enthusiasm.

Ability	All students (n = 24)			Native English-speaking students (n = 18)		
	Entering	Graduating	t	Entering	Graduating	t
Oral Communication	4.25	6.25	5.54***	4.56	6.50	4.36***
Enthusiasm	3.00	3.96	4.18***	3.17	4.06	3.33**

Note: Significance levels reported are for paired-sample t tests as one-tailed tests (*p < .05; **p < .01; ***p < .001).

Table 3. 1990–1992 Comparison of Entering
and Graduating Students with the Group Discussion Exercise.

	All students (n = 19)			Native English-speaking students (n = 18)		
Ability	Entering	Graduating	z	Entering	Graduating	z
Efficiency Orientation	.316	.632	−1.60*	.333	.667	−1.60*
Planning	.526	.842	−1.43+	.556	.889	−1.43+
Initiative	.895	1.316	−1.42+	.944	1.222	−1.05
Attention to Detail	.105	.158	−.45	.111	.167	−.45
Empathy	0.0	.158	−1.60*	0.0	.167	−1.60*
Persuasiveness	.105	.211	−.73	.111	.222	−.73
Networking	0.0	.211	−1.83*	0.0	.222	−1.83*
Self-Confidence	.368	.579	−1.83*	.389	.611	−1.83*
Group Management	.053	.158	−1.34+	.056	.167	−1.34+
Developing Others	0.0	.105	−1.00	0.0	.111	−1.00
Systems Thinking	.158	.211	−.40	.167	.167	.00
Pattern Recognition	.211	.474	−1.83*	.222	.500	−1.83*
Total	2.79	5.05	−3.31***	2.94	5.11	−3.18***
Number of Abilities	2.37	3.95	−2.95**	2.50	4.06	−2.79**

Note: Significance levels reported are for Wilcoxon matched-pairs, signed-ranks tests as one-tailed tests (+p < .10; *p < .05; **p < .01; ***p < .001). The Wilcoxon test was appropriate because of the nonnormal distribution of the behavioral coding in the GDE.

Table 4. 1991–1993 Comparison of Entering
and Graduating Students with the Learning Skills Profile.

	All students (n = 55)			Native English-speaking students (n = 46)		
Skill scale	Entering	Graduating	t	Entering	Graduating	t
Leadership	25.0	27.1	−2.62**	25.0	26.9	−2.13*
Relationship	29.3	30.5	−1.88*	29.0	30.5	−2.30**
Help	27.8	28.8	−1.30	27.5	28.5	−1.25
Sense-Making	26.2	28.4	−3.51***	25.7	28.2	−3.49***
Information Gathering	25.9	27.9	−2.42**	25.6	28.0	−2.56**

Table 4. 1991–1993 Comparison of Entering
and Graduating Students with the Learning Skills Profile, Cont'd.

Skill scale	All students (n = 55)			Native English-speaking students (n = 46)		
	Entering	Graduating	t	Entering	Graduating	t
Information						
Analysis	26.3	29.2	−4.66***	26.2	29.1	−4.32***
Theory	22.9	27.2	−5.55***	23.1	27.1	−4.96***
Quantitative	21.5	27.5	−6.86***	21.1	27.3	−6.62***
Technology	20.7	25.2	−4.38***	20.5	25.4	−4.24***
Goal Setting	27.0	28.9	−2.30**	26.3	28.6	−2.44**
Action	29.2	30.1	−1.30	29.0	29.5	−.66
Initiative	27.7	29.1	−1.81*	27.9	29.0	−1.34
Total	310	340	−5.12***	307	338	−4.64***

Note: Significance levels reported are for paired-sample t tests as one-tailed tests ($*p < .05; **p < .01; ***p < .001$).

Table 5. 1991–1993 Comparison of Entering
and Graduating Students with the Presentation
Exercise on Oral Communication (Total Score) and Enthusiasm.

Ability	All students (n = 16)			Native English-speaking students (n = 13)		
	Entering	Graduating	t	Entering	Graduating	t
Oral						
Communication	4.69	5.31	1.99*	4.77	5.54	2.13*
Enthusiasm	1.93	2.40	1.97*	1.92	2.67	4.18***

Note: Significance levels reported are for paired-sample t tests as one-tailed tests ($*p < .05; **p < .01; ***p < .001$).

Table 6. 1991–1993 Comparison of Entering
and Graduating Students with the Group Discussion Exercise.

Ability	All students (n = 30)			Native English-speaking students (n = 27)		
	Entering	Graduating	z	Entering	Graduating	z
Efficiency						
Orientation	.400	.867	−2.05*	.444	.963	−2.05*
Planning	.267	.700	−2.33**	.296	.667	−1.96*
Initiative	1.33	1.30	−.17	1.37	1.37	−.07

Table 6. 1991–1993 Comparison of Entering
and Graduating Students with the Group Discussion Exercise, Cont'd.

Ability	All students (n = 30)			Native English-speaking students (n = 27)		
	Entering	Graduating	z	Entering	Graduating	z
Attention to						
Detail	.067	.100	−.37	.074	.111	−.37
Empathy	.000	.067	−1.34+	.000	.074	−1.34+
Persuasiveness	.300	.400	−.84	.333	.444	−.84
Networking	.000	.067	−1.34+	.000	.074	−1.34+
Negotiating	.033	.033	.00	.037	.037	.00
Self-Confidence	.433	.633	−1.53+	.482	.667	−1.33+
Developing						
Others	.033	.000	−1.00	.033	.000	−1.00
Systems Thinking	.033	.167	−1.50+	.037	.185	−1.47+
Pattern						
Recognition	.100	.400	−2.12*	.111	.407	−1.96*
Quantitative						
Analysis	.000	.100	−1.34+	.000	.100	−1.34+
Social Objectivity	.033	.000	−1.00	.037	.000	−1.00
Total	3.03	4.73	−2.56**	3.26	5.00	−2.37**
Number of						
Abilities	2.33	3.73	−2.68**	2.52	3.93	−2.44**

Note: Significance levels reported are for Wilcoxon matched-pairs, signed-ranks tests as one-tailed tests ($+p < .10$; $*p < .05$; $**p < .01$). (See the rationale for the Wilcoxon test in the Methods section of Chapter Five.) Self-Control, Oral Communications, and Written Communications were not coded in the GDE. No person was coded as showing Flexibility, Group Management, or Use of Technology in either the entering or graduating GDEs.

Table 7. 1991–1993 Comparison of Entering
and Graduating Students with the Individual Interview.

Ability	All students (n = 34)			Native English-speaking students (n = 28)		
	Entering	Graduating	z	Entering	Graduating	z
Efficiency						
Orientation	1.26	1.91	−2.84**	1.21	1.86	−2.48**
Planning	1.35	2.00	−2.73**	1.43	2.04	−2.49**
Initiative	.68	1.24	−2.37**	.71	1.29	−2.17*
Attention to						
Detail	.44	.29	−1.18	.54	.36	−1.18
Self-Control	.09	.35	−1.78*	.11	.39	−1.61*

Table 7. 1991–1993 Comparison of Entering
and Graduating Students with the Individual Interview, Cont'd.

Ability	All students (n = 34)			Native English-speaking students (n = 28)		
	Entering	Graduating	z	Entering	Graduating	z
Flexibility	.06	.38	−2.42**	.07	.29	−1.68*
Empathy	.47	.82	−1.89*	.54	.89	−1.70*
Persuasiveness	1.59	1.44	−.72	1.71	1.64	−.36
Networking	.24	.74	−3.10***	.18	.64	−2.86**
Negotiating	.03	.06	−.53	.04	.07	−.53
Self-Confidence	.38	.65	−2.40**	.42	.68	−2.07*
Group Management	.03	.24	−2.37**	.04	.29	−2.37**
Developing Others	.53	.38	−1.03	.57	.42	−.91
Oral Communication	.00	.09	−1.60*	.00	.11	−1.60*
Systems Thinking	.29	.56	−1.92*	.32	.68	−2.20**
Pattern Recognition	.21	.56	−2.30**	.21	.57	−2.03*
Use of Technology	.35	.59	−1.34+	.21	.64	−2.13*
Quantitative Analysis	.00	.24	−2.20*	.00	.25	−2.02*
Social Objectivity	.12	.32	−1.41+	.14	.29	−.89
Total	8.12	12.85	−4.83***	8.46	13.39	−4.44***
Number of Abilities	5.71	8.71	−4.68***	5.93	9.04	−4.32***

Note: Significance levels reported are for Wilcoxon matched-pairs, signed-ranks tests as one-tailed tests (^+p < .10; $^*p$ < .05; $^{**}p$ < .01; $^{***}p$ < .001). The Wilcoxon test is appropriate because of the nonnormal distribution of the behavior coding from the Individual Interview.

Table 8. Comparison of Graduating Full-Time and Part-Time Students with the Presentation Exercise on Oral Communication (Total Score) and Enthusiasm.

Ability	All students			Native English-speaking students only		
	Full-time (n = 24)	Part-time (n = 15)	z	Full-time (n = 18)	Part-time (n = 15)	z
Oral Communication	6.25	4.53	−2.22**	6.50	4.53	−2.36**
Enthusiasm	3.96	3.27	−1.87*	4.06	3.27	−2.00*

Note: Significance levels reported are for Mann-Whitney U tests as one-tailed tests ($^*p$ < .05; $^{**}p$ < .01). Means are presented for visual comparison.

Table 9. Comparison of Graduating Full-Time and
Part-Time Students with the Group Discussion Exercise.

Ability	All students			Native English-speaking students		
	Part-time	Full-time	z	Part-time	Full-time	z
Efficiency						
Orientation	.37	.63	−1.24	.37	.67	−1.37+
Planning	.63	.84	−.90	.63	.89	−1.08
Initiative	1.32	1.32	−.02	1.32	1.22	−.24
Attention to Detail	.00	.16	−1.43+	.00	.17	−1.47+
Empathy	.11	.16	−.47	.11	.17	−.54
Persuasiveness	.32	.21	−.45	.32	.22	−.37
Networking	.00	.21	−2.09*	.00	.22	−2.15*
Self-Confidence	.32	.58	−1.61*	.32	.61	−1.78*
Group Management	.00	.16	−1.43+	.00	.17	−1.47+
Developing Others	.00	.11	−1.00	.00	.11	−1.03
Systems Thinking	.42	.21	−.80	.42	.17	−1.10
Pattern Recognition	.53	.47	−.12	.53	.50	.00
Total	4.05	5.05	−1.37+	4.05	5.11	−1.46+
Number of Abilities	2.84	3.95	−1.40+	2.84	4.06	−1.54+

Note: Significance levels reported are for Mann-Whitney U tests as one-tailed tests ($+p < .10$; $*p < .05$). Means are presented for visual comparison. All students: full-time, $n = 19$; part-time, $n = 19$. Native English-speaking students: full-time, $n = 18$; part-time, $n = 19$. Not coded in the GDE were Self-Control, Oral Communications, or Written Communications. No person was coded as showing Flexibility, Negotiating, Use of Technology, or Quantitative Analysis in either the entering or graduating GDEs.

Part Three

KEY LEARNINGS
AND DREAMS

Nine

REACTIONS
FROM THE STAKEHOLDERS:
THE TRIALS AND TRIBULATIONS
OF IMPLEMENTING
A NEW PROGRAM

*Richard E. Boyatzis, Scott S. Cowen,
and David A. Kolb*

In this chapter, we provide an interim report on the process of implementation, sharing what we have been learning as vision and concept meet day-to-day realities. Most of the observations will focus on the early years of implementation, in particular the first three years. Implementation is, in many ways, a first test of the generalizations proposed in Chapter Three. After outlining our progress, we will summarize what we have learned to date.

Program Implementation: How Are We Doing?

A wide range of issues are worth discussing.

Value-Added Considerations
from the Perspective of Stakeholders

One of our primary objectives was to design an educational experience that would meet the needs and interests of the school's

An earlier version of this chapter appeared as "Implementing Curricular Innovation in Higher Education: Year One of the New Weatherhead MBA Program," *Selections,* 9(1), 1992, 1–9.

stakeholders: current and prospective students, faculty, school and university administrators, employers and prospective employers, professional colleagues in other schools, and the field of graduate and higher education in general. This experience was to be outcome oriented and focused on significantly enhancing our students' skills and knowledge.

The most visible stakeholders — the students — express their views of the new MBA program in many ways. The number of applications is a measure of the reaction of prospective students, while actual enrollment is a measure of the reaction of new students. Since the inception of the program, applications for the full-time program have risen by 85 percent, and enrollments have increased by 15 percent.

The profile of the applicant pool for the full-time programs indicates that, compared with applicants to the earlier program, new applicants are older; have more work experience; are more diverse in terms of gender, ethnicity, and undergraduate major; and have considerably higher GMAT scores. However, the profiles of enrolled students, past and present, provide a more conservative comparison. Students in the new full-time program are slightly older (an average age of twenty-seven, compared to twenty-five), have substantially more work experience (up from 2.5 to 4.5 years), are more diverse in undergraduate major (up from 26 to 43 percent with liberal arts degrees), and scored slightly higher on the GMAT. These data indicate that the new program is being considered by a different type of student, with many deciding to attend our program because of its underlying philosophy and approach. The differences in applications, enrollment, and student profiles appear for the full-time program only, with the new program appearing to have had little impact on these factors for part-time students. In that program, geographic convenience, perceptions of comparative status of MBA programs, and cost may continue to have significant impact.

The reactions of students enrolled in the new program take many forms. Most evident is increased student involvement and activism, with students voicing their opinions and views more strongly and frequently than in the past. Active

student representation now exists on three key faculty committees, in contrast to one during the old program (although all
three were always constitutionally open to the students). The
number of clubs has increased from five to eight, with many
students now involved in more than one club. The students
started a newspaper, *The Weathervane,* which has a professional
format and style. A group was even formed to provide the "alternative" view by reflecting less popular, more controversial
views than those represented by the Graduate Student Association and *The Weathervane.*

Student activism has continued in many forms. For example, during the winter and spring of 1992–93, a group of students decided to improve the initial MBA residency program
(that is, the Orientation Program) on their initiative. They conducted a survey of the students and raffled off a free dinner to
someone who completed the survey. They met and eventually
took a major role in the new residency program. Among other
things, their efforts resulted in a day for the students from countries other than the United States at the beginning of the week,
two half days of social activities (for example, a "Wacky Olym-
pics"), and a day of community service.

Students' course evaluations and responses to specific components of the new program have been mixed. Initial reactions
included a theme of not wanting to be "guinea pigs" and of wanting "debugged" innovations rather than experimentation. Redesign based on such feedback has resulted in significant improvement. Employers, executive advisors to the Executive Action
Teams, and recruiters have been enthusiastically involved in
the new program. They have participated in half-day workshops
involving case studies and other learning activities for students.
While we originally had to search for executive advisors each
semester, approximately 90 percent of the advisors had volunteered for the second year, and now there is a waiting list. Several
recruiters who are familiar with the school and its programs had
indicated that the second-year students in the new program were
distinctly different and much more impressive than second-year
students in previous years.

The school's curriculum development efforts have also

received attention from other schools on the Case Western Reserve campus. The changes at the Weatherhead School of Management (WSOM) have not only provided an example for other faculty interested in curricular revisions, but they have also given those of us at the business school the opportunity to discuss educational improvement with our colleagues across the campus.

There is a perception on the part of various stakeholders of an increase in the value added of the WSOM program. Since such a perception is affected by the expectation of innovation and change, the question of whether we are experiencing a Hawthorne effect or a truly sustainable change in the perception of value added remains unanswered. Even if the Hawthorne effect is somewhat responsible for the observed perceptions, this can be considered a part of the process of innovation and change rather than a threat to it. Among skeptical — and often critical — professional groups, a positive expectation of change is a welcome relief and may be a major contributor to sustainable change.

Focusing on Learning Outcomes

One advantage of a focus on outcomes is that it facilitates continuing discussion among stakeholder groups about the objectives of education. Such discussion at the WSOM has centered on two efforts. The first involves the increased interaction of students with recruiters and prospective employers; the other involves the creation of an expanded portfolio for students to use in searching for employment.

In the fall of 1991, representatives of twenty-nine companies participated in a career day at the school. Following a brief introduction to the new program by faculty members, three students conducted a two-hour case study on the assessment of managerial abilities, utilizing a videotape and small-group discussions among recruiters and second-year students. The second-year students then processed the results for the group (about eighty people) and described how skills are evaluated and developed in the program. The second effort, known as the Second Transcript/Portfolio Project, is an attempt to determine whether the various stakeholders would value the development of a document that would complement the résumé and the school transcript in summarizing a student's abilities. The project has received enthusiastic support and interest from every group except the students, most of whom view it as yet another time-consuming task in an already burdensome schedule. However, eight students participated in a workshop to develop such documentation about themselves on an experimental basis. It is currently envisioned as a possible workshop to be held during the week prior to the beginning of the fall semester.

A less visible, but nonetheless important, element in the focus on learning outcomes is the fifty-year, longitudinal MBA Career Progress Study. In this study, graduating students are assessed on their knowledge, abilities, and values, and the results are compared with their capabilities at program entry (see Chapter Eight). Follow-up studies will commence in 1997, with alumni to be assessed on knowledge, abilities, values, career, and life changes. To examine the lifelong process of development, the study will follow graduates throughout their work lives.

The program's focus on learning outcomes has begun to reorient the thinking of all key stakeholders, especially faculty, students, and recruiters. The orientation is shifting from what faculty are teaching to what students are learning and how this relates to professional progression and success. This outcome perspective is consistent with the program's value-added orientation, and it provides a sharp focus for continuous improvement in program design and content.

Shifting from a Teaching to a Learning Perspective

This shift involves two main elements. One is the new focus on student-centered learning processes; the other is the new view of faculty as managers. The goal of a student-centered approach is to create an active learning community, while at the same time tailoring the program to meet students' individual needs. The increased involvement and activism of students in the governing of the school and in student-sponsored activities shows how eagerly they respond to a personalized approach.

In contrast, faculty are not so excited about assuming a manager-of-learning role. Many have had years of socialization into the teacher-as-expert approach, in which faculty are expected to dispense knowledge and students to absorb it. Such experience often results in a commitment, whether conscious or unconscious, to a particular educational philosophy and didactic methodology. This can be very difficult to change. Many of the WSOM faculty are still struggling with the identity, role, and responsibility changes inherent in the shift being made at the school. As one faculty member said, the shift requires "giving up the limelight and center stage in the classroom . . . changing how I think I am contributing to [the students'] development . . . trusting that they will change . . . and covering less material than should be covered in order to spend more time focusing on what material they are learning."

An unintended consequence of the training and team teaching to deliver the Managerial Assessment and Development course has been the socialization of faculty into elements of a learning perspective. In addition, the advanced doctoral students involved are also getting socialized into a different orientation than typically provided to them during their early years in the profession. The faculty and doctoral students work closely and personally with the MBA students. The focus of design considerations and discussions about progress during the course centers on what and how the students are learning — not what we are teaching. The faculty and doctoral students work with the Executive Action Teams and even use subgroups within the teams to manage interaction, involvement, and excitement. During the course, the training to deliver it, the weekly debriefing meetings, and the monthly "intellectual review and discussion meetings" about course subjects, there is a focus on stimulating the student's self-directed learning and development. With the invitation to students to rewrite papers and increase their grade, and hopefully increase their insight as well, there is continual emphasis on developmental feedback to students with high standards.

A focus on learning has resulted in the formation of two new committees. The faculty involved in teaching the required courses are members of a committee called the Core Learning Committee. They meet several times each semester to discuss course context, process, potential overlaps, opportunities for integration, and the mood of the first-year class. A parallel committee, called the Student Core Learning Committee, was formed by representatives from each of the Executive Action Teams. Members meet during the first year to discuss course and program issues. The objective is to provide vehicles for corrective action before the experience is over and the only benefit will be to future classes.

Liberalizing the Vocational Focus

There were three components to our pursuit of this design principle: the perspectives courses, globalization of the curriculum, and intellectual/value themes. All of the originally intended perspectives courses — Managing in a Global Economy, The History of Industrial Development, and Technology and Society: Progress and Problems — were developed and debugged and continue to be taught. A new perspectives course has been designed and is being offered regarding general systems theory and its applications in life and work. But while students have appreciated the subject matter, difficulties have emerged in the design and execution of the courses.

The liberalizing component of the new program requires the significant involvement of faculty from across the campus in the design and delivery of these courses. To date, however, the courses have been a frustrating experience for both students and faculty, since the teaching methods and styles of faculty from other disciplines are frequently very different from those of management faculty. The faculty of all three courses have expressed concerns about "inefficiency" and a "lack of control of group process and intellectual material covered." Serial teaching (different faculty leading different class sessions) and team teaching (pairs or trios of faculty in one class session) have been tried, but the desired process has not yet been achieved. We expect that the implementation problems will be alleviated through continued innovation and iteration.

Prior to the globalization of our curriculum, we had only one formalized international student exchange program; we now have seven. In addition, a dramatic increase has occurred in the number of students taking foreign language courses within the university. The school is conducting interdisciplinary projects in Romania, Russia, and the Netherlands, and numerous projects are being conducted in foreign countries by individual faculty.

A major component of the international program was added in 1993. Each summer, one to three groups of students, full-time and part-time, spend a three- to four-week period on a study tour of several countries. During these tours, they have classes, meet with executives and government officials, and explore working in each country, as well as examining global management issues.

The third component of our liberalization effort has been the development and use of five intellectual/value themes, centered on the overarching theme of "creating economic, intellectual, and human value." Faculty in the required courses have responded variously in their incorporation of these themes, from redesigning an entire course around the concepts to simply mentioning the themes several times during the semester. While the faculty remain committed to this effort, the conversion of that commitment into specific activities has been less than desired. We hope that the feedback received from the new course evaluation form is helping address this problem. In addition, creating new opportunities for debate about the intellectual meaning and importance of these themes has and should continue to increase the faculty's understanding of them, and thus the likelihood that faculty will incorporate the ideas into their courses.

Using Adult Learning Technologies

The following adult learning technologies were identified for use in the new program:

- Competency-based assessment
- Learning contracts

- Learning teams
- Experience-based learning
- Lifelong learning
- Machine technology (for example, computers and video)

The first three are initially addressed through the required Managerial Assessment and Development course (see Chapter Four).

Interestingly, a number of teams have continued to meet on a regular basis outside class, although this is neither a required nor a structured part of the program. Several groups, including those from part-time evening classes, meet once a month for social and personal development activities. Portions of some groups continue to pursue developmental activities.

Team members often comment that if it were not for the random assignment, they never would have gotten to know and appreciate many of the people in their groups. They would, they say, have been more likely to seek out individuals who seemed similar to themselves. A detailed study of the value of Executive Action Teams is under way, and early indications point to the ongoing value of the teams in enhancing the social and intellectual aspects of the MBA experience.

A number of design changes were made in the course after the first full semester of implementation. Results have been encouraging, as evidenced by student evaluations.

Numerous anecdotes among the faculty, students, staff, and executives involved with the program demonstrate the positive effects of the Learning Plan on virtually every aspect of students' decision making processes concerning school and career. For example, several students have reported that the plan precipitated major changes in their choice of major and intended career and helped them to set priorities early. Academic advisors indicate that students are increasingly making and justifying course selection decisions on the basis of their Learning Plans. In addition, the school's placement director claims that students are entering the placement market better prepared and with a much clearer sense of job desires and expectations. This sentiment has also been echoed by recruiters interviewing students for summer internships and permanent placement.

As of the winter of 1993, numerous examples of the abilities and Learning Plan have appeared in the daily life of the school. Here are two of them: (1) In the spring of 1993, one of the MBA students running for the presidency of the Graduate Student Association used "Coded for Group Management by Boyatzis Himself" as one of her campaign slogans. She was elected, but probably for her full range of abilities and enthusiasm, not just for being coded for Group Management. (2) One of the computer information screens appearing as anyone logged onto the school computer system in 1993 said, "WHAT IS HARVARD GRAPHICS? Remember 'Use of Visual Aids' from the Oral Communication section of MGMT403??? This class is designed to get you started with Harvard Graphics."

Experience-based learning is used in most courses in the form of projects requiring work in companies and/or with managers in these companies. Almost every required and elective course calls for a field-based project, and most of these projects require students to visit facilities and collect raw data. Experiential learning is also being used in workshops for the development of certain abilities. For example, to begin working on Social Objectivity, students can attend a one-day experiential workshop titled "Appreciating Diversity."

Lifelong learning has been approached in several ways. In one sense, the overall objective of the Managerial Assessment and Development course (see Chapter Four) — to help students develop both methods for assessing their capabilities and plans for continuing to grow throughout their careers — helps to establish the value of lifelong development. Students incorporate learning goals into a plan that extends five or more years and explicitly considers contingencies for changes in career or life direction.

The WSOM faculty and administration have pursued the lifelong learning technology through extensions of the school's professional development programs. For example, in the spring of 1991, the faculty developed the Professional Fellows Program. This program supplements the existing executive MBA program and is designed to facilitate continuing growth for advanced professionals. The multiyear, part-time curriculum incorporates many of the features of the new MBA program.

The Professional Fellows Program is in its third year of implementation. Physicians, lawyers, engineers, and faculty participating in it are active members of the newly formed Professional Fellows Society. The enrollment increased to sixteen in the second year of the program from eleven in the first year. Plans are being made to alter the format to allow for students from anywhere in the United States to participate in the program.

Plans are also being developed for a unique executive doctorate program aimed at professionals who wish to develop advanced capabilities in applied scholarship, knowledge integration, and global thinking. The planned curriculum is one that is beyond the MBA experience but is not normally part of traditional doctoral programs.

The Executive Doctorate in Management program was approved by the faculty in the fall of 1993. The process for the new degree has begun. The first class is expected in the fall of 1995.

The use of machine technology has always been an important component of the MBA experience at the WSOM. However, the new program has increased the demand for tools to assist students in enhancing their knowledge and skills. Video, interactive software, and teleconferencing are just a few of the technologies that are now in wider use at the school.

Faculty-Led Curricular Change

Curricular change requires continuous improvement, and faculty must be leaders in this ongoing process. Several of the faculty committees that worked on the design and development of the new curriculum have continued to stimulate innovation, even though their membership has changed. One faculty effort resulted in the acceptance, by full faculty vote, of the new course evaluation form. The effort, which took eighteen months, included field tests and comparative statistical analyses. The school's faculty are sensitive to student evaluations, not only for all the usual reasons of wanting to do well and to serve the needs of WSOM's stakeholders, but also because the information is used in promotion and salary considerations.

The new evaluation form (shown in Appendix 9.1) includes sections asking students to comment on which of the twenty-two assessment abilities and five intellectual/value themes were addressed in the course. These additions to the form were intended to focus faculty attention on the new program's intellectual and developmental objectives. For each course, student evaluations are summarized and given to the faculty member and the department chairperson, and they are also entered in a book available to all students.

A second faculty-led venture has been the development of electives designed to foster specific abilities in addition to addressing certain knowledge areas (the reverse of the usual priorities in elective courses). Efforts are also under way to expand the intellectual content and the use of feedback on abilities in many courses.

As previously mentioned, the faculty have been a major force in extending the principles of the new MBA program into other existing programs, such as the undergraduate program, and in developing new executive and degree programs.

Resource Consistency

While we have been able to implement the new program with existing faculty and staff, and most activities have remained within the budget of the old program, several elements of the new program have resulted in an increase in expenses. This increased dollar investment has been offset by an increase in enrollments. It is not clear whether the latter can be sustained given the lessening of MBA fervor in the United States and periodic, recessionary, economic forces.

What Have We Learned?

We will now address the question of whether our experience and evaluation to date will result in changes in the six generalizations we proposed in Chapter Three.

1. Curricular change is initiated by strong signals from stakeholders.

2. Faculty have primary responsibility for curriculum and change.
3. Strong leadership is necessary.
4. Moving from a teaching to a learning perspective is important.
5. Creation of integrative learning mechanisms is difficult.
6. A norm of continuous improvement emerges.

Following is an assessment of the current status of each generalization proposed.

Curricular Change Is Initiated by Strong Signals from Stakeholders

Once the environmental signals from stakeholders have been transformed into a strategy, that strategy must be vigilantly maintained. It is the context for the new curriculum, and it provides the philosophical and pedagogical roots of the changes and of their intended effects. But implementation is not exciting, and those involved can easily forget the rationale and purposes of the change. Resource allocations and reallocations accompanying the new curriculum must be assessed in terms of the strategic priorities. Continuous discussion, evaluation, and feedback about the new program are essential for maintaining momentum, making improvements, and increasing acceptance. The school must constantly seek opportunities for discussion of the new program's intellectual and practical underpinnings, its importance to the school's development, and its role in developing a culture of continuous improvement and quality enhancement. If it does not do so, complacency and inertia could cause curricular recidivism.

Information must be kept flowing from all stakeholders, and at the same time, stakeholders must be kept informed of progress. It must be remembered, however, that evaluation of the new program is a delicate job, requiring continuous examination and the avoidance of premature conclusions.

A modification to the earlier generalization is that the weight and importance of input from various stakeholders must be considered in the context of strategy. For example, stakeholders have high expectations of the new program and a desire to make immediate changes if something does not seem to be working. There is, therefore, a challenge to the balance between an academic, long-term view and a shorter-term, customer-focused perspective.

Faculty and administrators are, and should be, considering the needs of both current and future students. Current students, as well as recruiters, may view the program changes in the context of the job market, creating a short-term perspective. In contrast, the faculty may take a view of the knowledge, abilities, and values needed to reform the structure and functioning of organizations and build toward a better society, thus creating a longer-term perspective. While an immediate job focus may lead to a vocational training perspective, a "new-society" focus may lead to preparation of students for a world that will exist after all the current students have made their contributions.

Although it would appear self-evident, the costs of maintaining the strategic vigil must be made explicit. The new program empowers stakeholders to assume more responsibility for program success; consequently, they expect more involvement in the school and in its process of improvement. This expectation has many potential benefits for the institution, but it also has risks. For example, stakeholders may become frustrated and discouraged if their expectations are not met and the school is unwilling or unable to respond to their concerns as quickly and decisively as they would like. This risk is most apparent with respect to the senior executives who serve as advisors to the Executive Action Teams. Because their general impressions of the school are shaped by student comments, it is important that they also have strong, constructive, and open relationships with the faculty and staff.

Faculty. Have Primary Responsibility for Curriculum and Change

Faculty comportment related to the new curriculum ranges from concurrence to commitment. Intercolleague respect, along with accepted norms, may result in the faculty's voting to support a set of changes. This is especially likely if faculty members believe that some of their colleagues want the changes, but that they themselves will not be directly affected. However, concurrence is not the form of faculty involvement that will perpetuate the new curriculum or sustain the effort through the difficult early stages of transition. It is the views of the faculty, as stakeholders, that must be the most heavily weighted. If not, course revisions, adherence to the new curricular principles, course evaluations, feedback among faculty regarding performance standards, and so forth simply will not happen.

While the faculty as a whole must continue to lead the change and its necessary improvements, the primary responsibility will typically rest with a few faculty, with others trusting and following them. As universities become more customer oriented, a cultural change may be needed within the faculty with regard to their role in curricular change. For example, the need to make elements of the new program compatible with the existing academic structure may lead to design capitulations. Earlier, we had thought that workshops would be useful in helping students to develop abilities not addressed in courses and projects. However, it has become clear that both credibility and student reaction require that the necessary developmental activities be provided by faculty.

Required and elective courses must be developed that incorporate the new skills and abilities. For example, to assist students in learning how to work with others in groups, it is necessary to add some integrative or reflective activity connected explicitly with group processes and behaviors into many courses (especially where the course content objectives are not related to organizational or human behavior).

Curricular changes often require faculty to reorient their time from research to teaching. In a research institution such as ours, this reorientation is often questioned by the faculty and can result in foot dragging or other forms of resistance. It is important that there be ongoing dialogue concerning the justification and importance of the changes. Further, faculty performance evaluations and reward systems must be realigned, either temporarily or permanently, to reflect the school's strategic shift.

Interventions such as these serve to minimize faculty dissent regarding teaching and research during a period of significant change.

Strong Leadership Is Necessary

Effective leadership during the implementation process requires the willingness to continually ask what else can be done, along with the courage to listen to feedback in its full, and often raw, form. To say that such tasks are at times painful and fatiguing is an understatement. Inertia can set in early in the implementation process, since at this point it is still easier to go back to the old, comfortable ways, even for the leaders of the design and development efforts. If the organization is to remain focused on the new strategy, the network of leadership must be visible and active during implementation.

Leadership must not be solely an administrative task. Continuation of the effort requires that others, too, assume leadership roles, or curricular change will quickly dissipate and become a low priority for all.

Individuals involved in leadership roles in the early stages of implementation may lose the patience and excitement about experimentation necessary to sustain and expand the change process. Also, the frequency and severity of feedback sessions with many stakeholders can result in a reactionary posture among those in leadership positions. The best way to avoid these difficulties is to broaden the leadership and revitalization tasks so that leadership is spread among multiple efforts.

Delegation, prioritization, and frequent strategic reviews can aid in the avoidance of blind spots that could potentially ignite a series of crises and divert attention from innovation.

Moving from a Teaching to a Learning Perspective Is Important

The move to the new program involves a shift of values, style, and pedagogy that must be constantly reinforced among faculty and staff as well as students. As noted earlier, training and socialization into the professorial, academic culture creates strong commitments to pedagogical methods that sustain the expert-teacher model of faculty behavior. An outcome orientation implies measurement and increased accountability. Faculty often focus on those outcomes most easily measured rather than on those that are more qualitative and longer term.

Among students, those who may have difficulty making the shift include younger students (those aged twenty-one to twenty-three), those without sufficient work experience, and those who see the entire experience as merely a ticket-punching exercise. These groups are not likely to be accustomed to the degree of student involvement in the educational process and the concrete feedback they receive in an outcome-oriented program. For example, during the first offering of the Managerial Assessment and Development course, we overestimated the students' capacity to accept sometimes-negative feedback about their knowledge and skills. The result was a backlash of student resentment toward the faculty and school. In our redesign of the course, we explicitly considered how, when, and by whom feedback was to be given to students.

The empowerment of students and other key stakeholders does not occur suddenly. Rather, it is a slow, iterative process, achieved through the ongoing involvement of stakeholders and a sustained commitment to continuous improvement.

Creation of Integrative Learning Mechanisms Is Difficult

Since the structure of most schools is geared toward specialization and compartmentalization, the maintenance of integrating mechanisms is difficult. This is particularly true during the early stages of implementation — the point of maximum vulnerability. In our situation, such mechanisms were in place in the form of special committees, task groups, perspectives courses, the Managerial Assessment and Development course, the intellectual/value themes, and the staff groups. Integrative mechanisms can facilitate learning, not only for the students but also for the faculty, staff, and administration. This atmosphere of learning is an essential component of the change process.

Integrative devices are unnatural in academia. Even if a structure were already present to facilitate interaction across disciplines (for example, in the form of certain standing committees), the usual types of collaboration across departments, disciplinary units, and staff groups would not be sufficient for the needs of the new program. Many aspects of organizational life in a university are counter to the ongoing use of such integrative mechanisms as accounting for faculty time and effort, rewarding and recognizing collaboration on design, and team teaching.

A Norm of Continuous Improvement Emerges

The excitement that springs from an environment of learning automatically creates a culture of change, helping to perpetuate an atmosphere of innovation and experimentation. The gradual shift in culture spreads easily into other programmatic areas. Once the new MBA program had been implemented, it was a simple matter to move into innovation in executive education.

The focus on continuous improvement has also led to changes in noncurricular areas such as placement, student advising, and student activities. In addition, the emphasis on improvement helps to keep all stakeholders focused on strategy, quality, outcomes, and accountability.

The experiences of other schools in using elements of our new program suggest that sustained development is difficult to achieve. Assessment courses have a tendency to die when the first innovator leaves or shifts direction, and learning teams are difficult to manage, staff, and maintain as a program focus. It cannot be repeated too often that constant vigilance and reinforcement are essential to a sustained effort.

Conclusion

When we began the curricular change effort at the WSOM, we had the objective of actually transforming our MBA program rather than simply making incremental changes to the old model.

This effort was motivated by the belief that MBA education was in need of a radical change in orientation and of new intellectual and philosophical underpinnings. These underpinnings were developed following years of data gathering and analysis and of extensive intellectual dialogue about each design principle.

Unfortunately, during the new program's implementation phase, the frequency and fervor of discussions wane, and implementation is often viewed as an administrative task distant from the mainstream activities of most faculty. This tendency must be resisted if the intellectual justification of the program is to be realized. Otherwise, transformative changes will deteriorate into small, incremental changes. It is important to develop mechanisms that provide stakeholders with opportunities to discuss and debate the intellectual purpose and principles of the new program, as well as to evaluate its effectiveness and its extension to other areas of the school.

Sustained program implementation is, in sum, hard work. It is complex and unglamorous, but it is absolutely critical for attaining program objectives. It is no wonder that there have been so few radical innovations in management education in this country in the last four decades. Yet, while the process can be enormously frustrating at times, requiring a great deal of perseverance and dedication, it is rewarding almost beyond belief when it works. A number of U.S. schools are now attempting to make significant curricular changes based on a sound theoretical framework, rather than simply tinkering at the margins of their current programs. These efforts should be encouraged, applauded, and continually evaluated to determine their efficacy and value. We believe it will take at least another year to fully implement (that is, follow through) concepts and practices intended to be part of our new program, and a decade beyond that to determine its long-term effectiveness and significance. Nonetheless, we are encouraged by the early results. We are wiser for having tried, and we are convinced that we now have our important stakeholders involved in a different type of partnership with the school, one that we expect will lead to continuous improvement of the education we provide.

Summary of Learning Following Implementation

1. Curricular change is initiated by strong signals from stakeholders.
2. Faculty have primary responsibility for curriculum and change.
3. Strong leadership is necessary.
4. Moving from a teaching to a learning perspective is important.
5. Creation of integrative learning mechanisms is difficult.
6. A norm of continuous improvement emerges.

Appendix 9.1. Case Western Reserve University
Weatherhead School of Management
Course Evaluation Questionnaire.

Course/Section:_____   Instructor(s): _____

Expected Grade: Ⓐ   Ⓑ   Ⓒ   Ⓓ   Ⓕ

1. Please comment on what you felt went particularly well in this course.

2. Please comment on what you feel needs to be improved in this course.

3. Please evaluate and comment on the teaching materials and activities (e.g., textbooks, case materials, group projects, written assignments, computer exercises, experiential exercises, etc.)

4. Please comment on the use of class time (i.e., was it used effectively?).

225

Weatherhead School of Management
Course Evaluation Questionnaire, Cont'd.

Weatherhead School of Management—Course Evaluation Questionnaire

STUDENT INFORMATION			COURSE INFORMATION	
PROGRAM NAME	**CONCENTRATION**	**PROGRAM TYPE**	Instructor(s) Name	
○ EMBA	○ BAFI	○ 60 Hour	**DEPARTMENT**	**NUMBER**
○ MACC	○ ECON		○ ACCT	
○ MBA	○ HSMC	○ 42 Hour	○ BAFI	
○ MNO/CNM	○ LHRP		○ ECON	⓪ ⓪ ⓪
○ MSMS	○ MIDS		○ HSMC	① ① ①
○ MSODA	○ MKMR		○ LHRP	② ② ②
○ MBA/JD	○ OPMT	**STUDENT TYPE**	○ MAND	③ ③ ③
○ MBA/MSMS	○ OPRE		○ MGMT	④ ④ ④
○ MBA/MSN	○ ORBH	○ Full-Time	○ MIDS	⑤ ⑤ ⑤
○ PhD	○ PLCY		○ MKMR	⑥ ⑥ ⑥
○ Undergraduate	○ Other/None	○ Part-Time	○ OPMT	⑦ ⑦ ⑦
○ Other	○ Undecided		○ OPRE	⑧ ⑧ ⑧
			○ ORBH	⑨ ⑨ ⑨
			○ PLCY	**SECTION**
			○ QUMM	
			○ Other	① ② ③ ④ ⑤ ⑥

Poor ◄————► Excellent

I. What is you overall rating of the course?   ① ② ③ ④ ⑤

II. What is your overall rating of the instructor?   ① ② ③ ④ ⑤

III. Evaluate the course in terms of: Not Applicable / Not Valuable ◄————► Valuable

- Text no. 1 _____ ○ ① ② ③ ④ ⑤
- Text no. 2 _____ ○ ① ② ③ ④ ⑤
- Lectures ○ ① ② ③ ④ ⑤
- Class discussions ○ ① ② ③ ④ ⑤
- Projects ○ ① ② ③ ④ ⑤
- Computer exercises ○ ① ② ③ ④ ⑤
- Case materials ○ ① ② ③ ④ ⑤
- Written assignments ○ ① ② ③ ④ ⑤
- Experiential learning exercises ○ ① ② ③ ④ ⑤

IV. Evaluate the extent to which the instructor: Poor ◄————► Excellent

- Defines course objectives clearly ① ② ③ ④ ⑤
- Fulfills course objectives ① ② ③ ④ ⑤
- Imparts enthusiasm ① ② ③ ④ ⑤
- Knows subject ① ② ③ ④ ⑤
- Is well prepared for class ① ② ③ ④ ⑤
- Provides adequate feedback to students ① ② ③ ④ ⑤
- Presents material with clarity ① ② ③ ④ ⑤
- Is sensitive to student's level of understanding ① ② ③ ④ ⑤
- Is open to student opinion ① ② ③ ④ ⑤
- Grades fairly ① ② ③ ④ ⑤
- Is available outside of class ① ② ③ ④ ⑤
- Uses class time efficiently ① ② ③ ④ ⑤

Light ◄————► Heavy

V. Workload compared with other courses: ① ② ③ ④ ⑤

**Weatherhead School of Management
Course Evaluation Questionnaire, Cont'd.**

Sections VI, VII, and VIII ARE FOR MBA COURSES ONLY: Refer to your syllabus or the instructor's comments regarding the specific abilities and themes intended to be addressed in this course.

VI.   Please fill in the bubble to the left for any ability enhanced or developed during the course. Please leave the bubble blank for any ability not applicable.

- ○ Efficiency orientation
- ○ Planning
- ○ Initiative
- ○ Attention to detail
- ○ Self-control
- ○ Flexibility
- ○ Empathy
- ○ Persuasiveness
- ○ Networking
- ○ Negotiating
- ○ Self-confidence
- ○ Group management
- ○ Developing others
- ○ Oral communication
- ○ Use of concepts
- ○ Systems thinking
- ○ Pattern recognition
- ○ Theory building
- ○ Using technology
- ○ Quantitative analysis
- ○ Social objectivity
- ○ Written communication
- ○ Other: Please specify _____
- ○ Other: Please specify _____
- ○ Other: Please specify _____

VII.   Indicate which of the following themes were addressed during the course by filling in the bubble to the left of the theme.

- ○ Creating economic value
- ○ Creating intellectual value
- ○ Creating human value
- ○ Stimulating professionalism, integrity, and social responsibility
- ○ Innovating in the use of information and technology
- ○ Managing in a complex, diverse, and interdependent world
- ○ Developing the manager as team leader and team member

VIII. How did the course help you work toward fulfilling your learning goals and your learning plan?

Ten

CONCLUSION:
WHAT IF LEARNING
WERE THE PURPOSE
OF EDUCATION?

Richard E. Boyatzis, Scott S. Cowen, and David A. Kolb

In this final chapter, we would like to share with you some of our observations along the way and envision where we might go next. During the eight years of work together on this project, we have had many conversations. Some of these were moments of celebration, as when the faculty unanimously (with one abstention, of course) passed the proposal for the new program. Others were depressing. To our way of thinking, teaching interests dictated many required courses, while learning interests favored a more individualized approach. The teaching interests won. The challenge of continuous improvement seems overwhelming. In institutionalizing the program, erosion of innovation by traditional structures, interests, and perspectives is a relentless force. To paraphrase George Bernard Shaw, "Sometimes we looked at the way things are and ask 'Why?' Other times we looked at the way things might be and ask 'Why not?'"

We are grateful to David Justice, Dean of DePaul University's School for New Learning, for his contributions to an earlier draft of this chapter.

Finding a Purpose

Both perspectives are essential for educational reform. Why we conduct education as we do is a puzzling question. How to do it better is a big challenge. For us, the idea that learning should be the primary purpose of education has been a beacon. Ask a child why he or she goes to school and the spontaneous answer is likely to be, "To learn." Ask the same question of graduate students in medical school, law school, nursing, or management, and the most common answer will probably be, "To get a degree." Or some will say, "To become a doctor [or lawyer, nurse, or manager]." We might all agree that learning is a purpose of education — but is it the primary purpose?

From a societal perspective, education has at least four primary functions or purposes. One is human resource allocation, the certified sorting and matching of individuals by ability and interest to meet the needs of society. This sorting takes place on two dimensions. The horizontal dimension helps individuals find their niche in society — the field of knowledge that best suits their talents. The vertical dimension, explicitly legitimized by an ethic of meritocracy, attempts to match the best and the brightest with the most important and privileged positions in society. A second purpose concerns the transmission of cultural values and beliefs at the local and societal level. A third purpose of education is the development of human potential, helping individuals to actualize their talents and interests. The fourth purpose is what Mortimer Adler (1982) calls the "maieutic" function. Educational institutions are the birthing ground of new ideas and visions for the future of the world, of enlightenment and emancipation. Note that these functions are listed in increasing order of emphasis on learning and decreasing order of priority in current practice. Therefore, to make learning the primary purpose of education as reflected in these functions is, literally, to turn the educational establishment upside down.

At the level of specific educational institutions, other purposes become important. Research, for example, is a major objective for many universities. For many, education is a business important for jobs and economic development in the community. When we look at these institutions more purposes appear, based on the interests of different subgroups and specialities. Faculty, staff, and administration all have their particular portfolio of priorities, as do different disciplines and programs.

Promotion of learning becomes an objective that must compete with all of these objectives for primacy. It often seems to be lost among them. Observation of the current state of education would suggest that education is about everything but learning — about research, about teaching, about budgets and taxes, about drugs and discipline, about religion and values, about political correctness and political connections. So what would an educational institution whose primary mission was the promotion of learning look like? Is there a place for such an institution in today's world and the emerging world of the twenty-first century?

What Is Learning?

Defining learning may be a good place to start, since it is hard to promote something if you do not know what it is. Since learning is arguably the most studied topic in the hundred years of American psychology, one might think this would be an easy question to answer. Sad to say, this is not the case. The great majority of these studies have followed the path of psychological behaviorism, which effectively promoted the view that human learning was a simple, unitary process of accumulating associations. The meta-message was that when it comes to learning, humans are no better than rats.

However, in the last twenty years, new views of learning have been emerging. In a sense, they have been there all along in the works of Dewey, Lewin, James, Piaget, and Vygotsky — strong voices that have been silenced. As knowledge has become globalized, and diversity recognized, a new paradigm is emerging: *Learning is a big concept that is broad and deep.*

The human species is distinguished by its capacity to learn, to make meaning from experience. This unique ability to learn is what makes us human. How one learns from experience can be divided into two basic questions: "How does what is outside get in?" and "How does what is inside get out?" In Piaget's formulation, the answer to the first question is accommodation, the shaping of internal meaning-making structures by experience, a process he called *imitation*. The inside-out process is assimilation, the imposition of internal meaning structures on experience. This process he called *play*. Piaget (1980) believed that "equilibration" of assimilation and accommodation was the central problem of intellectual development. Learning from experience thus involves balancing surrender and mastery, or taking in experiences and others' views of them and expressing one's own conclusions in thought and action.

Learning is a solitary act that occurs in relationship with others. Through learning together the human community is created and recreated. Yet ultimately the choice of when and what to learn is a private one. To paraphrase Annie Dillard, be careful what you learn, because that determines what you know.

Jürgen Habermas's (1984, 1987) tripartite typology of knowledge is a major example of the new learning paradigm. He characterizes the breadth dimension in two basic categories: instrumental knowledge and communicative knowledge. His third category, emancipatory knowledge, describes the transformative, deep-learning dimension.

In this broad and deep perspective on learning, experiential learning theory (Kolb, 1984) is proposed not as a single universal method of learning, but as a map of learning territories, a frame of reference within which many different ways of learning can flourish and interrelate. It is a holistic framework that orients the many different ways of learning to one another.

Learning is a broad concept encompassing many ways of knowing. In the new learning paradigm, intelligence as the single, universal measure of the capacity to learn is replaced by recognition of diversity in ways of knowing. All of these are different ways of learning that every individual combines to form a unique learning style. For example, Howard Gardner described seven different kinds of intelligence. In *Creating Minds*

(1993), he describes how these intelligences were expressed in the lives of seven modern geniuses: Freud (intrapersonal), Einstein (logical-mathematical), Picasso (visual-spatial), Stravinsky (musical), T. S. Eliot (linguistic), Martha Graham (bodily kinesthetic), and Gandhi (interpersonal).

The scope of learning includes the many different things there are to know. Research on the nature of expertise suggests that learning is more contextual than universal: "A very intelligent person might be that way because of specific local features of his knowledge, organizing knowledge rather than because of global qualities of his thinking" (Minsky and Paapert, 1974, p. 59).

Deep learning refers to the fact that sometimes learning creates profound transformation in the life of the learner. Such learning opens doors through the barriers of class, race, gender, and ethnic identification. It opens eyes and hearts to the views of others. It transforms the child's awkward hand into the surgeon's steady blade. Kant's concept of enlightenment is perhaps the most influential modern idea of deep learning. His answer to the question "Was ist Aufklärung?" describes an age of enlightenment that requires a community of world citizens where all have unlimited freedom to use their own reason and express their own judgments and views for public testing. Habermas's emancipatory knowledge is a neo-Kantian version of this idea, emphasizing communicative reason in an "ideal speech situation." Other learning and development theorists define deep learning as liberating (Freire, 1990), integrating (Kolb, 1984), and transformative (Mezirow, 1991).

The idea of deep learning is in some ways analogous to Arne Ness's (1973) distinction between shallow and deep ecology. Shallow ecology is the self-interested protection of the environment to maintain our way of life, while deep ecology refers to a fundamental transformation in perspective from human centeredness to a large sense of identification and connectedness with the whole planet and all of life.

Deep learning is not only transformative but possibly transcendent. It is possible that an attitude of deep learning can reveal Deep Truth. Paolo Freire (1990, p. 72) contrasts the shallow learning that results from the banking concept of education with the transcendent, deep learning that results from problem-posing education: "Problem posing education is revolutionary futurity. Hence it is prophetic. . . . Hence it affirms men as beings who transcend themselves. . . . Hence it identifies with the movement which engages men as beings aware of their incompletion."

Deep learning is never having the same experience twice. Learning requires change, but change does not always imply learning. It is difficult to conceive of learning that does not result in a change in someone's behavior, attitude, perspective, interpretation, motivation, or approach to the next situation. To be open to the change, a person must be flexible. One of Louis XVI's biographers said that he never learned and never forgot anything. Although the two seem odd together, the act of never forgetting may lead to an intractability. So we must consider that learning requires flexibility, which may involve forgetting and probably forgiveness in work and family life.

Reflect on your own life. Have you had learning experiences that have fundamentally changed you? Has learning helped you find meaning and purpose in your life? Thomas Wolfe's (1991, p. 80) description of one person's reflections beautifully portrays the deep-learning process:

> For he had learned some of the things that every man must find out for himself, and he had found out about them as one has to find out, through errors and through trial, through fantasy and delusion, through falsehood and his own damn foolishness, through being mistaken and wrong and an idiot and egotistical and aspiring and hopeful and believing and confused. As he lay there he had gone over his life, and bit by bit, had extracted from it some of the hard lessons of experience. Each thing he had learned was so simple and so obvious once he had grasped it that he wondered why he had not always known it. Altogether, they wove into a kind of thread, trailing backward through his past and out into the future. And he thought now, perhaps he could begin to shape his life to mastery, for he felt a sense of new direction deep within him, but whither it would take him he could not say.

Teaching and Learning

Jacques Barzun began his book *Begin Here: The Forgotten Conditions of Teaching and Learning* (1991) with the words, "Forget EDUCATION . . . Let us talk rather about Teaching and Learning." We share his view that the educational establishment that has grown up around the core task of teaching and learning threatens to strangle it. In the process the natural connection between teaching and learning has been twisted and severed. When we speak of a journey from teaching to learning, we do not wish to imply an opposition between the two processes. As Erik Erikson (1961, pp. 159–160) pointed out, they are deeply connected: "For we are a teaching species. . . . Only man can and must extend his solicitude over the long parallel and overlapping childhoods of numerous offspring united in households and communities . . . parenthood is, for most, the first, and for many, the prime generative encounter; yet the continuation of mankind challenges the generative ingenuity of workers and thinkers of many kinds." In this respect as teachers, we are truly in loco parentis; for many, it is a deep calling.

But it is a mistake to assume that teaching and learning are the same thing: What you teach is not necessarily what I learn, and what I learn may be other than what you teach. Our view is that education has tended to focus on teaching, often assuming learning rather than promoting it. So, for example, we address a need for managerial knowledge or skill, say ethical judgment, by asking, "Is it covered in our current curriculum?" If not, we introduce a course on ethics and assume we have done our job.

When learning is promoted from the teaching perspective, it almost always occurs within the confines of the educational "black box." Most educational innovation begins by assuming the very structures and processes that should be questioned: the course, class, grades, examinations, classroom, credit hours, lectures, and so on.

As we consider the concept of learning, the view is that each student, especially each graduate student in a professional school, is not "tabula rasa" when he or she enters our programs and classrooms. Students have experiences, models and theories, expectations, and even a personal theory of learning. Respecting these experiences and thoughts, and bringing them into the classroom or educational setting, are essential to link the potential new learning to their lives and worldview, possibly to facilitate unlearning or relearning.

You can lead students to an experience, but you cannot make them learn. Engaging their views and ways of knowing appears fundamental to stimulating the motivation and desire to learn. As experiential learning theory describes, learning requires experience, reflection, integration and conceptualization, and then application, either in the form of thought or action.

Design Principles Emphasizing Learning

So let us return to the question we began with: "What would an educational institution whose primary purpose is learning look like?" We have seen pieces of this vision in the efforts of institutions that have attempted serious educational reform and by innovators outside of the educational establishment, but for the most part our feeling is that we have not yet asked deeply enough why things are as they are, nor creatively envisioned how they might be. The following design principles for an educational institution whose primary purpose is learning are offered as guidelines for critique and creative innovation:

1. Evaluating educational structures and processes by promoting learning criteria
2. Conducting outcome orientation to allow analysis of learning value added
3. Becoming a learner-centered institution
4. Carrying out continuous inquiry about the learning process
5. Developing an institutional learning strategy based on stakeholder conversation

Each principle will be discussed in turn.

1. *Evaluating educational structures and processes by promoting learning criteria.* To begin, we propose a zero-base assessment of

current institutional practices and procedures by asking the question, "How does this structure promote or inhibit learning?" Some of these structures literally have been in place for centuries with no explicit rationale. The course, for example, is probably the most overused educational intervention of all time. When the inside of this educational "black box" is examined, there is an astounding regularity of procedure, also unjustified.

The course is typically a discourse without recourse. As the teacher, I make the discourse. As the student, you are evaluated by how accurately you can repeat it back to me. If there is a discrepancy, it is assigned a number or letter that you as the student are required to carry with you for the rest of your life and report when any important decisions are made about your job and career. No standard psychometric questions are ever asked about the reliability or validity of these grades, and they assume that the discrepancy is the result of student failure to learn, not faculty failure to teach.

Grades are a questionable procedure. We have found no study that shows they promote learning and much anecdotal evidence about how they inhibit it by fostering unproductive competition among students, a focus on getting the answer instead of learning the concept, and a risk-averse strategy that stifles experimentation and creativity.

Other questions come to mind: How is it that every subject can be covered in exactly fifteen weeks? Why are classes so large? Why are classrooms arranged the way they are? Why are credit hours the measure of progress toward a degree? Does the Carnegie unit (seat time) assume that teaching equals learning? Why does one have to assume the subservient role of student in order to learn at an educational institution? Wouldn't member be a better role?

Promoting learning criteria in evaluating institutions and processes encourages concepts used in quality improvement efforts. Are the processes timely, responsive, innovative (so that they add value), flexible, and durable? In education, durability of learning and timeliness have been elusive measures to discuss. Experiential learning theory would contend that "storing" knowledge and abilities long before they are used will not result in learning, but merely cobwebbed, overfilled storage bins in the mind. Computer-interactive and video-interactive technology offer new possibilities for just-in-time learning. Responsiveness requires a multiple-stakeholder perspective and maintaining a constant flow of information with stakeholders. The "faculty-as-expert" assumption inherent in the focus on a teaching orientation diminishes the value of time and energy spent exchanging views with stakeholders. Flexibility can be translated into a question of allowing for diversity in the ways people learn. Beyond access for currently working students, using learning criteria asks questions about the methods, pacing, assignments, and pedagogy for students with various learning styles, interpersonal styles, cognitive and spiritual preferences, and so forth.

2. *Conducting outcome orientation to allow analysis of learning value added.* Generally, educational institutions seek to maximize their prestige by increasing the inputs to the teaching and learning process (for example, student SAT scores, faculty publications, library, buildings and endowments). They seek to maintain quality by controlling the throughputs. This is the rationale for the Carnegie unit, to measure educational quality by contact hours with Ph.D. professors. An institution whose primary purpose was learning would have an outcome orientation, measuring its success by the learning value added—retained learnings, if you like. The great advantage of measuring quality through output is that throughputs are free to vary in search of better output. Throughput quality control freezes the structure, producing the routinized educational black box. In the process, educators are absolved of any responsibility for outcomes.

To be sure, there are significant challenges in making the outcome orientation work. Assessment of learning becomes critical. A corollary to Mason Haire's maxim, "What gets measured, gets managed," is "What gets mismeasured, gets mismanaged." If there is one conclusion to be drawn from the psychological assessment literature it is that the best predictor of the ability to do something is the actual doing of it—not multiple-choice answers about what to do, or knowing what to do, or saying what I will do, but the actual in-context performance of a song, an essay, a research project, a speech, or whatever. An outcome orientation thus draws education closer to real life.

Assessment also plays an important role in determining learning value added on the input side. Harold Hodgekinson has suggested that productivity in higher education could be improved by 50 percent simply by not teaching people things they already know. The use of assessment technology to give academic credit for prior learning is one example of this growing trend in higher education. Do not teach people things they already know; teach them what they need to know.

3. *Becoming a learner-centered institution.* If its primary mission is the promotion of learning, then it follows that the institution should be most responsive to those who are most directly involved in the learning process and have the most influence over it: the learners themselves. A big challenge here is recognition and responsiveness to learner individuality. While a teaching-centered institution seeks economies of scale by large classes and standardized treatment of all students, a learner-centered institution seeks economies of scope by attuning its learning methods to the individual learning styles of its students. Efforts are made to put individual learners in charge of their own learning through learning plans and contracts and coaching on learning how to learn.

Sperling and Tucker (1993) identified a number of characteristics of "adult-centered" universities. They included: (1) have education of working adults as the primary mission of the institution; (2) ensure that faculty and courses are academically and professionally qualified; (3) require students to work in groups; (4) compress instructional formats by 20 to 50 percent to use the adults' experiential base; (5) offer instruction at times and places convenient to the students; and (6) continuously collect information from students and all stakeholders about the quality and impact of the programs and, of course, use this information for continuous improvements.

Another challenge for the learner-centered institution is the creation of a social context conducive to learning. It is not surprising that Paolo Freire, for whom education is politics, would see power as the central issue in the creation of this social context. He argues that the learner-centered institution must replace the authority-based monologue of teacher discourse by dialogue among equals where all have equal opportunity to name their own experience.

Social context appears vital to learning for at least three reasons. First, all prelearned insights and discoveries require application to complete the learning cycle. In most professions, the application most often occurs in a context with others. Second, an increasing amount of work in today's organizations is in small groups — formal or informal, long-term or short-term, for maintenance or innovation. Third, social interaction appears essential to the ways of knowing and ways of learning for many students in today's professional programs. It is not surprising, therefore, that numerous studies of educational impact recommend increased use of groups as study groups, learning teams, tutorials, or project teams (Sperling and Tucker, 1993; Harvard Assessment Project, 1990; Porter and McKibbin, 1988).

The challenge is to create a social context conducive to learning, and not one that unnecessarily complicates or interferes with the learning process. Peer learning requires a collaborative spirit — a shared commitment to the others in the group and their learning. Collaboration may occur in a noncompetitive environment in which students are not always forced to assume that everyone around them is a direct competitor. Grading on a curve, which makes sense to faculty teaching difficult material and supposedly gives students a chance to do well relative to others, fosters competition among students. Competition against standards of excellence in which students compete against their own goals, or standards established by a faculty member, can provide a context for learning free of the assumed zero-sum competition among students.

Research on learning indicates that access to learning opportunities is enhanced with the possibilities of imitation. That is, observing others helps a person "picture" how the new, desired, or potential ideas, behavior, processes, or analysis may appear in use. Developmental psychologists called this availability within the individual's proximal zone of development.

The social context of learning is helped when settings are created in which people can build on each other's ideas, not merely respecting each other's autonomy. How often have you sat in faculty meetings and said, "If you want to do XYZ, go ahead. I'll support that," and sotto voce said, "As long as I don't have to do anything!" Creating these settings also requires disagreement and conflict. Often, open disagreement among faculty means a veto or the beginning of a fifteen-year feud. Among students, open disagreements may mean wasted time, a commitment to spend even more time with another person they consider a jerk "to process or work out" the difference, or fear of being ostracized by social or opinion leaders. So, we swallow our differences of opinion and deny the opportunity of building on conflicting ideas to create new insight.

4. *Carrying out continuous inquiry about the learning process.* We referred earlier to Ernest Boyer's reflection on the sorry state of the telephone if AT&T had invested as little on communication R&D as education has invested in learning R&D. Learning is the core technology of education. Research to improve the learning process will do much to create the learning-focused institution of the future. An important implication of the idea that learning is a broad concept is that learning is not one topic within a single field, but a topic in every field. In his influential book *Scholarship Reconsidered: Priorities of the Professoriate* (1990), Boyer recommends expanding the current narrow definition of research to include the scholarship of teaching (we would say learning). In other words, a topic central to every field of study is how one learns it. Scholarship focused on this topic is just as important as the traditional scholarship of discovery.

To say that technology has a big role to play in the improvement of learning is an understatement. Learners of the future will spend a great deal of time commuting on the information superhighway. Education should be at the forefront of these developments.

5. *Developing an institutional learning strategy based on stakeholder conversation.* An institution cannot make the promotion of learning a priority without itself being a learning organization. In Chapter Two, we outlined a process of institutional strategy formulation based on a model of organizational learning in which learning is seen as a process of continuing conversation among organization stakeholders. We emphasized an outside-in ap-

proach to strategy formulation that ensures that the often-absent voices of outside stakeholders are heard.

These differences appear at many levels in the institution, including the vision, mission, and strategy communicated by the dean. Regardless of how and when and with whom it is developed, the nature of the vision, mission, and strategy will contribute to the atmosphere of the school. Larwood, Kriger, and Falbe (1993) studied vision statements from deans of business schools and discovered three types of visions: reactive communicators, reactive loners, and proactive visionaries. Reactive communicators were 10 percent of the deans; they described their own vision as "less changing, less flexible, less risky, less difficult to describe" and more conservative than other deans' vision statements. Reactive loners were 53 percent of the deans and described their vision as "less descriptive of what is taking place, less detailed or less focused, less formalized, less planned, and less understood" than the other deans' vision statements. The 37 percent classified as proactive visionaries described their vision as "action oriented, inspirational, integrated with the vision of others, long term, strategic" as compared to others' vision statements. If these differences appear in deans' descriptions of their own vision statements, one can imagine the lost opportunities to build on stakeholder resources within the institution for the approximately two-thirds of the schools whose deans were reactive communicators or reactive loners!

Another commonsense model of organizational learning is that the learning organization is one in which all of its members are engaged in a continuous process of lifelong learning.

Process Principles to Advance the Primacy of Learning

The process principles are as follows:

1. Conceptualizing management as an interdisciplinary phenomenon
2. Respecting and linking to the traditional departmental and disciplinary structure

3. Developing the whole person
4. Providing lifelong learning in the context of varying life and career stages, cycles, and modes
5. Creating a contagion of curiosity
6. Helping faculty and staff shift to a focus on learning

1. *Conceptualizing management as an interdisciplinary phenomenon.* Management, as it is practiced, is a multidisciplinary phenomenon. Typically, a manager does not encounter a marketing problem that does not have a human resource or management information component. Faculty, because of the specialization of their disciplines, tend to compartmentalize and give priority to their discipline. This narrow focus, from a manager's perspective, is exaggerated within a school of management because the disciplines often correspond to the departments; you then have a political structure supporting and possibly protecting a structure of intellectual specialization. Conceptualizing managerial phenomena as managers face them may appeal to students and assist them in learning how to function with one set of concepts in the context of other concepts. This shift is similar to the shift to organ-based learning characteristic of medical schools for the past several decades. This builds on the observed need for integrative learning mechanisms mentioned in Chapter Nine.

2. *Respecting and linking to the traditional departmental and disciplinary structure.* Although multidisciplinary concepts and integrative learning are important, the traditional disciplinary and departmental structure also play an important part in our institutions. Completely dismantling the departmental structure may seem like a politically expedient approach to overcoming perceived faculty resistance or political coalitions. But it would also dismantle the primary structure for perpetuating and advancing the university's prime intellectual resources, the faculty.

The disciplines provide the framework for training new professionals (that is, future faculty). The development of expertise requires some specialization as well as integration. The departmental and disciplinary structures are vehicles for dissemination of knowledge and insight (conferences, journals, and book mailing lists are easily organized around disciplines).

The generation of new knowledge might be threatened if we were to dispense with disciplinary identification. It would become difficult to identify and study complex phenomena without having vehicles for specialized inquiry and dialogue. These first two process points are placing an emphasis on not adopting either solely the disciplinary structure or solely an integrated, multidisciplinary structure.

3. *Developing the whole person.* Graduate management education should be seeking to develop knowledge, abilities, and values, as discussed in Chapters Three and Four. Currently, knowledge development probably constitutes 87 percent of the time students are in formal developmental experiences provided by our institutions. Ability development is probably about 10 percent, and value awareness development is probably the remaining 3 percent. In programs where assessment and ability development courses are taught, they shift about 5 percent of the students' time in formal program activities to ability development (that is, one out of twenty courses). If an ethics course is taught, it adds 5 percent to value awareness development.

What should the distribution of time be? Should we be apportioning the courses or classroom time differently? Should we think in terms of the total time the student is in the program rather than class hours? What would a student's schedule look like if we devoted 40 percent of the time to knowledge development, 40 percent of the time to ability development, and 20 percent of the time to value awareness development?

One possible approach is to lower the expectations about the *amount* of material to be covered in a course while raising the standards as to learning. A recent study of the durability (or retention) of accounting knowledge taught through a traditional course revealed that six weeks after taking an exam, students retained only about 40 percent of the material, as reflected in test grades (Specht and Sandlin, 1991). Although this may sound cavalier, suppose we reduced the "content" material to be covered in a course by 50 percent and focused on the students' learning, retention of the material, and integration with other material and abilities and values? How much would this affect their ability to function as managers after graduation?

Development of knowledge, application of knowledge, development of abilities, and awareness and choicefulness of values and value orientations should be integrated into *all* activities. Ability development and value awareness should be integrated into traditional courses and knowledge into internships. Alverno College has had impressive success in just this way.

4. *Providing lifelong learning in the context of varying life and career stages, cycles, and modes.* There are various theories of life stages, life cycles, career stages, and career cycles. All of these theories postulate that people are different — that they have different interests, anxieties, motivators, objectives, and concerns in each of these stages or cycles. And yet we typically offer material and experiences to our students in similar ways!

A twenty-seven-year-old entrant into an MBA program may be trying to get a jump shift on a career or to find one. A forty-two-year-old may be seeking to identify the career and environment that provides satisfactions not available in previous environments. A thirty-six-year-old engineer, recently laid off with no idea of what to do or where to go next, may also be seeking to identify new environments and opportunities. A fifty-five-year-old professor may be looking for new sources of excitement or variety. The factors that motivate each of these potential "management students" are different at each of these career transition points (Kolb, 1984; Boyatzis and Kolb, 1993; Levinson, 1978; Erikson, 1982; Loevinger, 1976; Schein, 1978; Dalton and Thompson, 1986; Perry, 1970; Kohlberg, 1976; Gilligan, 1982). How are we prepared to structure developmental experiences differently? What pedagogy and educational processes are best for each stage or cycle?

An ideal institution devoted to learning would not have the answers to these questions but would be considering them and experimenting. Research into the developmental issues and how to stimulate learning would be occurring. Discussions among faculty would focus on ways to respond to the pluralism of the prospective management student body, not just in terms of gender, ethnoreligious group, undergraduate major, occupational history, and cognitive cycle, but also with respect to stages and cycles in our lives and careers.

5. *Creating a contagion of curiosity.* Discussions with faculty and deans from professional schools about programs devoted to learning often are brought to an abrupt conclusion with the complaint that "faculty just don't want to change. How do you make them change?"

Our experiences in the journey and those of many colleagues in other institutions who have also implemented significant curriculum change points toward the following observation: If you create a contagion of curiosity, faculty will volunteer to join in the process and create change!

The process begins with the realization that faculty enjoy discussing and exploring ideas. To engage faculty in examining ideas is to engage their hearts and minds. Creating opportunities for faculty to reflect, study, discuss, argue, and in other words, join together in intellectual play, stimulates a rejuvenation and excitement about learning and the purpose of education. Many schools have found that by beginning with two or three faculty members interested in conducting various types of outcome studies, the collection and analysis of the data becomes a seminar about learning and education. Other faculty members hear about it and often want to join. How many times have you had faculty members volunteer to join a committee? In these schools, it has occurred.

Studying our own educational processes and impact becomes a source of intellectual discovery. Providing a voice for all faculty in this type of process appears to stimulate a degree of design inventiveness not considered possible in most schools. The faculty often exceed the administration's wildest dreams.

These types of discussions, committees, or seminars also provide insights into the school's strategic distinctiveness (see Chapter Two). Finding the local strengths on which to build a new program allows for natural differentiation to other programs prospective students might consider.

6. *Helping faculty and staff shift to a focus on learning.* Faculty and staff would not need special training and development in our ideal institution. They would be learners! As learners, the institutional and educational processes would be helping them to be in a learning frame of mind. What is often called a spirit

of co-inquiry would permeate all activities. As mentioned in an earlier section of this chapter, faculty, staff, and students would all be "members" of the institution. Of course, each would have somewhat different roles and responsibilities, but each would be committed to and excited by learning.

If faculty reward systems recognized and encouraged learning, exploring, and experimenting with the learning process, there would be an integration of research and teaching. Even if the faculty member's primary research was focused on a specific topic, learning about the topic should become part of his or her research agenda. After all, the difference between a university and many nonprofit research institutes is the educational purpose of the university. Both types of organizations are committed to research, but only one has a developmental agenda with students. The challenge is not to develop courses or training activities for faculty to "help" them make the shift from a focus on teaching to a joint focus on teaching and learning. We should create settings, events, and processes in which faculty and staff can rediscover learning, and in particular, explore learning about learning.

Summary of Design and Process Principles of an Ideal Educational Institution

Design Principles:
1. Evaluating educational structures and processes by promoting learning criteria
2. Conducting outcome orientation to allow analysis of learning value added
3. Becoming a learner-centered institution
4. Carrying out continuous inquiry about the learning process
5. Developing an institutional learning strategy based on stakeholder conversation

Process Principles:
1. Conceptualizing management as an interdisciplinary phenomenon
2. Respecting and linking to the traditional departmental and disciplinary structure

3. Developing the whole person
4. Providing lifelong learning in the context of varying life and career stages, cycles, and modes
5. Creating a contagion of curiosity
6. Helping faculty and staff shift to a focus on learning

Conclusion

Reform is a necessary but not sufficient condition for change. It is time to rise above a business-as-usual approach and to join together in bringing about a transformation in human learning by focusing our educational system on its primary mission — the promotion of learning.

> What you can do, or dream you can, begin it,
> Boldness has genius, power, and magic in it.
> — Goethe, *Faustus, a Dramatic Mystery,* as translated by John Anster (1835)

REFERENCES

Abramson, J., & Franklin, B. (1986). *Where are they now?* New York: Doubleday.

Adair, S. M. (1990). Educational outcomes: Their impact on graduate pediatric dentistry education. *Journal of Dental Education, 54*(3), 188–190.

Adler, M. (1982). *The Paideia proposal.* New York: Macmillan.

Albanese, R., Bernardin, H. J., Connor, P. E., Dobbins, G. H., Ford, R. C., Harris, M. M., Licata, B. J., Miceli, M. P., Porter, L. W., & Ulrich, D. O. (1990, August). *Outcome measurement and management education: An Academy of Management Task Force Report.* Presentation at the annual Academy of Management meeting, San Francisco.

American Assembly of Collegiate Schools of Business. (1987). *Outcome measurement project: Phase II report.* St. Louis, MO: Author.

American Assembly of Collegiate Schools of Business. (1989). *Report of the American Assembly of Collegiate Schools of Business Task Force on Outcome Measurement.* St. Louis, MO: Author.

Argyris, C. (1985). *Strategy, change, and defensive routines.* Boston: Pitman.

Astin, A. W. (1992). *What matters in college? Four critical years revisited.* San Francisco: Jossey-Bass.

Astin, H. S., & Leland, C. (1991). *Women of influence, women of vision: A cross-generational study of leaders and social change.* San Francisco: Jossey-Bass.

Atkinson, J. W. (ed.). (1958). *Motivation in fantasy, action, and society.* New York: Van Nostrand Reinhold.

Bakan, D. (1966). *The duality of human existence.* Skokie, IL: Rand McNally.

Banta, T. W. (Ed.). (1988). *Implementing outcomes assessment: Promise and perils.* New Directions for Institutional Research, no. 59. San Francisco: Jossey-Bass.

Banta, T. W., & Associates. (1993). *Making a difference: Outcomes of a decade of assessment in higher education.* San Francisco: Jossey-Bass.

Bardwick, J. (1980). The season of a woman's life. In D. McGuigan (Ed.), *Women's lives: New theory, research, and policy* (pp. 35–37). Ann Arbor: University of Michigan, Center for Continuing Education of Women.

Barnett, R., & Baruch, G. (1980). On being an economic provider: Women's involvement in multiple roles. In D. McGuigan (Ed.), *Women's lives: New theory, research, and policy* (pp. 69–83). Ann Arbor: University of Michigan, Center for Continuing Education of Women.

Baruch, G., Barnett, R., & Rivers, C. (1983). *Life prints: New patterns of love and work for today's women.* New York: New American Library.

Barzun, J. (1991). *Begin here: The forgotten conditions of teaching and learning.* Chicago: University of Chicago Press.

Bateson, M. C. (1989). *Composing a life.* New York: Atlantic Monthly Press.

Belenky, M., Clinchy, B., Goldberger, N., & Tarule, J. (1986). *Women's ways of knowing.* New York: Basic Books.

Berzoff, J. (1985). *Valued female friendships: Their functions in female adult development. Dissertation Abstracts International, 46,* 3890.

Bettelheim, B. (1965). The problem of generations. In E. Erikson (Ed.), *The challenge of youth* (pp. 64–92). New York: Doubleday.

Bigelow, J. D. (Ed.). (1991). *Managerial skills: Explorations in practical knowledge.* Newbury Park, CA: Sage.

Bird, B., & Jordan, R. (1987, August). *A study to develop measures of time orientation and future time perspective.* Presentation at the annual Academy of Management meeting, New Orleans.

Bloch, J. H. (1977). *Sex differences in cognitive functioning, personality characteristics, and socialization experiences: Implications for education policy.* Report to the presidents of Smith, Wellesley, and Mt. Holyoke College.

Bly, R. (1990). *Iron John: A book about men.* Reading, MA: Addison-Wesley.

Boyatzis, R. E. (1982). *The competent manager: A model for effective performance.* New York: Wiley.

Boyatzis, R. E. (1994a). Stimulating self-directed learning through the Managerial Assessment and Development course. *Journal of Management Education, 18*(3), 304–323.

Boyatzis, R. E. (1994b). Rendering unto competence the things that are competent. *American Psychologist, 49*(1), 64–66.

Boyatzis, R. E., Cowen, S. S., & Kolb, D. A. (1991). Curricular innovation in higher education: The new Weatherhead MBA program. *Selections, 8*(1), 27–37.

Boyatzis, R. E., Cowen, S. S., & Kolb, D. A. (1992). Implementing curriculum innovation in higher education: Year one of the new Weatherhead MBA program. *Selections, 9*(1), 1–9.

Boyatzis, R. E., & Kolb, D. A. (1969). *Feedback and self-directed behavior change.* Unpublished working paper no. 394-69, Massachusetts Institute of Technology, Sloan School of Management.

Boyatzis, R. E., & Kolb, D. A. (1991). Assessing individuality in learning: The learning skills profile. *Educational Psychology, 11*(3&4), 279–295.

Boyatzis, R. E., & Kolb, D. A. (1993). *Performance, learning, and development as modes of growth and adaptation.* Unpublished manuscript, Case Western Reserve University.

Boyatzis, R. E., & Kolb, D. A. (in press). Beyond learning styles to learning skills: The executive skills profile. *Journal of Managerial Psychology.*

Boyatzis, R. E., & Renio, A. (1989). The impact of an MBA program on managerial abilities. *Journal of Management Development, 8*, 66–77.

Boyatzis, R. E., Renio, A., & Thompson, L. (1990). *Developing abilities in an MBA program.* Unpublished manuscript, Case Western Reserve University, Weatherhead School of Management.

Boyatzis, R. E., & Sokol, M. (1982). *A pilot project to assess the feasibility of assessing skills and personal characteristics of students in collegiate business programs.* St. Louis, MO: American Assembly of Collegiate Schools of Business.

Boyd, M. A., Bennett, I. C., & Bentley, K. C. (1991). Accreditation of predoctoral dental education: Clinical Outcomes assessment. *Journal of Dental Education, 55*(11), 729–734.

Boyer, E. (1987). *College: The undergraduate experience in America.* New York: HarperCollins.

Boyer, E. (1990). *Scholarship reconsidered: Priorities of the professoriate.* Princeton, NJ: Carnegie Foundation for the Advancement of Teaching.

Bray, D. W., Campbell, R. J., & Grant, D. L. (1974). *Formative years in business: A long term AT&T study of managerial lives.* New York: Wiley.

Briars, D. J. (1983). An information-processing analysis of mathematical ability. In R. F. Dillon & R. R. Schmeck (Eds.), *Individual differences in cognition.* Vol. 1. New York: Academic Press.

Brod, H. (ed.). (1987). *The making of masculinities: The new men's studies.* London: Allen & Unwin.

B-schools are failing the US. (1988, November 28). *Business Week,* p. 190.

Byrne, J. A., Norman, J. R., & Miles, G. L. (1988, November 28). Where the schools aren't doing their homework. *Business Week,* pp. 84–86.

Caie, B. (1987). Learning in style: Reflections of an action learning MBA programme. *Journal of Management Development, 6*(2), 19–29.

Campbell, J. P., Dunnette, M. D., Lawler, E. E. III, & Weick, K. E., Jr. (1970). *Managerial behavior, performance, and effectiveness.* New York: McGraw-Hill.

Case, S. S. (1987). Appreciating diversity: Exploring the impact of ethnic group membership in organizations. Paper presented at the annual International Conference on Women and Organizations at Tulane University, New Orleans, LA.

Case, S. S. (1988). Cultural differences not deficiencies: An analysis of managerial women's language. In S. Rose and L. Larwood (Eds.), *Women's careers: Pathways and pitfalls* (pp. 41–63). New York: Praeger.

Case, S. S. (1993). The collaborative advantage: The usefulness of women's language to contemporary business problems. *Business and the Contemporary World, 5*(3), 81–105.

Case, S. S., & Thompson, L. (1994). Developmental differences in MBA students: An examination of life stories and career histories. In L. Turner & H. Sterk (Eds.), *Differences that make a difference: Examining the assumptions of research in communication, language, and gender.* Westport, CT: Greenwood Press.

Chodorow, N. (1974). Family structure and feminine personality. In M. Rosaldo and L. Lamphere (Eds.), *Woman, culture, and society* (pp. 43–66). Palo Alto, CA: Stanford University Press.

Clawson, J. G., Kotter, J. P., Faux, V. A., & McArthur, C. (1991). *Self-assessment and career development* (3rd ed.). Englewood Cliffs, NJ: Prentice-Hall.

Coltrane, S. (1988). Father-child relationships and the status of women: A cross-cultural study. *American Journal of Sociology, 93*(5), 1060–1095.

Cowan, A. (1992, September 27). For women, fewer MBA's. *New York Times,* Section 3, p. 4.

Crooks, L. A., Campbell, J. T., & Rock, D. A. (1979). *Predicting career progress of graduate students in management.* Princeton, NJ: Educational Testing Service.

Curry, B. K. (1992). *Instituting enduring innovations: Achieving continuity of change in higher education.* ASHE-ERIC Higher Education Report No. 7. Washington, DC: Association for the Study of Higher Education.

Dalton, G., & Thompson, P. (1986). *Novations: Strategies for career development.* Glenview, IL: Scott Foresman.

Derr, C. B. (1986). *Managing the new careerists: The diverse career success orientations of today's workers.* San Francisco: Jossey-Bass.

Development Dimensions International. (1985). *Final report: Phase III.* St. Louis, MO: American Assembly of Collegiate Schools of Business.

Douvan, E., & Adelson, J. (1966). *The adolescent experience.* New York: Wiley.

Dreyfus, C. (1991). *Scientists and engineers as effective managers: A study of the development of interpersonal abilities.* Unpublished doctoral dissertation, Case Western Reserve University, Cleveland, OH.

Eccles, J. (1987). Gender roles and women's achievement-related decisions. *Psychology of Women Quarterly, 11,* 135–172.

Eichenbaum, L., & Orbach, S. (1988). *Between women.* New York: Viking.

Eisler, R. (1988). *The chalice and the blade: Our history, our future.* San Francisco: HarperCollins.

Ely, R. (1991, August). *Gender difference: What difference does it make?* Paper presented at the annual meeting of the Academy of Management, Miami, FL.

Erikson, E. (1961). The roots of virtue. In J. Huxley (Ed.), *The humanist frame.* New York: HarperCollins.

Erikson, E. (1968). *Identity: Youth and crisis.* New York: Norton.

Erikson, E. (1982). *The life cycle completed.* New York: Norton.

Flanagan, J. C. (1954). The critical incident technique. *Psychological Bulletin, 51,* 327–335.

Fraser, N., & Nicholson, L. J. (1990). Social criticism without philosophy: An encounter between feminism and postmodernism. In L. J. Nicholson (Ed.), *Feminism/postmodernism* (pp. 19–38). New York: Routledge.

Freire, P. (1990). *The pedagogy of the oppressed.* New York: Continuum.

French, M. (1985). *Beyond power: On women, men, and morals.* New York: Ballantine Books.

Friedman, G. (1989). *Women in management: Competence and career development.* Unpublished doctoral dissertation, Case Western Reserve University, Cleveland, OH.

Fuchsberg, G. (1990, June 6). Business schools get bad grades. *Wall Street Journal,* pp. B1–B2.

Fuchsberg, G. (1992, September 25). Female enrollment falls in many top MBA programs. *Wall Street Journal,* pp. B1, B6.

Gallese, L. (1985). *Women like us.* New York: Signet Books.

Gallos, J. V. (1990). Exploring women's development: Implications for career theory, practice, and research. In M. Arthur, D. Hall, & B. Lawrence (Eds.), *Handbook of career theory and development* (pp. 110–132). New York: Cambridge University Press.

Gallos, J. V. (1993). Women's experiences and ways of knowing: Implications for teaching and learning in the organizational behavior classroom. *Journal of Management Education, 5*(1), 7–26.

Gardner, H. (1993). *Creating minds.* New York: Basic Books.

Genthon, M. (1989). Why does it take forever to revise the curriculum? *Accent on Improving Teaching and Learning.* Ann Arbor: University of Michigan, National Center for Research to Improve Postsecondary Teaching and Learning (NCRIPTAL).

Giele, J. (1982). Women's work and family roles. In J. Giele (Ed.), *Women in the middle years* (pp. 115–150). New York: Wiley.

Gilligan, C. (1977). In a different voice: Women's conception of self and morality. *Harvard Education Review, 47,* 481–517.

Gilligan, C. (1980). Restoring the missing text of women's development to life cycle theories. In D. McGuigan (Ed.), *Women's lives: New theory, research, and policy.* Ann Arbor: University of Michigan, Center for Continuing Education of Women.

Gilligan, C. (1982). *In a different voice: Psychological theory and women's development.* Cambridge, MA: Harvard University Press.

Goethe, J.W.V. (1806). Prelude at the theater. Pt. I of *Faustus, a dramatic mystery.* Translated in 1835 by John Anster. London: Longman, Rees, Orme, Brown, Green, and Longman, 303.

Goleman, D. (1985). *Vital lies, simple truths: The psychology of self-deception.* New York: Simon & Schuster.

Gutek, B., Repetti, R., & Silver, D. (1988). Nonwork roles and stress at work. In C. Cooper & R. Payne (Eds.), *Causes, coping, and consequences of stress at work.* London: Wiley.

Habermas, J. (1984). *The theory of communicative action.* Vol. 1. Boston: Beacon Press.

Habermas, J. (1987). *The theory of communicative action.* Vol. 2. Boston: Beacon Press.

Halper, J. (1988). *Quiet desperation: The truth about successful men.* New York: Warner Books.

Hancock, E. (1989). *The girl within.* New York: Ballantine Books.

Hardesty, S., & Jacobs, N. (1986). *Success and betrayal: The crisis of women in corporate America.* New York: Franklin Watts.

Harvard Assessment Project. (1990). *Explorations with students and faculty about teaching, learning, and student life.* Cambridge, MA: Harvard University Press.

Hayes, R. H., & Abernathy, W. J. (1980). Managing our way to economic decline. *Harvard Business Review, 58*(4), 67–77.

Hegelson, S. (1990). *Female advantage: Women's ways of leadership.* New York: Doubleday.

Hennig, M., & Jardin, A. (1978). *The managerial woman.* New York: Pocket Books.

Hochschild, A. (1989). *The second shift.* New York: Viking Press.

Howard, A., & Bray, D. (1988). *Managerial lives in transition: Advancing age and changing times.* New York: Guilford Press.

Hunt, D. E. (1987). *Beginning with ourselves: In practice, theory, and human affairs.* Cambridge, MA: Brookline Books.

Johnston, W., & Packer, A. (1987). *Workforce 2000: Work and workers for the 21st century.* Indianapolis, IN: Hudson Institute, Inc.

Johnstone, D. B. (1993). Enhancing the productivity of learning. *Bulletin of the American Association of Higher Education, 46*(4), 3–5.

Josselson, R. (1987). *Finding herself: Pathways to identity development in women.* San Francisco: Jossey-Bass.

Justice, D., & Marineau, C. (1988). Self-assessment: Essential skills for Adult Learners. In P. Hutchings & A. Wurtzdorff (Eds.), *Knowing and doing: Learning through experience.* San Francisco: Jossey-Bass.

Keele, R. L. (1986). Mentoring or networking? Strong and weak ties in career development. In L. L. Moore (Ed.), *Not as far as you think: The realities of working women* (pp. 53–68). Lexington, MA: Lexington Books.

Keys, B., & Wolfe, J. (1988). Management education and development: Current issues and emerging trends. *Journal of Management, 14,* 205–229.

Knowles, M. S. (1986). *Using learning contracts: Practical approaches to individualizing and structuring learning.* San Francisco: Jossey-Bass.

Kohlberg, L. (1976). Moral stages and moralization: The cognitive-developmental approach. In T. Lickona (Ed.), *Moral development and behavior: Theory, research, and social issues* (pp. 54–69). Troy, MO: Holt, Rinehart & Winston.

Kohlberg, L. (1981). *The philosophy of moral development.* San Francisco: HarperCollins.

Kohlberg, L., & Kramer, R. (1969). Continuities and discontinuities in child and adult moral development. *Human Development, 12,* 93–120.

Kolb, D. A. (1971). *A cybernetic model of human change and growth.* Unpublished working paper no. 526-71, Massachusetts Institute of Technology, Sloan School of Management.

Kolb, D. A. (1984). *Experiential learning: Experience as the source of learning and development.* Englewood Cliffs, NJ: Prentice-Hall.

Kolb, D. A., and Boyatzis, R. E. (1970a). On the dynamics of the helping relationship. *Journal of Applied Behavioral Science. 6*(3), 267–289.

Kolb, D. A., and Boyatzis, R. E. (1970b). Goal-setting and self-directed behavior change. *Human Relations, 23*(5), 439–457.

Kotter, J. P. (1982). *The general managers.* New York: Free Press.

Kotter, J. P. (1988). *The leadership factor.* New York: Free Press.

Kurfiss, J. G. (1988). *Critical thinking: Theory, research, practice, and possibilities.* ASHE-ERIC Higher Education Report No. 2. Washington, DC: Association for the Study of Higher Education.

Larwood, L., & Gutek, B. A. (1987). Working toward a theory of women's career development. In B. A. Gutek & L. Larwood (Eds.), *Women's career development* (pp. 170–183). Newbury Park, CA: Sage.

Larwood, L., Kriger, M. P., & Falbe, C. M. (1993). An investigation of the vision construct-in-use of AACSB business school deans. *Group and Organization Management, 18*(2), 214–236.

Lee, M. D. (1993). Women's involvement in professional careers and family life: Themes and variations. *Business and the Contemporary World, 5*(3), 106–127.

Levinson, D. (1978). *The seasons of a man's life.* New York: Knopf.

Loevinger, J. (1976). *Ego development: Conceptions and theories.* San Francisco: Jossey-Bass.

Louis, M. R. (1990). The gap in management education. *Selections, 6*(3), 1–12.

Luthans, F., Hodgetts, R. M., & Rosenkrantz, S. A. (1988). *Real managers.* New York: Ballinger.

Maccoby, E., & Jacklin, C. (1974). *The psychology of sex differences.* Stanford, CA: Stanford University Press.

McCall, M. W., Jr., Lombardo, M. M., & Morrison, A. M. (1988). *The lessons of experience: How successful executives develop on the job.* Lexington, MA: Lexington Books.

McCarty, P. A. (1986). Effects of feedback on the self-confidence of men and women. *Academy of Management Journal, 31,* 633–653.

McClelland, D. C. (1973). Testing for competence rather than intelligence. *American Psychologist, 28*(1), 1–40.

McClelland, D. C. (1975). *Power: The inner experience.* New York: Irvington.

McClelland, D. C. (1985). *Human motivation.* Glenview, IL: Scott, Foresman.

McClelland, D. C., & Boyatzis, R. E. (1982). The leadership motive pattern and long term success in management. *Journal of Applied Psychology, 67*(6), 737–743.

McClelland, D. C., & Winter, D. G. (1978). Thematic analysis: An empirically derived measure of effects of liberal arts education. *Journal of Educational Psychology, 70*(1), 8–16.

McConnell, R. V., & Seybolt, J. W. (1991). Assessment center technology: One approach for integrating and assessing management skills in the business school curriculum. In J. D. Bigelow (Ed.), *Managerial skills: Explorations in practical knowledge.* Newbury Park, CA: Sage.

McGill, M. E. (1985). *The McGill report on male intimacy.* New York: HarperCollins, 1985.

Magner, D. (1989, February 1). Milwaukee's Alverno College for 16 Years a Pioneer in Weaning Students from Dependence on Teachers. *Chronicle of Higher Education,* pp. A10–13.

Melchiori, G. S. (Ed.). (1988). *Alumni research: Methods and applications.* New Directions for Institutional Research, no. 60. San Francisco: Jossey-Bass.

Mentkowski, M., McEachern, W., O'Brien, K., & Fowler, D. (1982). *Developing a professional competence model for management education.* Final report to the National Institutes of Education. Milwaukee, WI: Alverno College.

Mentkowski, M., Rogers, G., Deemer, D., Ben-Ur, T., Reiseter, J., Rickards, W., & Talbott, M. (1991, April 5). *Understanding abilities, learning, and development through college outcome studies: What can we expect from higher education assessment?* Paper presented at the annual meeting of the American Educational Research Association, Chicago.

Mentkowski, M., & Strait, M. (1983). *A longitudinal study of student change in cognitive development, learning styles, and generic abilities in an outcome-centered liberal arts curriculum.* Final report to the National Institutes of Education. Milwaukee, WI: Alverno College.

Mezirow, J. (1991). *Transformative dimensions of adult learning.* San Francisco: Jossey-Bass.

Miller, J. B. (1986). *Toward a new psychology of women.* Boston: Beacon Press.

Minsky, M., & Paapert, S. (1974). *Artificial intelligence.* Condon Lectures. Eugene: Oregon State System of Higher Education.

Mintzberg, H. (1973). *The nature of managerial work.* New York: HarperCollins.

Morgenstein, W. M. (1990). Outcome measures in dental education: We've only just begun. *Journal of Dental Education, 54*(6), 308–310.

Muller, H. J., Porter, J. L., & Rehder, R. R. (1988, October). Have the business schools let down U.S. corporations? *Management Review, 77*(10), 24–31.

Mullin, R. F., Shaffer, P. L., & Gelle, M. J. (1991). A study of the assessment center method of teaching basic management skills. In J. D. Bigelow (Ed.), *Managerial skills: Explorations in practical knowledge.* Newbury Park, CA: Sage.

Ness, A. (1973). The shallow and the deep, long range ecology movement: A summary. *Inquiry, 16,* 95–100.

Newmann, F. M., & Archbald, D. A. (1992). The nature of authentic academic achievement. In H. Berlak, F. M. Newmann, E. Adams, D. A. Archbald, T. Burgess, J. Raven, & T. A. Romberg (Eds.), *Toward a new science of educational testing and assessment.* Albany: State University of New York Press.

Packham, R., Roberts, R., & Bawden, R. (1989). Our faculty goes experiential. In S. Weil & I. McGill (Eds.), *Making sense of experiential learning.* Philadelphia: Society for Research on Higher Education (SRHE), Open University Press.

Pascarella, E. T., & Terenzini, P. T. (1991). *How college affects students: Findings and insights from twenty years of research.* San Francisco: Jossey-Bass.

Pellegrino, J. W., & Goldman, S. R. (1983). Developmental and individual differences in verbal and spatial reasoning. In R. F. Dillon & R. R. Schmeck (Eds.), *Individual differences in cognition.* Vol. 1. New York: Academic Press.

Perry, W. G., Jr. (1970). *Forms of intellectual and ethical development in the college years.* Troy, MO: Holt, Rinehart & Winston.

Piaget, J. (1980). *The equilibration of cognitive structures: The central problem of intellectual development.* New York: Basic Books.

Piotrkowski, C., Rapoport, R. N., & Rapoport, R. (1987). Families and work. In M. Sussman & S. Steinmetz (Eds.), *Handbook of marriage and the family.* New York: Plenum Press.

Porter, L., & McKibbin, L. (1988). *Management education and development: Drift or thrust into the 21st century?* New York: McGraw-Hill.

Powell, G., & Mainiero, L. (1992). Cross-currents in the river of time: Conceptualizing the complexities of women's careers. *Journal of Management, 18*(2), 215–237.

Prideaux, G., & Ford, J. (1988a). Management development: Competencies, contracts, teams, and work-based learning. *Journal of Management Development, 7*(1), 56–68.

Prideaux, G., & Ford, J. (1988b). Management development: Competencies, contracts, teams, and work-based learning. *Journal of Management Development, 7*(3), 13–21.

Raven, J. (1992). A model of competence, motivation, and behavior, and a paradigm for assessment. In H. Berlak, F. M. Newmann, E. Adams, D. A. Archbald, T. Burgess, J. Raven, & T. A. Romberg (Eds.), *Toward a new science of educational testing and assessment.* Albany: State University of New York Press.

Revans, R. *The origins and growth of action learning.* London: Chartwell-Bratt, 1982.

Rhee, K. (1992). *A study of critical incident interview: A close look at factors that influence the interview.* Unpublished paper, Case Western Reserve University, Cleveland, OH.

Riordan, T. (1993, May). Focusing on student learning changes the nature of teaching. *Alverno Magazine,* pp. 4–7.

Roberts, P., & Newton, P. (1986). *Levinsonian studies of women's adult development.* Working paper, Wright Institute, Berkeley, CA.

Roberts, T. (1991). Gender and the influence of evaluations on self-assessments in achievement settings. *Psychological Bulletin, 109*(2), 297–308.

Roberts, T., & Nolen-Hoeksema, S. (1989). Sex differences in reactions to evaluative feedback. *Sex Roles, 21,* 725–747.

Rosener, J. B. (1990). Ways women lead. *Harvard Business Review, 70,* 119–125.

Rosenthal, R., Hall, J. A., Archer, D., DiMatteo, M. R., Rogers, P. L., DePaulo, B. M., Eisenstat, R. A., & Finkelstein, S. (1979). *The PONS Test Manual: Profile of Nonverbal Sensitivity.* New York: Irvington.

Schaef, A. (1981). *Women's reality: An emerging female system in a white society.* Minneapolis, MN: Winston.

Schein, E. (1978). *Career dynamics: Matching individual and organizational needs.* Reading, MA: Addison-Wesley.

Schein, E. (1982). *Individuals and careers.* Technical report no. 19. Washington, DC: Office of Naval Research.

Sekaran, U. (1986). *Dual-career families: Contemporary organizational and counseling issues.* San Francisco: Jossey-Bass.

Specht, L., & Sandlin, P. (1991). The differential effects of experiential learning activities and traditional lecture classes in accounting. *Simulations and Gaming, 22*(2), 196–210.

Spencer, L. M., Jr., & Spencer, S. M. (1993). *Competence at work: Models for superior performance.* New York: Wiley.

Sperling, J. G., & Tucker, R. W. (1993, spring). Adult-centered universities: Education's least-cost way to a world class workforce. *Adult Assessment Forum,* pp. 3–13.

Stark, J. S., Lowther, M. A., & Hagerty, B.M.K. (1986). *Responsive professional education: Balancing outcomes and opportunities.*

ASHE-ERIC Higher Education Report No. 3. Washington, DC: Association for the Study of Higher Education and George Washington University.

Stewart, L., & Gudykunst, W. (1982). Differential factors in influencing the hierarchical level and number of promotions of males and females within an organization. *Academy of Management Journal, 25,* 586–597.

Stoltenberg, J. (1990). *Refusing to be a man.* New York: Meridian.

Tannen, D. (1990). *You just don't understand: Women and men in conversation.* New York: Morrow.

Thompson, L. (1989). *Gender differences in MBA student development: A pilot study.* Unpublished raw data, Case Western Reserve University, Cleveland, OH.

Thornton, G. C. III, & Byham, W. C. (1982). *Assessment centers and managerial performance.* New York: Academic Press.

Townsend, B. K., Newell, L. J., & Weise, M. D. (1992). *Creating distinctiveness.* ASHE-ERIC Higher Education Report No. 6. Washington, DC: Association for the Study of Higher Education.

Valliere, P. (1986). Perceived academic competence in women in Ph.D. programs: Effects of feedback, self-esteem, and academic discipline. *Dissertation Abstracts International, 47,* 4528.

Velsor, E., & Hughes, M. (1990). *Gender differences in the development of managers: How women managers learn from experience.* Greensboro, NC: Center for Creative Leadership.

Veroff, J., & Feld, S. (1970). *Marriage and work in America.* New York: Van Nostrand Reinhold.

Whetton, D. A., Windes, D. L., May, D. R., & Bookstaver, D. (1991). Bringing management skill education into the mainstream. In J. D. Bigelow (Ed.), *Managerial skills: Explorations in practical knowledge* (pp. 23–40). Newbury Park, CA: Sage.

White, J. W., and Gruber, K. J. (1985). Gender differences in leisure-need activity pattern. *Sex Roles, 12,* 1173–1186.

Winter, D. G. (1973). *The power motive.* New York: Free Press.

Winter, D. G. (1979). *Correcting projective test scores for the effect of significant correlation with length of protocol (unpublished technical note).* Boston: McBer and Company.

Winter, D. G., McClelland, D. C., & Stewart, A. J. (1981). *A new case for the liberal arts: Assessing institutional goals and student development.* San Francisco: Jossey-Bass.

Wolfe, T. (1991). *Readings from the Hurricane Island Outward Bound School.* Hurricane Island, ME: Outward Bound.

Zoffer, H. J. (1981). *New dimensions in the process of lifelong learning for management education.* Paper presented at the 9th International Congress on the Assessment Center Method, Lincolnshire, IL.

INDEX